BACKPACKING C[

A Northern Irishman's Journey
Through 100 Countries

dontstopliving.net
a lifestyle of travel

by JONNY BLAIR

Backpacking Centurion:

A Northern Irishman's Journey

Through 100 Countries

Volume One: Don't Look Back In Bangor

by Jonny Blair

Backpacking Centurion: A Northern Irishman's Journey Through 100 Countries by Jonny Blair

Backpacking Centurion:
A Northern Irishman's Journey
Through 100 Countries

Volume One: Don't Look Back in Bangor

by Jonny Blair

Photos: All photos were taken by, or taken with permission of the author Jonny Scott Blair unless otherwise accredited. All photos are owned by the author Jonny Scott Blair.

Editing and formatting by Jonny Scott Blair.

Cover designed by: http://www.bookbaby.com/ and Scott Eldridge: http://www.eldowebdesign.co.uk/

Additional artwork by Ilona Skladzien: http://www.mylogoi.com/

Author's websites: http://dontstopliving.net and http://www.northernirishmaninpoland.com/

Author Biography and Contacts

Jonny Blair is a Northern Irish travel writer based in Poland. Jonny was born in Newtownards in 1980 and grew up in Bangor in Northern Ireland. Since leaving his hometown in 2003, Jonny has travelled far and wide, detailing his journeys on his one man travel blog, Don't Stop Living. Jonny has visited over 180 countries across all seven continents including Iran, Ethiopia, Andorra, China and Suriname. Jonny has also travelled to some lesser known places such as the Republic of Uzupis, Podjistan, Nauru, Kugelmugel, Sark, Antarctica, Nagorno Karabakh, Iraqi Kurdistan and The Empire of Austenasia. As well as working as a freelance writer, editor, teacher and copywriter, Jonny has also worked in bars, hotels and restaurants as well as on ferries, in farms, in schools and in offices. Jonny writes every day in some capacity and is also a poet and a football fanzine editor. Aside from travel, Jonny is a passionate football supporter of Glentoran FC, AFC Bournemouth, Klub Piłkarski Starogard and Northern Ireland. Jonny aims to inspire other people to get out there and see the world with their own two eyes.

Author's websites:
http://dontstopliving.net/
http://www.northernirishmaninpoland.com/
https://www.twitter.com/jonnyblair/
https://www.facebook.com/donotstopliving/
https://www.facebook.com/northernirishmaninpoland/
https://www.facebook.com/Jonny-Blair-Poetry-623933877981938/
https://www.instagram.com/jonnydontstopliving/
http://www.youtube.com/user/jonnyscottblair/
jonny@dontstopliving.net

Backpacking Centurion
Volume One - Don't Look Back in Bangor

1980 - 2008

35 chapters

"Slip inside the eye of your mind" - Noel Gallagher.

When Jonny Blair's 100-country book "Backpacking Centurion" was completed in August 2015, it was supposed to be released soon after that, and as a one-off book. That didn't exactly happen the way it was intended. Over the next five years, as Jonny continued on his travels, it became clear that chapter after chapter needed to be re-edited, re-positioned and in some cases, removed, delayed or in other cases – posted faster and onto the online travel blog "Don't Stop Living", which meant they didn't make the book as they made the blog.

In those five years, unfortunately depression kicked in and was the major reason for the book's delay. It was even possible that the book would never see the light of day at all. In 2019, it became clear that the book needed to be split into three volumes, and not all released at the same time. These three volumes are more or less in chronological order and are now being released one by one. The first one, here with its volume title "Don't Look Back In Bangor" is finally here in print.

Don't Look Back in Bangor, the first volume of Backpacking Centurion begins where it all began for Jonny Blair. That means the seaside town of Bangor in Northern Ireland. The year is 1980. Jonny will take you on a "fool circle" here as he details his childhood with footballic zest. Jonny's topsy turvy time at Bangor Grammar School is encapsulated in an enthralling chapter trilogy of teenage angst.

Delve into Jonny's early tourist days of visiting The Netherlands, France and significantly Bournemouth in 1994. Seaside beach towns beginning with B on the brain, it was here in an unlikely ice cream hut where this nationalistic Northern Irishman found a hunger for global travel.

Weekend trips to Burnley, Colchester and Portsmouth soon became backpacking adventures to Belarus, China and Poland. The odyssey really kicked off when Jonny was in his twenties, which is where this first volume ends to prepare us for volume two. This is a real life journey of ups and downs.

Expect some regretful bad boy behaviour, unashamed nudity and vintage banter as Jonny injects humour, sincerity and openness to his life of tears, fears and elation.

By the end of this volume, Jonny will have gone through failed romances, an arm break, a leg break and some wacky trips to lands afar watching the Northern Ireland football team. He will have you gagging for volume two, where in essence the real 100 country quest begins to dominate proceedings.

The volume's title and much of its theme reflects on Jonny's desire not to look back at what has been and gone. Doors are closed and his Bangor hometown was left behind. In true poetic Noel Gallagher fashion, Jonny's soul slides away, but don't look back in Bangor, we heard him say.

For A.M.

#ulsterczyk #dontstopliving #backpackingcenturion

Chapterski

Chapter 1
Fool Circle

La Linea de la Concepcion, SPAIN (April 2015)

"And across the dark Atlantic, Belfast lies asleep"
- Tim Wheeler.

Wacaday. Life has gone full circle for me and I cried my eyes out. Your life might go full circle for you and you might cry your eyes out, too. On the grand scheme of things, it ain't a bad old world. As I write this on a bus in southern Spain (the Costa del Sol, *baby*), I'm reminiscing. I'm jotting down memories that come into my head. Memories from an inadvertent spot of travelling which was never intended to end up the way it did. I never meant to go backpacking around the world the way I have done. And this moment of realisation and sentimentality would have to come in Spain, wouldn't it? The *"Arconada...Armstrong!"* country. I'm a total fool and I've gone in a complete circle here. Hence, you know, fool circle, there are no errors, but there might be deliberate spelling mistakes. "Fool Circle" should have been the title of this book you know and it was destined to be that for the most part, but it just wasn't bold and brave enough. The book had three working titles, "Don't Stop Living: The Book" (too boring), "Backpacking Centurion" (that's me), "Fool Circle" (better as a chapter). Move over, Bud Light year. I'm a backpacking centurion. There ain't no time to waste. This is only the beginning. This is "Don't Look Back in Bangor". It's something I heard you say.

What is the Jonny Blair of today's world doing? Here I am on route to Malaga from the town of La Linea de la Concepcion (which nicely borders Gibraltar) on just a normal bus on a normal day in a normal country. There is no new planet in the solar system (in fact there is one less as poor Pluto recently got deleted) and there is nothing up my Slieve, Donard. As I flick through some pages of my passport and sip an ice cold cerveza by my window seat, I know it's not a dream anymore. Because I have done it now. Uruguay have done it. Brazil have done it. They won the World Cup. It feels like I won that one too. But my World Cup. My crazy World Cup. Everything you see is real and you can have it all. A tear rolls down my Northern Irish cheek as a lonely sun sinks slowly over today's chosen horizon in mainland Spain. I've seen the same sun sink over enough different horizons a large quantity of times to realise it's genuine. This is as real as it gets, my friends. I sniff the air for a second and it smells good. I think we have a winner. I raise a wry smile.

You see, I hadn't been back to Spain properly since 2003. Hence why this moment completes my full circle, well actually, my fool circle. It was back then, as a curious 23 year old, that I realised I had never spent more than 3 consecutive weeks outside of Northern Ireland, my home country. That's right - I had never been away from my homeland properly until that point – that fact remains. Yet, now in April 2015 I have been away for 12 years on a journey that wasn't planned and I'm back where it all began. I've gone full circle in the last 12 years. I'd have been a fool to have predicted that back in 2003. I wouldn't have believed you if you'd told me back then, where I'd end up in the forthcoming dozen of dozen months. Last month I finally joined the real 100 club. I turned myself into a backpacking centurion. I created the term "Backpacking Centurion" before I even stepped in country 100. It's been a long and crazy journey. Over one hundred countries, over one thousand towns or cities, all seven continents. At times it has been absolutely ridiculous. I often travelled on my own bereft of loneliness. I travelled without purpose, timeframe or ambition most of the time. I just travelled because it seemed the best thing to do. I get bored of the same place. I always want something and somewhere new. I need a break from the mundane. Routines don't excite me. They're too fucking repetitive. You can say that again. I don't have to.

Travelling to 100 countries is a fake Ulsteric justification for the writing of this book of course, but it still doesn't explain the reason **why** I've travelled this much. As I sip another swig of this golden Spanish cerveza, I realise that there is no reason. It's just the way my life happened, and your life is just the way your life happened. You can't explain it, nor can I. You can't plan it or predict it. Nothing in this book was planned on that 2003 visit to Spain. What happened in those 12 years scares the living daylights out of me. I can't explain it, however at least in the forthcoming chapters of this humungous document, and through my one man internet-based travel blog ("Don't Stop Living") I'll tell some of the stories from those journeys. It's important to note that everything written in this book really happened and I was there for it. Some of you reading were also there for it. I can't guarantee 100% memory or accuracy on every single detail and we do forget things, but I've done my best. My Mum and Dad taught me honesty from an early age and they were right. I didn't always listen to them, but now I do. They were right. Honesty, it made me and it ruined me, because I made mistakes just like you and in my younger years, I did dishonest things. We live and we learn. John Lennon's notion of "Instant Karma" could well have been delayed for me. Mistakes I made came back to bite me years on and I have cried a lot in my life. Maybe even more than Paul Gascoigne gurned on a night in Turin.

Here in Spain, on this bus to Malaga, a song comes onto my iPod (which in 2003 would have been a Walkman cassette player with barely charged double A batteries on the verge of chewing up my bootleg mixtape). Today's random song is 'Seventh Circle' by Northern Irish rock band Ash.

And it makes me cry.

Everytime, that song makes me cry.

It's beautiful. It's the guitar sweep, it's the vibe of the song, it's the Ulster inspired lyric, it's Tim Wheeler's muttering of the Belfast and Quoile lines that get me emotional. It's the memory of the time I first arrived in Hong Kong in 2011 and the same song came on random play when I sat putting on unstrong enough sun cream at Tsuen Wan harbour. It sends a shiver down my spine and I can't hide. I'm overtly sentimental. Today, yesterday and potentially tomorrow. If God spares us. My Granny's words…

"If God spares us" – Mary Blair (my Granny).

I normally have a book with me on my journeys. A physical book. Today I also have one.

Today it's Diego Armando Maradona's autobiography that I'm reading and it's excellent. I'm really enjoying it.

I turn another leaf of Diego's journey. I swallow another drip of beer before the warmth of the sun kills its glory, but not Diego's.

Burrachaga's onside.

I raise a childish smile to myself. I think of my family and friends from my journeys and I know I'll see them all again soon. And I know they'll believe me and stand by me when I tell them I went travelling around the world and I had fun. I have ups and downs but I'm not sad today. I'm content. I feel happy enough to write this **last chapter of my book, this is chapter 100 right**? In fact, no. It doesn't belong at the end. It needs to be at the start. I'll make this the first chapter. It kind of fits, it's the fool circle I created yet never craved. Again, I'm the fool. How can the last chapter be the first? I don't really know, but it's here now, so roll with it…

This book isn't the end of my journeys or travel writing though, it's a closing of the 100 country chapter. It's something which had to be released now as it has been delayed time and time again. There are so many stories that are still untold. I've plenty more ambitions to achieve here on planet earth but right now it's the best time to get this typed up and released. I thought I'd type it all up before I forget what happened when I went backpacking the world. Because I had nothing else to do.

My bus pulls into Malaga bus station in the Hispanic darkness and I'm alone. With my backpack. I pull out my paper and pen and I get writing. I find a bar by the bus station and I order the cheapest cerveza they have (it was always what Jonny Blair did), which tonight is Sammy Magill on tap, (known locally as San Miguel). I start to finish the final chapters of this book and then I get distracted. There's a Barcelona match on the TV. I have to watch it.

So, I put my book away, I join some locals and I watch the match. Suarez scores a screamer and Andres Iniesta salutes the fans as I take another swig of the Sammy Magill. The lads shout me another beer and the Spanish I learnt during my time in Uruguay, comes in damn handy. So much for writing that book. The journey continues. There ain't no time to waste, and for the record…

Burrachaga scored. But that was 1986.

Who else but Diego had played him through…?

"Times running out the door you're running in"
- Ian McCullough.

Chapter 2
My Childhood Sweetheart

Newtownards and Bangor, NORTHERN IRELAND (The 1980s / March 1980 until 1991)

"Looking in your eyes, I see a paradise. This world that I've found is too good to be true" – Starship.

Let's start at the start. The good old 1980s. Growing up in a 1980s Northern Ireland was a joy. Yes, you hear all these news reports about the "troubles" but at the end of the day - people are people and always will be. Most of these people, you'll find are good people. People got hurt, people lost loved ones, people "gat shat" (got shot, were fired at using a gun), buildings got bombed, but life does what it always does - it carries on regardless.

"Don't know what I'm doing here, I'll carry on regardless"
– The Beautiful South.

I was born in the town of Newtownards, some 12 miles from the pulsating Northern Irish capital city - Belfast. But we'll kick things off in nearby Bangor, my home town. I attended Kilmaine Primary School in Bangor. Bangor is widely regarded as a middle class unionist seaside town in County Down, Northern Ireland. It's a fairly safe large coastal dormitory town, a brisk thirty minute drive from Northern Ireland's inspirational breath thefter, Belfast. Looking back now, Bangor was a cool spot to grow up in. I lived with my Mum and Dad in Marlo and was born at the turn of the decade. Conceived seemingly in Spain (Canary Islands) in 1979, born in Northern Ireland in March 1980, I'm now into my sixth decade from embryo status (70s,80s,90s,00s,10s,20s). Yet I'm still 'mid' 30s at the time of writing this. My brother Marko and sister Cathy are twins and they arrived on the scene in 1984. A decade later my youngest brother Daniel was here to complete our family in 1994 – but a whole load of crazy stuff happened before that and if you didn't see it with your eyes, you can read some of it here. A few home truths will come out, I told it all. I've travelled a bit as well, so no doubt the away goals rule will apply at some point too, Glentoran didn't always win.

Make no mistake about this - I loved the 1980s. No internet, no mobile phones, no flashy computer games. Maradona, Maggie Thatcher and Madonna. Meneminem du du du du du. Life was all about school, family, children's TV, toys and football. I loved my Primary School. **Loved it. Kilmaine Primary School** was massive in the 1980s and I mean huge. With over 1,000 children, at one point it was the largest Primary School in the United Kingdom. There were a few cool people who came through the ranks too. Former Miss Northern Ireland Zoe Salmon was in my year and a cool girl to know. At school she always had short blonde hair; she later made her name on Blue Peter with long blonde hair. Hull City striker Josh Magennis who helped set up the second Northern Ireland goal against the Ukraine at France Euro 2016 and had scored 7 Norn Iron goals by October 2019, also came through the ranks at the same school.

My schoolmate, Douglas "Dougie" Gordon has run more marathons than any other Northern Irish male around. He completed the world marathon majors with aplomb, humility and zero self-praise. Dougie is a personal friend and an inspiration to many. Kilmaine is a school of hard work, local talent and pride. There was something magic in the air as a child. Break times and lunch times were crazy in the playgrounds though - there were so many kids about. There wasn't much health and safety in those days though! We dived in the mud, we ended up in the adjacent river, "The Cotton", getting stung by nettles manys a time and we played football down the park daily, till the moon arrived – Linear Park was my Windsor Park or Dean Court. We often nicknamed it

"Lineker Park" after 1986 World Cup golden boot winner Gary Lineker, who scored 6 goals in a World Cup where incidentally England scored zero in their first two matches. I'd get stung by nettles daily in the summer before finding solace in a docken leaf. I started Kilmaine Primary School in P1 with Miss Melanie Preston (later Mrs. Thompson) as my teacher. I cried on my first day at school, my Mum recalls. I was shy and scared. But I got into it thick and fast and I loved it. Whether we want it to be or not, most of our first decade on planet earth is centred around education. And why not? We all want to learn stuff, so grab a book and hang on tight for a bumpy ride.

"Libraries gave us power" - Manic Street Preachers.

In my 7 years at Kilmaine my best friends were Graham Irwin, Stuart Hutchinson, Mark McCullough, Claire McKee, Magoo (also known as Peter McIvor), Gareth "Robbo" or "Coco" Robinson, Dougie Gordon and Scott Callen. Yes only 1 girl on that list, and a good one at that. A few of these names will crop up again in the story, others may be introduced along the way. Outside of school I was in the local Boys Brigade (10th Bangor B.B.) and I went to church every Sunday - Ballycrochan Presbyterian Church. This was actually a Protestant Church. This might come as a surprise to those who know that I now attend Catholic Churches in Poland but I was mostly at Protestant Church as a child. I have no qualms with attending either and I am in Catholic Churches much more often than Protestant ones. My love for God has remained the same throughout. I also pray in Orthodox Churches and Armenian Churches. I am at ease with my own religious beliefs. This isn't a book about that.

However, the 80s were the 80s. I played football on Saturday mornings for the BB Junior Section. I started going to watch Glentoran and Northern Ireland football matches around 1990, with Michael and Gavin McClelland who lived two doors down.

Football wise, most people who know me through that sport are aware that I support AFC Bournemouth, Glentoran FC and Northern Ireland, and have been to over 100 matches of each team, at least 20 of them away from home. But it wasn't always like that with Bournemouth, as my love affair with the Dorset seaside town didn't begin until 1994, nor did it take off and fly until 2003. More on football and Bournemouth in later chapters though. Glentoran and Northern Ireland were my first two football loves. My Dad is a Tottenham Hotspur fan and after Glentoran and Northern Ireland, I used to watch Gascoigne, Lineker, Nayim, Sheringham and Thorstvedt with him. I previously has a curiosity for the unknown (at the time) "Bournemouth" for three reasons – firstly in the 1986 World Cup, Northern Ireland's last goalscorer in the tournament, Colin Clarke played for Bournemouth. Secondly George Best's last British league match was for Bournemouth. The third reason came when thanks to my parents we ended up in Bournemouth in 1994 on a family holiday. Something with the town stuck and Dad eventually realised that his Tottenham Hotspur influences on me had faded away and transferred to his other two sons. We're a football loving family. Back to the 80s first though!

In 1986, when I started P3, my new teacher was Mrs. McKee. It was Sally McKee. I knew her well as my Mum worked as a babysitter and childminder. My Mum loved it and she loves caring for children. My Mum and Sally McKee were friends and I was delighted to have Sally as my teacher. However, I was much more interested in her daughter, the lovely Claire. She may not know it (or need to know it, but it's being told anyway, now) but aged 6, Claire McKee provided me with my first ever crush. I thought Claire was stunningly beautiful, and so intelligent. She was; and is. I remember how good she always looked, how smart she was, how positive she would be. All the time. We hung out together almost every day after school. Claire and I were best friends for most of the mid to late 80s. We would do art together, play games, watch

TV, we even wrote books and comics together. As kids we also once used toilet roll tubes to check each other's private parts out through fake binoculars. Yes, not embarrassing at all and I have no shame to tell it – honesty wins in life. I guess in that case, Claire's fanny was the first I ever saw and my willy was probably one of the first she set eyes on (sorry Claire). Claire and I used to have days out in the summer to the seaside resort of Cloughy, where her family had a caravan near the beach and a dog called Pepe that I was always scared of. That was travel. The road from Bangor to Cloughy provided me with my earliest travel memories. There was always a buzz about Claire. She was a special girl and I'll never forget her. Claire had an insatiable magnetic charm. Claire McKee really gave me that big crush when I was only 6-8 years old. Surely it's too young for that type of thing. Claire was just unforgettable.

Claire and I would go down to Cloughy beach and listen to tapes on our ghetto blasters. By tapes I mean cassettes - the transition from vinyl to CD hadn't yet materialised - cassettes and watching Top of the Pops filled the void. Actually, there wasn't a void, but if there was, they would have filled it. Claire and I listened to Kylie and Jason. Kylie Minogue and Jason Donovan - Australian acting duo who starred in Neighbours and also released singles. It was all the rage in 1987 - 1989. I was a bit deluded in those days. I fancied Kylie Minogue. I used to think of myself as the Jason, and Claire as the Kylie. I was always convinced that Claire and I would stay friends forever, fall in love, get married, live happily ever after. But life is just not like that. It's not a bowl of cherries and you pick the one you want. It probably would have been too perfect anyway – we looked more like brother and sister than lovers. Plus, we were young - aged 9, it's hardly the thing you want to say to a girl. It was more like "do you want to watch Ghostbusters?", "my Mum taped Neighbours, want to watch it?", "let's draw together". Claire was my first crush and she was my childhood sweetheart, even if the feelings never went mutual *(and I'd hazard a guess they weren't, nobody really knows and it's not really relevant anymore anyway).* I just remember how cool it was to hang out with Claire. Those are days I will never ever forget. Childhood memories linger long and we never lose them. Again, Claire McKee was unforgettable. Can you be in love when you are that young? I don't know, as I'm older now, and I forget what my feelings were like, but I guess so. Claire was my childhood sweetheart and I know I loved her. I guess now, that yes, I was in love with Claire McKee. "Definitely? Maybe"…but certainly too young for the "Morning Glory". And we don't need to "Be Here Now" to know that. Looking back, I was probably "Standing on the shoulder of a Giant" at the time.

When I look back at photos of Claire and I, we look so perfect, so similar. We even had identical hair colours and front fringes. Perhaps we look like brother and sister, rather than a couple. But why did I never up dating Claire? Well the truth is, from about 1989 onwards, things changed in many ways. I started to get a lot more occupied with football. It became an obsession. Claire wasn't round as often as before and my parents moved house - not very far but far enough for things to change dramatically. Initially Claire came round a few times to the new house and I went to hers - she lived in Beverley Hills (yes really, quirky Bangor has a Beverley Hills!) - I classed it as the "posh part" of Bangor. I loved the space she had in that house and the garden which backed onto the golf course and the big pink house next door which I nicknamed 'the castle'. Oh, what happened to Claire and I on that damp and lonely Thursday, years ago (with reference to Jarvis Cocker).

"Take me to the magic of the moment on a glory night"
– Scorpions.

But for some reason you could tell the 1980s was over and the new decade brought change. The Berlin Wall came down. Claire and I were not hanging out together anymore (or, ever again) - I was down the park playing football or at the Oval watching Glentoran. We both left Kilmaine Primary School on the same day and went to the separate Grammar Schools in town. Claire got the same grade as me in the "Eleven Plus" exam - we both got a Grade 1 (equivalent of an A grade back then). Claire went to Glenlola Collegiate - the girls school in town, where she studied with future Miss Northern Ireland and Blue Peter Presenter, Zoe Salmon and some of my other classmates from those days including Emma Nicholl (another mini childhood crush of mine – Emma was in my class), Coleen Morrison (now Matovu) and Sarah Quinn (now Bell).

After being rejected by Sullivan Upper School in Holywood (a school once attended by Rory McIlroy), I ended up studying at Bangor Grammar School (a school once attended by Keith Gillespie). I got the highest grade possible in my "Eleven Plus", the highest predictable grade possible, I had two awards for excellence at the school, I had written my own Glentoran football fanzine (with Michael and Gavin McClelland) and even my first travel blog (a diary on a school trip to Netherlands) but I was still rejected by the school in Holywood. A swanky Belfast suburb. Damn! My first failure in life – I didn't get into the Secondary School I had wanted to get into!

I then turned down Regent House Grammar School in my birth town of Newtownards – I am not sure why I turned it down, but I did. Not to worry - my mates were going to Bangor Grammar so I ended up going there. An instant changes your life and this one did. For better or worse, nobody can really tell. Having loved my Primary School, Kilmaine, things were about to change at Bangor Grammar. Bangor Grammar School is an all-boys posh Grammar School. A school which, in the words of my friend Ryan Smith, "took a load of smart people from Kilmaine and Ballyholme; and turned them into wasters". Ryan was right about the school, but as the story develops, you'll find that some of these "wasters" have become successful. Passion always wins. If you have passion for something and work hard at it - there are no limits anymore.

"Can't make head nor tail of passion, oh my love"
– Right Said Fred.

Whatever childhood friendship Claire and I had; it was over in a flash. I remember how everything changed from 1989 to 1991. It was like two different worlds. I had studied maps and geography in my spare time, drawing countries and dreaming of cities I presumed I'd never visit. I felt I was boringly different to others in my class about politics and geography. I felt I knew stupid facts about countries that nobody at school cared about (aged 7 I knew every capital city of every country in the Atlas I had – ask Mum and Dad), but yet I must have lagged behind in other aspects. I couldn't talk politics or geographic capitals with my best friends Magoo or Graham Irwin, my brain was outrageously warped and ironically in my proud Northern Irish nationalism, non-Northern Irish. I watched a lot of political stuff on TV outside Norn Iron. The Berlin Wall, the Wind of Change, the crumbling of the USSR. Perestroika. Glasnost. Rinat Dasaev. John Major. I knew what was happening. I knew of cities and football teams in countries my teachers had never heard of. While my teachers taught me Maslow, Bronte and Shakespeare, I was raving to them about Soviet Union goalkeeper Rinat Dasaev, Luton Town's Kingsley Black and Cyrille Makanaky of Cameroon. I bet you didn't know that Makanaky was born in Douala.

I wanted to backpack through Eastern Europe and the Former Soviet Union as a 9 year old. But I didn't quite understand everything as much as I did my own country. Northern Ireland was always my focus. Day after day we'd hear of deaths, shootings, petrol bombs, car bombs. Bangor didn't suffer as much as the rest of the Province, but I was in and out of Belfast at least once a week visiting Granny and Granda and my many cousins there. We were forced to evacuate shopping centres in Belfast City countless times in the 1980s. Car bombs were frequent. Bombscareless-days didn't exist. You couldn't walk through the city centres at night – they were closed. Ask any 1980s Northern Irish child about this kind of shit. It was normal life.

In a way, I kind of enjoyed it, as at least it was real, it was a real war.

It was honest.

I hate liars and dishonesty and I learnt to hate them more in the years leading up to the release of this book. The IRA used to phone you and tell you they planted the bomb and the UVF would delight that they "claimed responsibility for the shooting last night", fucking hell, a sad and grotesque world, but at least it was real. Slag Northern Ireland off all you want, but there was an honesty in this brutal life. It set me up for my later travels if not for a lifetime of unnecessary terrorist warfare.

I wasn't scared of anything, or anyone. Anymore.

We can all die in an instant – bang! Belfast hardly went a day without a security alert. Northern Ireland was a political war zone under what I always felt was covered up by religious excuses. No religious person in the world will wish death on another person, so how is my country experiencing a religious war? Anyway, much more on Northern Ireland to come but this isn't a book about politics, you should know that. By 1991, East and West Germany had combined, Yugoslavia was now at war, there were new reborn countries such as Latvia and Lithuania emerging from the "wreckage" of the Soviet Union. Rwanda was about to head into a deep period of genocide and unrest. Closer to home, "Maggie" had gone and Johnny Major was the new British Prime Minister. When the 80s disappeared from view, things would never be the same again. And I shed a tear as I knew the decade had faded rapidly into my dreamlike Northern Irish sunset. Cremola Foam would unwillingly slide out of view, too.

"Nothing's gonna stop us now" – Starship.

"Life is a mystery, everyone must stand alone"
– Madonna Ciccone.

"It was the hand of God" – Diego Armando Maradona.

And what about my childhood sweetheart? Since 1991 I have seen Claire McKee just once, yes it's really true. Once in 29 years! She popped in to buy some cheese and salad when I worked in the local shop in Steenson's in Ballyholme in 2002. We said hello, we didn't even have a conversation, she bought her salad and cheese and off she went. It's a strange world sometimes. I don't like to let the past slip away though. I'm a nostalgic sentimental person and I try to keep touch with everyone from my childhood. I've organised a few school reunions and get-togethers in the last few years, on my visits back to my hometown of Bangor. The internet brings us all back together again and I've been in touch with Claire again for a few years via Facebook, as she is important to me. Claire McKee travelled the world too, set up a business, got married and had babies. I kind of relate the Pulp song Disco 2000 to my crush and friendship with Claire back in the 80s:

"Let's all meet up in the year 2000, won't it be strange when
we're all fully grown. I never knew that you'd get married. I
would be living down here on my own…Would you like to meet
me Sunday maybe? You can even bring your baby."
- Jarvis Cocker (Pulp).

Claire and I had great fun. The 80s were a fantastic decade. They were good times. Thanks, Claire. Even if I never see you again, you changed my life completely and without doubt you made me a better man.

Chapter 3
Arconada…Armstrong!

Luis Casanova Football Stadium, Valencia, SPAIN (25th June 1982)

"Gerry Armstrong, what a worker he is" - John Motson, 1982.

The story on Valencia will come at the chapter's end. First up though, we kick things off in Northern Ireland. So, while growing up as a 1980s Northern Irish kid, what did we do? I lived in Marlo, a cool area of Bangor which had enjoyed a major baby boom. There were always kids on the streets. There was always someone to play with and hang around with. Childhood birthdays and Christmases had been kind and a big part of my childhood was playing in the street. Playing football, cycling, skateboarding. The strongest of these is of course football. The people's game. My childhood largely revolved around school, family and football. I like to think I had an equal mix of all three, but in reality, it was the third of those three entities that proved the most vital in my journey around the globe. It was football. It was football. It was twenty two buck eejits kicking a spherical piece of leather around a pitch with the hope of kicking it into a gap made from three rectangular posts, two vertical, one horizontal. Often accompanied, depending on cashflow by a net behind it. Supporters welcome, and we'll come as supporters.

It was obvious where my passion for football came from. My Dad, Joe Blair. Dad got paid to play football back in the 60s and 70s, making a load of appearances for Dunmurry Rec, Construction, Bangor Amateurs and at one point, Crusaders and Distillery (reserve team matches and friendlies for the last brace as my Dad recalls, though nobody can really remember – we can't even check the times of his goals on Facebook or Twitter – do any records even exist?). Aged 17, my Dad starred in a George Wilson Cup Final at the Oval in Belfast. He came onto the field as an early substitute for Crusaders Reserves against Glentoran Seconds in that match, losing 2-1 in front of 10,000 spectators. Attendances for even first team matches in Belfast (in 2019) don't even attract that size of crowd anymore and my first AFC Bournemouth match wouldn't have been attended by more than 8,000 people. Later on, while playing for a Crusaders Select team, my Dad nut-megged Derek Dougan in a match at Seaview in Belfast and got man of the match. The match was a Crusaders Select v. a Northern Ireland Select. So, my Dad actually played against Northern Ireland, getting man of the match in a match that was played behind closed doors!

Yes, my Dad played *against* Northern Ireland.

Things could have been different for my Dad as well, when he represented Northern Ireland Phones Team (while working for BT) in a match against a Manchester Based BT team. Watching the match was Stan Mortensen, then a scout for Manchester City. Stan Mortensen goes down in history as the first ever man to score a goal for England at a World Cup tournament. My Dad took the ball round a couple of players and smacked it against the crossbar from 30 yards. The story goes, after the match Stan Mortensen asked who the wizzkid was, then said to my Dad "If you'd have scored that one son, I'd have signed you". And we're talking Manchester City here. My Dad did get to see Maine Road, but of course returned to Northern Ireland. I still have a paper clipping of a time my Dad scored a hat-trick while playing for Construction, the third "a bullet". My Dad also played for Dunmurry Recreation, 2nd Bangor, Bangor Amateurs and 10th Bangor Old Boys amongst other teams he "forgot the names of". Fans of Dunmurry Rec still cite my Dad as one of the club's best ever players, a fact confirmed during a chat with the lads in Nice, France before the Northern Ireland v. Poland match in June 2016. In 2017, I organised a five a side match in Belfast. Everyone who played was in their 20s or 30s. Except Dad. Dad was 68 at the time and was still the best player on the pitch. I kid you not.

Without my Dad even telling me to like football, I got into it myself and it was obvious from the early 80s that football would play a major part in my life. This book will be unfootballic at times too though, so don't worry your wild pigeons.

At this point though, my Dad (from Ravenhill Road in East Belfast) had already met my Mum, Muriel (a beautiful blue-eyed brunette from Comber), aged 19 at a Christmas Eve Ball in Belfast's Floral Hall in the late 60s. The Beatles were around in those days. Looking back at my Dad's hair styles, I personally see a McCartney-Harrison influence. After living together in a few different places and getting married, my Mum and Dad moved to Bangor and by 1980 were living in Marlo Drive, where I grew up.

There was a significant moment in June 1982 which has inspired and influenced my journeys ever since. That moment came in Valencia in Spain at the 1982 World Cup. I was two years old, and of course there is no way I could have remembered that moment at the time. However, in November 1982 my Dad went to watch Northern Ireland play West Germany at home in Belfast. Karl Heinz Rummenigge, world superstar that he was, was apparently scared of the crowd and was nervous going into the match against my country at Windsor Park. Northern Ireland won the match 1-0 thanks to an Ian Stewart goal. I was lying in bed that night and one of my first ever memories in life, is of my Dad walking in and handing me a programme of the match and telling me that we beat the Germans. I still have that programme with my Dad's handwritten etching of "Stewart 17" on it. Stupidly, I ripped the front cover of the programme off because I was 2 and didn't know better! To put things in perspective - we beat the team that had just been in the World Cup Final (and that would be in the next two World Cup Finals as well!). Just wow!

My Dad also met World Cup hero Pat Jennings in a café in Belfast in the mid-1980s and got me his autograph on a handkerchief. Of course, I don't know where that hankie is now, but I have the memory.

By 1986, my Dad had bought me a Northern Ireland kit and a Mexico 86 scarf, he worked bloody hard to give his children a good life. I also collected Panini stickers and cousin Alison helped me complete my 1986 Panini Sticker Album by "swapping stickers with boys"… "in exchange for sweets and kisses" at Harding Memorial School in the Cregagh, Belfast. It was amazing. Northern Ireland qualified for the World Cup in 1986, drawing with Algeria, losing narrowly to Spain and bowing out in style to a Josimar and Careca inspired-Brazil. I watched all three matches with my Dad and his friends. I remember the first match we watched it on a small black and white TV with Raymond Fitzsimmons and his son Neil. Norman Whiteside was my first hero. He scored the goal and we drew 1-1 in hot conditions with Algeria. We should have won the match, and in the second match we should have got at least a draw with Spain. We lost 2-1 to Spain, and then 3-0 to Brazil but I was hooked. I also completed my entire Mexico 86 sticker album. But there was a sad moment with this - I later lost the album. I looked for it one day and couldn't find it. Around the time of 1990 - 1991 was when I lost it. I was gutted and even cried a bit. I want that album now - it's not the money it's worth. It's the memories. I won't mention it again as it pains me, but if you have it, find it or know where it is, please bring it back to me. Any way you look at it, from the 1986 World Cup onwards, I was now a massive football fan.

I'd play football in the back garden, I'd play in the street, I'd play Subbuteo, I'd play down the park, Linear Park mostly but also at Millbank House. Millbank was owned by Ryan Brown's Dad. Ryan later went on to play for Bangor FC and Northern Ireland Juniors. My mate Michael McClelland set up a team to compete in what we called "The Streets League" where one street (or area) would play against other streets. It wasn't very official. It would be like 4 a side sometimes but it was great fun. We called ourselves Marlo Rangers. David Gherardi and I (who lived behind us) also decided to set up a rival team disguising it as a "Sports Society" encompassing tennis, cricket and rounders into the equation. David and I called it M.S.S. (Marlo Sports Society) and once only we played a match against Marlo Rangers, my ex-team. Of course, the M.S.S. record books cite a 12-11 win for M.S.S. The Marlo Rangers books cite a 12-11 win for Marlo Rangers, so nobody really knows who won. Though my cousin Gary was down from Belfast for the weekend and starred for our team, leaving Michael McClelland to claim we had fielded ineligible players who were not from Marlo! A loophole would show that Gary stayed overnight in Marlo at the time of the match, I can just imagine me saying to Michael "it was a one match loan deal, he's gone back to the Cregagh now". Probably Mike would even laugh about that shit now, or we'd have a "thirty years later penalty shoot-out" to decide the actual winner. That match was the end of the era and probably the last Marlo Rangers match I played in. It happened in 1992, long after I had left Marlo. But those 6 years of football on the streets, football on TV and football at matches were amazingly inspired. Nobody had heard of the internet. Come to think of it, nobody had heard of Marlo Rangers either. But it was a 'real' team and I played for them.

We thought we were all heroes back then. We were just kids playing football down the park, dreaming of playing in an Irish Cup final, an FA Cup Final or a World Cup Final. Aside from this "make believe" streets league, there was real football to be played. I played Boys Brigade football on Saturday mornings for 10th Bangor BB. Managed by Brian Liggett, we had a kit - Maroon shirts and light blue shorts. We were sponsored by Allied Dunbar and we had a decent team. I can still name the team and subs right now! I can even recall some politically incorrect nicknames that somehow seemed acceptable in a 1980s Northern Ireland, yes "black baby":

1. Russell Tollerton (Russ)
2. David Montgomery (Dougal)
3. Paul Ormsby (Ormo)
4. Michael McClelland (Mike)
5. Michael Whitford (Whitty)
6. Keith Freel (Freaky)
7. Jason Patterson (J)
8. Jonny Blair
9. Ricky Armstrong
10. Michael Harte
11. Colin Walker.
Subs: Gary Rainey, Garth McGuigan, Steven Wilson, Jonny Savage (Black Baby).

Actually, it was normally Jonny Savage or Steven Wilson that would be number 8 instead of me and by the mid-90s it was always Gary Rainey. I wasn't very good but this is my book and I want to always be on the team. "Black baby" as a nickname? Don't even ask. Seriously, but you have to remember it was 1990 and things were different then, if not socially acceptable or politically correct. Whatever happened to Jonny Savage? He was our black baby! Darkest Ulsterman on the pitch in those days…yet he was white with a "foreign look". I have one vivid recollection of drawing a match 1-1 on a sunny day and our central defender Dougal scored both goals – an own goal and a 20 yard strike for us! The rest of the early days of that team are a blur.

The Junior Section of that BB had about 100 people in it back in the late 80s and early 90s. It was massive. By 1998, our BB team which now included Peter McIvor (Magoo), Ricky Barr (Barrso), Brian Hutchinson (Bru) and Alan Thompson (Tompo) won the Northern Ireland National BB Cup. It was a high. I set up our third goal and won the corner for our last goal in the final at Loughgall's stadium and we got gold medals in a 4-4 draw. We were the Champions of Northern Ireland, yet we shared it with a Portadown team – they decided against a pelanty (penalty) shoot out after extra time couldn't settle the match.

I'm still quite proud of that – we were national champions, in football, I was aged 18. Nonetheless, apart from a few kick abouts down the park after that and charity games, I hardly played a proper football match again!

But for one match only, I played on the same team as my Dad in a competitive match for 10th Bangor Old Boys team against a Belfast side. It was in February 1999 and I played right back and my Dad played centre back. I cannot remember the score but the match was played at Bloomfield Playing Fields in Bangor. I was 18 at the time and my Dad was 49. **I'm still quite proud that for one match only, my Dad and I played a competitive organised match on the same team together.** I think I missed an open net after he set me up, in the second half when I was pushed up front. As crazy as it sounds, neither my Dad nor I can remember the final score!! But neither of us thinks we lost, and I personally think it was a 2-2 draw and my miss cost us the 3-2 win. I know I missed a sitter and I think Daryl Freel came up to me after and said something like "yer Da woulda stuck thatun away". He was right of course.

So, I was hooked on football and though I played it every week up until I was aged 19, my real passion lay as a supporter and follower of the game. Although I was only 2 years old, I'll link all my football passion back to that night in Valencia in 1982…

The World Cup was in Spain that year and Northern Ireland had defied the odds and qualified for the tournament from a tough group – including Sweden and Portugal – yes we knocked them both out!! Neither country qualified for 1982 because of mighty Northern Ireland! Our best players in those days were Pat Jennings, Martin O'Neill and Gerry Armstrong. Not included in the squad was 36 year old George Best, yet included in the squad was 17 year old uncapped Norman Whiteside. My first hero.

"Most of my mates went to prison. I went to the World Cup" – Norman 'my hero' Whiteside (1982).

At the tournament itself, we had a tough group - Yugoslavia, Spain and Honduras. We started off with a 0-0 draw against Yugoslavia and despite once leading 1-0 against Honduras, we drew 1-1. We were as good as out. Everyone had written us off. Two boring draws and we still had to play the host nation Spain, in Valencia. Yugoslavia were clear favourites to finish second, with Spain expected to walk all over us and win the group. People often ask me if there is a difference between being Northern Irish, Irish or English. I usually tell them: "we don't use the word "can't" in Northern Ireland, we don't like that word, we always find a way to try and do something. And unless it's political, we don't say "no" very often. We hate being ignored and we don't like those who shun or snub us. We're fighters. We abhor defeat and we don't give up. I'm Northern Irish. I won't give in. I won't give up. I'm relentless. I'm not British, I'm not Irish. I'm Northern Irish. And I am a Northern Irish nationalist at that. What's your next question?"

"Gerry Armstrong, what a worker he is" - John Motson.

The newspapers had written the next day's headlines already! Spain were going to whop us! We were going to lose 3-0. 4-0, 5-0, you name it! "Northern Irish bow out proud after 3-0 defeat to hosts" – The Sun (for example). However, at half time it was still 0-0 and we had our fair share of the action. In the 47th minute, our hard working striker Gerry Armstrong intercepts a Spanish pass in the centre of the park. He knocks the ball wide to Billy Hamilton and makes a surge for the penalty area. Billy Hamilton shrugs off Spaniard Tendillo his marker, and crosses the ball ferociously intill the box.

The Spanish goalkeeper Luis Arconada blunders and drops the ball at big Gerry's feet. Northern Ireland's number 9 Gerry Armstrong blasts the ball hard and low into the net, nutmegging a brace of buck-eejit Spanish 'defenders' on the way in. It's the 47th minute and we are 1-0 up away to Spain.

So far - Spain 0-1 Northern Ireland (Armstrong, 47)

Nobody gave us a hope of holding a 1-0 lead when we had a few hundred fans against their thousands, in their home stadium in Valencia, with their Real Madrid and Barcelona superstar players. At one point we had a player from Coleraine FC on the pitch (Felix Healy) and a Linfield FC goalkeeper on the bench (George Dunlop). Our left back Mal Donaghy got sent off and we were hanging on for dear life, playing the rest of the match with 10 players. Spain hounded us for the last half an hour, but the legendary Pat Jennings would let nothing past him in nets. We hung on to a remarkable 1-0 win and Northern Ireland had not just beaten Spain in Spain, we had won the group! We now had two more World Cup matches to play!

Final score - Spain 0-1 Northern Ireland (Armstrong, 47)

And it was that moment, that final whistle, every time I looked back on it, that inspired me. It might be a Northern Irish thing. This small unknown country. But proud, punching above our weight and producing shocks, giving us local world champions and heroes. Of which I had many local heroes. George Best is still widely regarded as the best footballer of all time. He grew up round the corner from where my Granny and Granda lived in the Cregagh Estate in Belfast. In snooker we had Alex Higgins and Dennis Taylor. In music we had Stiff Little Fingers and Van Morrison. In golf these days the likes of Graeme McDowell, Darren Clarke and Rory McIlroy are putting Northern Ireland on the map again. Mark Allen wins at snooker. Jonathan Rea is a Superbike Multiple World champion. Eddie Irvine came within a whisker of winning the 1999 Formula One championship. We punch above our weight in boxing too – pun intended with Carl Frampton and Wayne McCullough flying the flag.

The commentary for Gerry Armstrong's goal that night came from BBC journalist John Motson, whose words *"Arconada... Armstrong!"* have become immortalised by Northern Ireland football fans. In the early 1990s a Northern Ireland football fanzine called *"Arconada...Armstrong!"* emerged. Run by Coleraine and Crewe Alexandra fan David Alcorn. I wrote to David (who used the moniker/acronym Dr. Wa) and asked if I could contribute to the fanzine with articles. From 1995 - 1997 I had my first ever writing gig as a contributor to the fanzine. I also helped sell the fanzine on a few occasions with my friend Michael McClelland outside the matches at Windsor Park in Belfast, before we decided to launch our own Northern Ireland fanzine (Here We Go...Again) as 16 year olds in 1997.

I became an enormously proud Northern Irishman down the years and still get a shiver down my spine when I land back in Belfast or I see a picture of George Best in a bar in some far flung place like Thailand or Uzbekistan. And I'll never ever tire of watching a re-run of Gerry Armstrong's goal against Spain. Never. I could watch it a million times and I still love everything about the goal, the entire move is the work of genius. It was just magical. It kick-started my glorious love affair with the Northern Ireland international football team. A lot of people that follow my stories, do so because they know I'm proud of being Northern Irish. If you meet me, it's likely I'll mention my homeland in the first few sentences of our conversation. I want people to know where I'm from. I'm from Northern Ireland. I'm Northern Irish. I'll never be anything else. I'd never want to be anything else. It sends a shiver of pride down my spine. Every time. I'm Northern Irish.

"Northern Ireland, du du du du du"
– Northern Ireland football fans.

Chapter 4
My First Backpacking Adventure

Italia 90 (on TV) and NETHERLANDS (1990 - 1991)

"The flag stays down and the ball goes in"- A football commentator reporting on Costa Rica's goal against Scotland in the 1990 World Cup.

Despite the fact that Northern Ireland didn't qualify, World Cup Italia 90 enthused me just as much as Mexico 86. I was now older, wiser and about to head into my final year at Primary School. We did this thing called the "Eleven Plus" which is an exam in Northern Ireland that determines what secondary school you will go to. I loved Kilmaine Primary School though and didn't really want to leave. My final 18 months in the school featured three key turning points in my life. These were huge so let's bullet point them:

1. One was watching almost every match of Italia 90 on television.
2. Two was attending my first ever live Northern Ireland football match.
3. Three was my first ever backpacking adventure without my parents.

Yes, the third in that hat-trick is probably the premier catalyst as to why I backpacked the world and one reason as to why this book exists, but the other two sure played their integral parts in my journey.

Aged 11, I went backpacking to the Netherlands. In April 1991, I headed on my first ever travel journey without my parents as I went on a school trip. I decided I would take a camera on the trip (some of the photos have sadly, obviously since been lost). I also decided I would collect leaflets, make notes in a notebook and write a travel blog on the entire trip. It wasn't known as a travel blog in those pre-internet days of course. It was simply a travel diary. It was all hand written and I later typed the entire book up almost word for word from the way it was back then and released it in the early months of 2015 as a mini e-Book. It's not meant to be a guide to backpacking the Netherlands. I'm no expert now, nor was I back in 1991. It was simply a written document of my personal journey to the Netherlands. In fact, that is what all my travel stories are - documents of my personal journey around the world. So, this chapter was partly written by an eleven year old, and some of the chapter was written in 1991, which means this book is a 29 year work in progress. It really took me 29 years to release this book, I started it in 1991 making this the oldest chapter in the book.

As chapter 2 (and probably a load of other chapters too) mentioned, I attended Kilmaine Primary School in Bangor, Northern Ireland. Kilmaine Primary School organised a trip abroad to the Netherlands for pupils and I told my Mum and Dad about it and I was very keen to go. However, at the time the trips were immensely popular and of course over-subscribed, so those who got chosen for the trip were drawn out of a hat, completely at random. I was delighted and lucky that my name came out of the hat and I was heading to the Netherlands. It was a twist of fate that for sure has changed my destiny in life. Whoever drew my name out of that hat, thanks!

I had been on family holidays abroad before, to England, Republic of Ireland, Scotland, Wales, France, Greece and Portugal. They were with my parents, my brother and sister (except Portugal was just Mum, Dad and I). But this was a step into the unknown for me. A brand new exciting adventure. Heading off on my own (well with the school) but without my parents. I was getting out to see the world, having turned 11 years old less than a month before the trip. As you can imagine, I was highly enthusiastic and buoyant at that age.

Also from my P7 class Mr. Rea's, there were 7 other students on the trip - Magoo (Peter McIvor), Bru (Brian Hutchinson), Simon Milligan (a bit of a wanker who bullied me and thought he was hard), Klins (Colin Davidson), Chrissy Bower, Louise Smith (both of whom later worked with me in Tesco Springhill) and Wendy Irvine. Plus, our teacher Mr. Billy Rea would be there. There were students from the other five P7 classes too, but I can't remember who they were. It was a long time ago. Incidentally Magoo and Bru were two of the players in our team the day we won the Northern Ireland BB Cup, some 7 years later, 3 of us had been in the same room on the same trip!

The trip would take place the last week in April and first week in May 1991. I remember this for three main reasons:

1. My Dad's birthday is the 30th April and it would be the first time I had missed being with him on that day in my life.
2. Northern Ireland were playing the Faroe Islands on the 1st May in a football match and I would miss the match, the first home match that season that I had missed (and I only missed a whoppaday further 3 matches at home in the next eighteen years! True bill!).
3. Kilmaine Primary School had got into the final of the Northern Ireland Primary Schools Radio Competition, "Put Away Your Books". I was on standby for the team, knowing that two others were heading to the Netherlands and I may have made the team that day had I been in Northern Ireland. But alas it was probably better that I headed on an adventure. (Plus, Kilmaine won the competition in my absence anyway).

So, we were all set for the mega trip. Passports, backpacks all ready to go and I was off. As an 11 year old, going on a journey like that is unforgettable. It is something that lingers forever and I often think how lucky I was to get chosen, and how grateful I am that my parents could afford to send me on the trip. I also pondered that if I hadn't gone on that trip, would I still have the same desire to travel effortlessly and endlessly the way I currently do? Nobody really can ever tell. But I stand by the fact that it was a catalyst for my obsession for travel and having independence and freedom from my parents for a while was such a positive thing while growing up in a war drenched society. Something felt like freedom here as I munched a chunk of Dutch cheese.

As far as the trip was concerned, it was a five day journey. We would fly from Aldergrove International Airport in Belfast to Schipol International Airport in Amsterdam in the Netherlands and back the same way. We stayed at the Deinstuif Hotel in Noordwijk and had full tours and buses organised for us where we visited Edam, Delft, Volendam and Amsterdam as well as some other locations in the Netherlands.

It was my first experience of hostel dorms as well - the six boys, we all shared a room, which had 3 sets of bunk beds and a window. I remember being on one of the top bunks. I was in Room 9 which I wrote down in my diary at the time, so hopefully someday I can go back to Deinstuif and see if the room which kick started a crazy wanderlust still exists. This chapter is a reproduction in its entirety of my first ever travel blog diary entry, lifted directly from the hand-written notes from the 1991 book. This is my day by day travel diary of that wonderful first journey to the Netherlands in 1991 that somehow set me off on a boundless journey to explore the planet. Please note that I sometimes refer to the country as "Holland" back then, before I was fully aware of the geography and politics involved. These days of course I am aware that Holland is not entirely synonymous with The Netherlands. In diary form here goes, the oldest chapter in this book, all written in 1991 as an 11 year old:

Sunday 28th April 1991
I got packed for going to Holland. Clothes, games, pens etc.

Monday 29th April 1991
We went over on the plane to Holland and there was a double decker bus with two TVs in it. We took around half an hour getting to Deinstuif and all the Dutch buildings were lit up. When we got to the hotel, we had supper and I got put in Room 9 with Brian, Peter, Chris, Colin and Simon. I went to sleep around a quarter past one and woke up at 5:52 a.m.

Tuesday 30th April 1991
We went on the bus to a flower garden on the Queen Beatrix's birthday. We then went to the cheese factory and guess what? I saw

a hill! We had our lunch before going into a town called Volendam. A shop we went into had an upstairs full of cigarette wrappers. Usually it would be roughly 4 Gilders to get into but as it was the Queen's birthday we got in free. It had over 6 million wrappers. Then we went to see how to make cloggs. We went back for tea. After, we went to go to the pool but it was closed so we went into Nordwijk and came back home then went to bed. The flower garden was called Franz Rosen Bulbfields.

Wednesday 1st May 1991
We got up and went to a miniature town called Madurodam. It had small buildings and planes and boats. Then we went shopping in Nordwijk and we went back for tea. Afterwards we went ten pin bowling then swimming before coming back to Deinstuif for supper.

Thursday 2nd May 1991
We got up and went to Amsterdam. First we went on a boat on a canal for about 50 minutes then we went to Anne Frank's House. We had lunch and then went to crazy golf and trampolines then came back and went to bed.

Friday 3rd May 1991
We got packed for going home and set off for the candle factory. We made our own candles which took about half an hour then went to Delft pottery and watched the man showing us how it is made. We had our lunch shortly after then we went to Schipol Airport and returned to Aldergrove Airport at roughly 17.00 hours.

It was such an inspiring trip. It must have been cool to see all these places as an 11 year old and we covered a lot of textbook Dutch attractions in five busy days. My memory seems to tell me that we only saw the entrance to the Madame Tussauds centre and didn't go inside, but I could be wrong. I also remember that we went swimming but perhaps it wasn't at Duinrell. I have jotted down some memories of the trip here in the next few paragraphs.

Colin Davidson in our class was 11 years old at the time, and the Home Alone films were popular back then. Colin looked remarkably similar to US child film actor Macaulay Culkin, star of Home Alone. During our time at Madurodam, a group of Chinese or Japanese tourists crowded round Colin begging for a photo with him and he obliged. They thought he was Macaulay Culkin! It was hilarious and makes me think about the stories that I write about my travels (losing $1000 in the river in Laos, doing a sh*t in a broccoli field in Tasmania, feeding hyenas at dusk in Ethiopia, showing my ass in a PR office in London). This story back in the Netherlands set the standard - every trip I've been on since had similar totally hilarious spontaneous moments. Colin milked the success of course and later earned the nickname "Klins" as he once had long hair and looked like German footballer Jurgen Klinsmann. In such a case, Colin probably could have made a career out of being celebrity lookalikes. Macaulay Culkin, Jurgen Klinsmann! I studied with Colin at Bangor Grammar School too and last spoke to him at Colin Walker's 18th Birthday party in 1998. To this day, I don't think any of us know whether the Asian tourists genuinely thought Colin Davidson was the real Macaulay Culkin, or they just wanted a photo because they could pretend to their mates that it was him. At any rate, it was a talking point and we were all in stitches.

On the Wednesday night Northern Ireland were due to play the Faroe Islands at Windsor Park in Belfast. One of the only upsetting things for me with this trip was that it coincided with the match and it was the first time in my life I'd face a scenario where I couldn't be in two places I wanted at the same time. I wanted to be Superman. On that night, I kept asking the teachers for the final score and they couldn't find out for me. There was no internet in those days and the TVs were all Dutch TV so the only way we could have found out would have been to have phoned home. I don't remember seeing any phones. The next morning over breakfast, they showed highlights of the England v. Turkey match, where England won 1-0 with a Dennis Wise goal. It then showed all the results and listed Northern Ireland as having drawn 1-1 at home to the Faroe Islands. I knew it was not true. We were expected to win by 3 or 4-0 so I didn't believe the score. I thought it was a mis-type or a joke, really! When I arrived back in Belfast, Mum and Dad had the newspaper for me (Belfast Telegraph) which did indeed show that Northern Ireland surprisingly did draw 1-1 at home to the Faroe Islands. They had also taped the highlights for me from BBC coverage.

It was a busy five days for sure and I remember thinking how cool it was that you could visit a flower garden in the morning, have lunch in a new town, then visit another town and go swimming in a different town before dusk. All on the same day. I loved the sheer diversity of it and without a doubt I was smitten with a lifestyle of unpredictable days. It took me a while in life to get to the stage where I have complete freedom to do what I want every day, but it all began in 1991 on this trip to the Netherlands.

We also visited a toy shop. In there I bought a football magazine, some presents for my family and a pair of Dutch football wristbands which I still have.

We also visited a candle factory where I made my own candles, two of them, and I brought them back to my family as a present. I have no idea where they ended up. Separately I also had an ice cream candle made of wax which had a real edible wafer on it. A few months later, we had a mouse in our house in Northern Ireland and the mouse ate the wafer and so I had to throw the wax candle into the bin after that!

In the town of Volendam there was a football stadium and myself and a few of the guys walked along to the outside of it as it was near our bus. I bought an FC Volendam football pennant in the club shop which my Dad still has somewhere.

We ate a lot of cheese and crackers and sandwiches on the buses.

I cannot find my full book of photos from the trip. I think I gave the photos as part of an album I left in Weston Super Mare when dating Liz Carter in 2007. Unfortunately, Liz wasn't a kind girl and she refused to give me the album back and I lost some of those photos forever. I must have taken either 24 or 48 photos on that trip, as camera films back then had 24 exposures. I included some of them in the travel blog book in 1991 (such as the page on Madurodam), and found some others, but the rest could be in a box somewhere or lost via Liz. I really hope someday I can find all the photos from this trip. If Liz is reading and still has that album – please return it – it's so sentimental to me. You weren't kind to me and you know it.

Back in 1991 on the trip, I grew in knowledge too – I became aware of the difference between Holland and the Netherlands and used both terms interchangeably in my articles. However, I cannot remember if we stayed in Holland only during the trip, or if we visited other regions of the Netherlands.

We visited a sweet shop one night and I bought a packet of local sweets, some of the sweets were like bits of wood which I was told Dutch people chew on them. It really happened but I don't remember anything else other than I didn't like them, or chewing wood. On my two trips back to the Netherlands since, I never saw this wood product again.

In the lads dorm there were six of us. Each night we would chat before bed, after dinner, some banter and having a shower. It was an introduction to dorm life. One night we got talking about what girls each of us fancied from our P7 class. I remember Magoo (Peter McIvor) went for Gemma Wilson and I picked Emma Nicholl. I can't remember who the other guys liked. Claire McKee, despite being my childhood sweetheart was never actually in my class. Just as well, as you can guarantee I'd have kissed her during a sweaty P.E. lesson or showed her my willy "by mistake" as we enjoyed our "milk break".

At the time I owned a "shell suit" and so did lots of the other pupils on the trip. It must have been in fashion back then.

After that trip in 1991, I thought nothing more about it, went to a different school and later headed off on my journey. I never visited the Netherlands again. Until January 2014 that was. It was then that I made a return to Amsterdam, and again in July 2016.

Having read over my travel blog from 1991 I was intrigued by it completely and I then compared it to my second visit to the Netherlands which incredibly wasn't until January 2014. Here are a few final thoughts from my second visit to Amsterdam.

On my return to Amsterdam in January 2014, I did a tour of the city with Sandeman's New Europe and stayed in a cool Irish Pub and Hostel called Durty Nelly's. On this occasion I was travelling alone, I was 33 years old, exactly three times older than back in 1991.

I found that the only thing that had really changed was my age. I was still immersed in the pure joys of travel. But this time I loved exploring Amsterdam as an adult and did the things that I wouldn't have done or been able to do back in 1991. I visited a microbrewery, I smoked some cannabis in Hunter's, I visited the Sex Museums, I tried Space Cake, I walked through the famous Red Light district, I visited the world's oldest condom shop, I went on a pub crawl. I loved it. I also visited the Amsterdam Arena, home of Ajax Amsterdam the football team. On the walking tour of the city we got to Anne Frank's House and everything had changed. This was an emotional moment on my travel journey.

In January 2014, Anne Frank's House wasn't as I had remembered it. The magic and beauty of my first visit had passed Amsterdam by. Anne Frank's House had a huge queue outside it, there were tourists everywhere. There was a coffee shop and a souvenir shop, and the entire building had become very commercial. I decided not to join the queue and go inside. I couldn't do it. I was content with my 11 year old memory of my marvellous visit to Anne Frank's House. With no long queues, my school friends and the building in its original state without any touristy add ons. I felt a bit sad that it had changed and life had moved on here in Amsterdam. Other than that, I loved the fact I was back as an adult and reminisced over some beer and cheese in the bars by the canals in the Red Light District.

My trip to Amsterdam in 2014 was also a secret trip. I hadn't told my parents or friends about it as I had been backpacking in Iraqi Kurdistan just before this and had told my Mum I would head back to Hong Kong. I wanted to surprise her as I hadn't been back to Northern Ireland for two years at that point. I also didn't publicise the visit on my website. It was an emotional one. Life had truly gone full circle for me, again as I walked unknowingly through my Mum's door to surprise her.

But it all started with that school trip to the Netherlands in 1991, that was my first trip away from Northern Ireland without Mum and Dad. But it was only thanks to them that I did it.

[Chapters 5, 6 and 7 Prelude to the Bangor Grammar School Trilogy]

"For tonight and every night, you're a superstar" – Love Inc.

Before I launch into Chapters 5, 6 and 7, I have something to say. This trilogy, these three chapters are about my life at Bangor Grammar School from 1991 – 1997. I didn't enjoy the school at the time. In fact, I hated it and wasn't really a happy teenager. However, since those days at Bangor Grammar School, I have become more at ease with my past and have also been approached by the school to contribute an article on my travels to their 2016 – 2017 School Magazine, The Grammarian. Which I gladly did and am proud of. I was delighted they got back in touch and **I no longer hold grudges.** I repeat, I don't have a problem anymore with Bangor Grammar School, but as a teenager, I didn't like it. That's the hard truth and these chapters are brutal.

There are no hard feelings anymore from myself towards the school or its teachers, so the next three chapters, you can take with a pinch of salt and with the mind of an angry teenager. But remember, I am honest. It was all teenage angst, but those things really happened at the school and I didn't really like my time there. For the sake of the book and the fact they are good stories from my life, I have kept it all in here and have been a tad harsh. I did consider deleting "Chapter 7: The OXI one", but this is my life and this is what I did. Without further ado, onto Chapter 5, arguably my favourite story from my journey so far, the Paddy Campbell inspired "The Great Exam Heist". We're a long time dead.

Chapter 5
The Great Exam Heist

Bangor Grammar School, NORTHERN IRELAND (16th May 1994)

"I, I sometimes lose myself in me, I lose track of time and I can't see the woods for the trees; you set them alight. Burn the

bridges as you've gone, I'm too weak to fight ya. I've got my personal hell to deal with" – Peter Cunnah.

Paddy Campbell and I sang along to it instead of doing an English project - the D:Ream song "Things Can Only Get Better" - that's how mature we were in a 1994 Northern Ireland. We played Fantasy Football in our notebooks instead of doing our science homework and we generally hated school teachers. Ironic that I later became one.

"Karma chameleon, you come and go. You come and go"
– Culture Club.

While I **loved** my time at Kilmaine Primary School, I **hated** my time at Bangor Grammar School.

My two major schooling experiences in life were polar opposites. There's a certain sense of what goes around, comes around. If you want my honest opinion, at the time, the school was a pretentious sh*thole. They still taught Latin (in a post-Berlin Wall break up, I'd have loved Polish, Russian, Serbian or German in First Form); they forced us to play rugby; football was not allowed in P.E. (Physical Education) or the stupidly named 'Games'; and you couldn't even eat an apple in a school corridor (I'm serious). As I backpacked through several ex-Soviet Union states in my adult life, I couldn't help but compare those in charge of Bangor Grammar to failed totalitarian extremists and dictators. At least there were no murders at the school, nor did we have to put up with communist propaganda. But Tommy Patton, the headmaster during my entire time at the school, it wouldn't have surprised me if we were forced to bow down to him every morning in front of a painting of the man himself.

I started Bangor Grammar School in September 1991. It was all change. My parents had moved house, further out of town, I lost touch with Claire McKee. I had a new best friend in the neighbourhood, Peter Bell. I had new friends in school. But somehow as an 11 year old, I conjured up evil thoughts in my mind about the school and its ways. I just didn't like the school from day one. First Form passed by uneventfully. I was in the class 1Y. I used to write it as *One Why?* in my school books and got told off for it. I refused to play rugby a few times, got put in detention too often and had a few new friends - Michael Whitford (Whitty), Michael Robinson (Snowball) and David Gherardi (who for some reason developed peculiar nicknames - we called him "Housey" for a while, then "Gherardhman" (with that strange spelling) and even "Dave" which never suited him).

Second Form saw a new kid in our class - Paddy Campbell replaced Stuart Leathem (who went to Sullivan in Holywood). It was a straight swap, long before the Bosman rule came into play. Our class was 2Y. I knew Paddy already though – it was to be another crazy twist. Back in the 1980s Paddy Campbell and I, you see, we were in hospital together. We both had eye operations and were in adjacent beds in Newtownards Hospital during the 1980s!! I used to tell people about my "mate in hospital called Patrick" and they didn't believe the story was true. You don't go to hospital to make friends, they thought I was crazy. I was. But so was Patrick. Paddy and I went to completely different schools though and after hospital I didn't see him again. Until 1992, when a new pupil walks into our 2Y class at Bangor Grammar School. A guy called Patrick Campbell. A guy that looked like he knew how to have a laugh but still cool enough to wear red glasses in Northern Ireland and get away with it. Bullying and name calling in Northern Ireland is sadly part of the childhood culture and upbringing. If you don't have thick skin, you might end up with no skin at all. Harsh, and not even fair. Paddy had red glasses and looked like a "geek".

But he wasn't.

You should never judge a cover by what's in the book. After a few weeks of getting to know Paddy, he became one of the popular dudes in the class. Class 2Y. A class oozing personality and talent incidentally - I know of people from our class who went on to big things – one became a millionaire, one a local business owner, one a global traveller, one a successful playwright, one a serial marathon runner and one a musician. Dougie Gordon broke records in the marathon world – he completed all the world major marathons with aplomb and is the most marathonic Ulsterman you will ever meet. Stuarty Leathem recorded a song for a Queen and Freddie Mercury Tribute album. One of the lads owns a big business in the United Arab Emirates. Scott Callen toured the world, working in numerous jobs and then set up a popular business back in Bangor. Paddy Campbell became a successful playwright. Michael Whitford promoted cancer charities, cancer awareness and wrote about trying to beat cancer. Michael Whitford is a hero to many of us – he died in 2016 after his long battle with cancer. A man of pure strength and a true gentleman. Respect to Whitty. A West Ham United, Glentoran and Northern Ireland fan, who I went to many a football match with, spanning three decades. Rest in peace, our Y-class hero.

Class 2Y was the best the school had, but they were too blind to see it. Passing us off as a disruptive set of immature lads and at one point we were told we were the worst class in the history of the school. It's funny that, at the exact same time, I came to the very opposite conclusion. We were the best they had. And similarly to Soviet dictatorships, the smart and cool crowd needed to be silenced. Oddly, most of the stuff in this chapter was told 20 years later. Perhaps some personal inspiration from my backpacking travels through every ex-USSR state which concluded with the totalitarian statelet of Turkmenistan.

Twenty years too late, back in 2014, I presented readers of my travel blog with a story – *"The Day My Best School Buddy Nicked The Exam Paper (And Got Expelled)"*, a story more commonly referred to as *"The Great Exam Heist"*, a phrase coined by the story's brainchild and full-time genius, Paddy Campbell himself.

Paddy named this chapter. It's his prodigy at work here.

This is a day that goes down in history as a defining moment in my childhood and teenage years. It is a significant moment that shaped my life and changed it forever. For better or worse? I'm completely convinced it was the former. On the 20 year anniversary of "The Great Exam Heist" I felt it was finally right to tell what really happened in May 1994 through my eyes, in form 3Y at Bangor Grammar School in Northern Ireland. The story goes, and everybody knows that Paddy Campbell - a smart, popular and crazy lad in our 3rd form class didn't make it into 4th form at Bangor Grammar. Nor was he allowed to sit all of his 3rd form exams, which at the time were important. Though trying to convince us all of that back then would have taken some doing.

"You'll never change what's been and gone" – Oasis.

I kept the story to myself for 20 years until I published it live on "Don't Stop Living" on the exact day 20 years on. This is what I wrote, fired up, sentimental and longing to meet my friend again, I've added some extra stuff in for the book though and removed the meaningless drivel that I concocted for the blog. I have met up with Scott Callen and Paddy Campbell since I published this story and they both admitted that the way I told it, is different from how they remembered it. I really don't know anymore. But this is the story as I told it and what rings true in my brain. I was 14 and trying to grow up.

Mum, Dad - yes this is what happened and I'm telling it now and I'm happy to tell it and I've moved on. It doesn't make me a bad person to tell this. We all make mistakes and we all learn from them. I was 14. But then again, was it all a mistake? Is it wrong to do something wrong? Was this the right thing to do? Is this why I later became depressed aged 36? Was it a 22 year late karma for me?

"An expert is a person who has made all the mistakes that can be made in a very narrow field" - Niels Bohr.

When you keep secrets for this long, a cloud hangs on your shoulder as it does for me on my self-titled "Paddy Campbell Day" every year (May 16th incidentally - the same date that I published the story twenty years on). There are many sides to this story, so this is mine. Ask the others for theirs.

"It's no secret because you told everybody" - Kylie Minogue.

"You can have it all if you like" – Stereophonics.

It's May 1994.

Paddy and I were good mates at the time – in fact I'd say that in 1993-1994 we were best mates at school. We never really met outside of school but as the 1994 World Cup approached we planned a big meet up to watch the opening game together, hang out away from school and also head down to the beach in Bangor to "get some girls" and have a few illegal tins of beer when the sun reared its head on this beach resort in Northern Ireland. We were both 14 – he was a month older than me. However, an event that occurred in May 1994 meant that Paddy and I would cease to be in touch, we wouldn't be friends again, we wouldn't watch the World Cup together and after 1994, Paddy and I would only meet once more in the next twenty years, for about one minute at a bus stop in

1997. From being best mates, we didn't keep touch. This chapter explains why.

"Man you should have seen us on the way to Venus, walking on the Milky Way" – OMD.

Before I start, this story is a sensitive issue for some and some names have been protected. But you know what, I don't really care anymore - I'm telling it now as I want to. I also must say that not all of this chapter can be 100% true - most of this shit actually happened but we were 14, we were young. I can't remember every detail. So please forgive the memory - this was over two decades ago so not all of the story can be remembered, but I've done my best.

"When I was younger, so much younger than today, I never needed anybody's help in any way" - The Beatles.

Paddy Campbell and I at school - The Unlikely Lads
Paddy and I weren't the best students behaviour wise. Academically I reckon we did well, but we messed around too much. We were teenagers having a laugh. We played fantasy football league during lessons and we had ridiculous competitions about funny stuff we could do. In one lesson Paddy had to say the word "trapezium" 100 times during a lesson in a gay accent ("Oh matron!"). He did it. In another lesson I would sit at the back of class with a box of pencils and make a pencil tower. We threw books from Bummer's English class into a strategically positioned bin outside the window. We'd then hoke in the bin after the lesson and count who put the most books in it. To see what we could get away with. For what reason we did all this shit, neither of us would ever know. We weren't very mature, but we did have fun. And thanks to Paddy, we knew what a trapezium was. Paddy was a genius.

"Trapezium" - Paddy Campbell, 1993.

<u>Third Form End of Year Exams, 1994</u>
In third form you do end of year exams, aged 14 – these were during May and June 1994. I never put education first though as you may have read before, but these exams would determine your groups for the next 2 years of Secondary School, with the higher graded students getting placed in higher level classes for the next two years. It wasn't actually a big thing you know, but I had my eye on getting into one of the top 2 classes out of the 6 available. I just liked the idea of doing that in a school that tried to diss so many of us. I gathered from an early age that prestige and the honour of being there was more important than how you got there (a theory that I stand by, to this day). i.e. If Einstein is the best physicist of all time, we all applaud that fact and ignore the journey that took him there. I wanted the prestige. Same goes for the story about Wimbledon FC winning the FA Cup in 1988, when 5 years earlier they were in the 4th division and 10 years earlier they were non-league. All people look at is the facts - in 1988 Wimbledon won the FA Cup. In 2004 Greece won the European Championships. In 1994 Jonny Blair was in one of the top 2 academic classes at Bangor Grammar School to study his GCSEs. It's the fact, not the journey.

"If you want more, scream it out louder" – Usher.

Even though I hated the school, academically I didn't do too badly in exams etc. I was good enough at English, French and Geography to get into the top 2 classes. I was let down by Science and History. I remember telling one of my history teachers "I'd rather study a subject called 'Present' than worry about the past!" (Mr. Mackie). Alas I was 13 at the time, and wrong. History is important as it forms the reasoning behind the present. I had to look back to find that out. I always wondered why Norman had so many castles, wasn't that a bit greedy? Away from school though, I knew a hell

of a lot about Soviet Union history and the recent break up of
the USSR.

"We're here because we're here"
- Northern Ireland football fans.

I digressed there, so back on topic - as you might have guessed
from this chapter's title, *we decided to steal an exam paper, Paddy
Campbell and I!!* Yes baby!

How to pinch a 3rd form History Exam Paper
It's a three step process my friends, it worked for us and it could
work for you too. I concocted the idea myself, before deciding to
confide in my best mate at school – Paddy Campbell. I made it
look like we both wanted to steal the exam paper somehow but the
reality is - the event didn't happen by chance - I planned the whole
thing. I told Paddy – "Paddy, let's nick the 3rd form history exam
paper and get decent grades." "How the hell do you plan to do
that?" Paddy said. "I have the plan", I said.

So, I told him my three steps. I made it sound easy and we
executed it to perfection. I needed an ally; Paddy was the ally.
What I didn't know was that he would become the scapegoat. That
was never the plan.

Three Easy Steps to Stealing a 3rd Form Exam Paper in 1994 in
Bangor Grammar School:

1. Find out which history teacher at the school is compiling the
    exam paper (we were told in advance it would be compiled by
    ONE teacher only)
2. Go to their classroom when they're not in it and find it.
3. Pinch it.

That was "Plan B" in fact. Over the next week, by chance I told Paddy of a "Plan A" which crept up by chance. During the next history lesson, I asked our teacher "which teacher will be making the history paper this year?" They told me – "Mr. Jones". We knew him as Jonesy and strangely in May 1993 my Dad had played football with him in Newtownards. Here, in 1994, for 2 lessons a week we would be in Jonesy's room for a period - I think it was Room 103 or 102. Even better Jonesy wouldn't be in the room, but his files and materials probably, and hopefully would still be. Already, we had got past step 1 and had a chance of making it to the next round. Next step was when we next had a period in Jonesy's room, Paddy and I went in early to scrummage for it. I can't remember how we did this – but we did – just two of us went in early, took the two seats at the front of the classroom right in front of his desk. It would look suspicious 1 of us going in on our own, but not two. Before the next teacher came in we had checked all the files and drawers and there it was - holy shit!

I found the exam paper.

I found it.

We had to confirm this was it though. I got Paddy to double check. But one thing we didn't do was nick it straight away. By this time, the other classmates were in the lesson, as was our teacher (not Jonesy – our lesson was in Jonesy's room but with another teacher). During the lesson I wrote on a piece of paper to Paddy – "nick it". The only reason I can give for not nicking it myself was that out of the two of us, Paddy was less likely to be caught. I was more vulnerable. I wasn't being selfish getting him to do it - I had the balls to nick it too, but we felt he was the safe bet and Paddy was a lot more nuts than me. He was particularly buzzing that day I recall. Failure or getting caught wasn't even on our minds. We were totally fired up. The lesson finished and Paddy nicked the paper. Job done. Step 3 complete and job done nice and easy. Only one problem – Jonesy would be back in his room and probably looking for the exam paper so we had to either:

1. Memorise the questions
2. Write out the questions
3. Photocopy it

There were probably other options but these were the 3 we came up with in the heat of the moment. We decided to bunk off the next lesson, run to Bangor Library on Hamilton Road (a 5 minute walk), photocopy the shebang and return it to where we found it – Jonesy's files. We racked up the 60 pence and got it photocopied. Buzzing at this point. That's right - two 14 year olds frantically buzzing at the theft of a nothing exam paper for a something exam at a nothing school. But you live in the here and now and yes we were buzzing. Like we were heroes.

"Teenage angst has paid off well, now I'm bored and old"
- Kurt Cobain.

Oh yeah my 3 step plan was cool and all but I forgot there was a Step 4 – returning the exam paper to the exact place we found it in, to make it look like nobody had nicked it. Because Paddy had nicked it, it was now obviously on my shoulders to return it. I had told him to nick it, and we were in on this together, so it was only fair that I should return it. The pressure was back on me. I came up with a plan – I had a friend (Magoo) who I knew had a lesson in that room just after and I'd go up and wait till their class came out, hopefully the teacher would too and I'd run in and return it as if I was part of that class or lesson. If the teacher came in and knew I wasn't and I was stopped, I'd say I thought I left my book in there during the earlier history lesson. Hardly rocket science but we were 14. It worked a treat. I placed the exam paper in the precise slot I found it in. I ran down to tell Paddy, we high five-d each other and we now had to make an agreement – neither of us would grass the other one up. We now had a copy each of the exam paper. Paddy nicked the paper, but it was my idea, although we were both in on it. We were 50-50 so far, though the reality and (forgive the irony) the history books tell you the entire event was my idea. Concocted from an evil mind against a school I had no time for.

"I fought the law and the law won" - The Clash.

Why Did I Not Just Revise Harder to get a good grade?
Because that's boring. And uninspiring. I didn't particularly like history at school and rarely read my history books outside lesson time. Geography and English – yes. Plus, in the mind of a 14 year old in a troubled Northern Ireland the thought of stealing an exam paper was like an incentive or an act of rebellion. I buzzed off the dangers of it and knew my sidekick Paddy would too. Now, at this point in the story, two of us had a copy of the third form history paper. Yeah we nicked it. This was "The Great Exam Heist".

"You and me, we're history" - Richard Ashcroft.

Then there was the "Business Plan"
Sat at our desks in third form history one day and Paddy and I no longer needed to listen to the lessons. We'd eliminated the need for it. We'd be able to get good grades easily as we knew the exam questions on the paper already. Fantasy football time. We'd sit and play cards. So, I came up with a plan – change Jonesy's exam paper into our own handwriting, photocopy it and sell them to other selected students in our year. We couldn't hand out photocopies as it was because, if caught they would know we nicked it - as it was an exact copy of Jonesy's papers with his writing on it. Plus, in those days none of us had computers and couldn't type it up or print it – my parents had a typewriter at home and an Amstrad monitor and printer but it would arouse too much suspicion. So, one of us had to rewrite it by hand, so that if anyone did report us, the actual page that they had would look like just one

of our own handwritten exam notes, we certainly weren't going to write "Exclusive! Nicked 3rd Form Exam Paper - your ticket to freedom!" on it. Putting it in our own handwriting was dangerous ground of course as if grassed up, and somehow they proved we had access to the paper, we could be suspended or expelled. But we didn't think of that. We buzzed off it. We hand-picked a selection of students in each class who we thought "won't grass us up".

"My baby's got a secret" – Madonna.

How to Make Money by Selling a Stolen Exam Paper
We'd charge 3 quid for the privilege of a copy of the paper, pocketing a massive £1.50 each and secretly gave the buyer a copy of the questions. But we couldn't exactly "advertise this"! Imagine the news "Hey Jonesy did you see the advert in the paper from Paddy Campbell and Jonny Blair selling your exam paper?". But we asked a few others to buy it. This was a stupid business plan that clearly went wrong. We had to stop selling the paper after about 10 students had a copy. If any more students got it, word would spread too easily. We confided in Scott Callen first off, and of course we didn't charge him - a good mate of mine through Primary and Secondary School, Scott loved it, buzzed off it too and we closed the box within a few days. Willy Dallas and Craig Lemon were also in on it. Dougie too and one who asked not to be mentioned. There were four or five others, one of whom must have been the "grass". I would say only about 10 of us knew about the stolen paper.

As good a "business idea" as it was, we decided we didn't want the money anymore – we just wanted the good grades. I wanted myself, Paddy and Scott to get good grades. We'd saved revision time and in essence created our own "4 hour work week" philosophy, aged 14. The whole thing was pretty cool at the time. It made me happy that we were rebelling against a school we just didn't like. My parents seemed to think the school was good, but of course they didn't see it from the inside like we did. We exposed a weakness.

"You gotta fight for your right to party" - Beastie Boys.

But the box wasn't totally closed. One day Scott said to me "are you sure this is the exam paper? because student "x" also now wants a copy". This was the last copy we gave out. Student "x" got a copy and paid up. I never revealed before who had copies of the stolen exam paper and actually I'll be honest - I can't remember all the students we sold them to but I think Nidge (Neil Young), Dougie Gordon, Colin Walker, Rick Willis, Ryan Smith, Lurgan Traffic (name changed), McKitts (Neil McKittrick), Wulldog McIntyre (name changed) and Tompo (Alan Thompson) all got copies. Paddy and I had fun the next 2 weeks – building up to the 1994 World Cup we had some footie mags and stickers. Paddy and I agreed to watch Germany v. Bolivia together – the opening match and we both banked on Milton Melgar for first goal. Good times. Everything was going well!

Remember Milton Melgar? He was the first sticker that Paddy and I got in the USA 94 World Cup Panini book!

"When the day arrives, we'll live on oceandrive"
– The Lighthouse Family.

History Exam Day
The day arrived – it was "history exam day" and Paddy, Scott and I met outside the Clarke Hall before the exam – "got yer answers already written up lads?" "Aye" said the hat-trick of us as we each pulled out our pre-written exam papers from our pockets. Winks, handshakes and a happy vibe all round. Genius. We'd written our answers to the entire exam already having had two weeks to write them - instead of the normal two hours! During a free period, we each compared notes to make sure our answers varied slightly.

Blair, Callen and Campbell – as the exams were done alphabetically we were sitting near each other for the exam!! We knew of which other students in the exam hall also had the paper or at least so we thought, however there was still a 5% doubt that the paper might not actually be the one Paddy had nicked, or that it could have been leaked year-wise to other classes via a "grass".

"Make the best of this test and don't ask why" - Green Day.

<u>What if someone had grassed us up and the paper was changed at late notice?</u>
They didn't and it wasn't – we were too smart. Within 2 seconds of seeing the exam paper I turned to Paddy and winked. "Good job mate". We pulled our already written answers out of our football soiled blazers and placed them on our respective desks. We sat doing nothing during the exam of course. I think I drew a picture of Teddy Sheringham and worked out that Colombia would win the World Cup - on scrap paper. I was looking forward to watching the World Cup with Paddy and having a beer with him – I hadn't drunk beer before, except at home with my Dad when he offered me a small glass on a Sunday football matchday. But that was the end of it all.

The beer with Paddy never happened.

Somebody squealed.

To this day, I have no idea who grassed us up or who squealed on us, but I know it wasn't me, Paddy or Scott. Of that I'm certain. Why would Paddy grass me up, when we were best mates? Why would I grass Paddy up for the same reason? It was my idea - he nicked it, I returned it, we both distributed it. Scott wouldn't have grassed us up either - it wasn't in his nature - he was just your cool trusted lad – he knew the score and was in on it with us. There were 3 of us. If you're reading and know who "told the teacher" please let me know – I won't be angry. Twenty years on I'll find it funny. Paddy Campbell might not...

The Aftermath: Expulsions and Suspensions

A week or so after the history exam, Paddy, Scott, myself, Dougie Gordon and a few un-named others are invited to meet the headmaster, Tommy Patton, for questioning. We knew something was going down. I saw it coming first when Paddy was called.

Deny it, deny it, deny it.

Winslow Boy case - no proof. Circumstantial evidence. That's what I said to the boys. I stood by Paddy. And I know Scott Callen would have too. I didn't grass him up – Paddy if you're reading this, I didn't say a word – I didn't tell them you stole it. Of course, I didn't. Because it was my idea. In my eyes, if you were expelled, I was expelled too. If I was expelled, you were expelled too. We were in it together. We both lose or we both win. I prayed for the win. I was sure of it. I valued our friendship at the time too much. I wasn't in the room when you got questioned though and I never spoke to you about it again, so I don't know what happened in there.

I saw you when you came out of the room.

Your expression said it all mate.

I knew you'd been expelled but I never had the chance to ask you.

I expected to suffer the same fate. I prepared for it. I knew Tommy Patton would do the same to me as he had done to you.

I was next to enter the Headmaster's office.

When I went in he asked me "Blair did you know about this exam paper in advance?". "No" I said - "I know nothing about it - I don't even like history lessons!". "You got 67% Blair", your normal average is 54 for history. "I studied hard, you can check my notes. I wanted to get into the higher class. I've no business stealing an exam paper I've no interest in. I'd rather watch football". And with that, he suspended me, issued me with 3 consecutive "Saturday detentions" and I was let go. I left the room and remember looking for Paddy – but on a day of sadness and at the point of no return, he had gone.

I went back to class and I knew that Paddy had gone.

He had gone.

Paddy had gone.

Patrick had gone.

My best mate had gone.

Paddy Campbell had gone.

Patrick Campbell had gone.

Aged 14 you don't cry losing a best mate and I didn't know that was definitely that. But I had a hollow feeling in me. We had done something horribly stupid and wrong. The fact of the matter is that he had nicked it, but I blamed myself because I told him to and we did the whole thing together. I encouraged him, I also put the exam paper back after we'd copied it. If fingerprinting in schools were done, mine were the last on it (despite being a Poirot fan, I didn't wear gloves putting an exam paper into a file). Yes - I cheated in the exam. Paddy and Scott also cheated in the exam. Bingo lads – nicely done!

Hey boys - I cheated and I passed. Sounds like a "Student 1-0 School" football fairytale to me.

I did get 67%. I deliberately didn't get higher as that would look suspicious to be too good wouldn't it? Or was I just not good enough? One of the students who had an advance copy pulled an 89% grade. Unexpected for him. 65% was the cut-off point in the end and I scraped into the second tier class for forms 4 and 5 to join Peter McIvor! Scott Callen made the cut of course as well, but into a different class and also got suspended and given multiple "Saturdays" (our term for "Saturday Detentions" where you had to attend school on Saturday mornings and miss football). But alas - the real news hurt us deep.

Paddy Campbell was expelled.

Outright. It was the end of an era. Every year since, I've been slightly haunted by the event but only when the 16th May comes round. Paddy Campbell Day. It should be a national holiday for everyone in Northern Ireland who hates pretentious schools. It's my selfish day to think of Paddy and the friendship we had; and the one we lost.

"Denial is the first sign of guilt" - Jonny Blair.

<u>Why did Paddy Campbell get expelled?</u>
Perhaps only Paddy can answer this. Maybe he admitted it straight up, though the pact we had was that we would both deny it. Therefore, I don't believe Paddy would have admitted it. In my heart I reckon I know how they knew – the handwriting – someone that we had sold a copy of it to had given it to the headmaster and it had Paddy's handwriting on it. Paddy - you were expelled before you could get a word in edgeways. I felt so guilty and responsible for your decline on that dark day. It hit me deeply and I cried.

Incidentally, Scott and Dougie were just in on it – they played no part in the theft, the photocopy or the business plan as far as I remember – Paddy and I kept the thing quiet for the most part. Paddy was gone and I had lost a friend, big time.

"It's over - you don't have to tell me" - Damon Albarn.

Meeting Paddy Campbell in Summer 1994

Perhaps the worst part of this whole event was that I randomly met Paddy Campbell and his sister Sophie while in Bloomfield Shopping Centre in my hometown of Bangor a few months later. I don't know why, but instead of me asking Paddy how he was and if he watched the World Cup and asking him what really happened that day, I got nervous and confused. I walked up to Paddy pointing "expelled" at him rudely and walked off. I really really do regret that and I have no idea why I did it. Teenage angst is an excuse but by my standards not an acceptable one. Sorry Paddy, I was in the game with you and we should have both been expelled. Or neither of us, which was the masterplan. I also felt that he might have thought that I grassed him up and that's why we never spoke again. I think and hope he knows me better than that.

Three Years Later:

Meeting Paddy Campbell in October 1997

In October 1997 I got off the train from Belfast to Bangor and saw Paddy Campbell waiting at a bus stop. It was a bit weird. I hadn't thought of Paddy for 3 years as we had both picked up the pieces and got on with our lives after the Great Exam Heist - I was now studying in Belfast, Paddy was in Holywood. Strangely though, I had seen Paddy in a dream I had that week and it was now 3 years since the exam paper episode and this was the first time I had seen him since the day I pointed "expelled" at him (an episode he later told my friend Colin Walker and one I regretted). However, it was now 1997. We were both 17 now. I said "hello" to Paddy and he replied. It wasn't awkward. We had a 1 minute chat before he boarded his bus. "How's things?" I said. Paddy replied - "All good mate – studying for my A-levels in Sullivan and just got a police caution for painting trains". Typical Paddy - nothing had changed. We just weren't mates anymore and could never go back. In the intervening years I myself had also now left Bangor Grammar School after a silly episode of "teenage angst" during my first year of A levels (that story is in Chapter 7). In 1997 I was studying media in Belfast by now. Paddy got on his bus, and boarded and since that day I had yet to see him since and the entire story remained forgotten. But then, in 2014 I decided to get back in touch with Paddy Campbell and I told the story on my blog about it.

Twenty Years Later:

<u>Hey Paddy, fancy a beer mate? - May 2014</u>
Twenty years on from "The Great Exam Heist", I knew I had to contact Paddy again, and I did through the article on my website. I typed "Paddy, if you're reading this, I want you back as a mate even just on e-mail - an explanation of what happened to you and I'll give you my take on it. Yes, it was 20 years ago, but they were good times until I stupidly decided we should nick the paper. Take me up on the offer – meet up with me for a beer sometime and we'll reminisce on what happened. We're older now. We're wiser. If you'll let me back in of course. If not, I fully understand".

"Somehow I've survived" - Jon Bon Jovi.

I posted the story on the twenty year anniversary on my personal Facebook feed and sipped a cold Guinness from my girlfriend Panny's flat in Hong Kong. It felt like a weight off my shoulders. I was ready to head to the World Cup in Brazil - which by coincidence Colombia were also in. Though professional football had, by now, passed Bolivian international Milton Melgar by.

The story got retweeted, it got shared by some other people and for the first time in history, my "travel blog" site Don't Stop Living amassed 1,500 daily hits for a single article. It was the most popular article on my travel blog! I was taken aback. A retweet on Twitter by fluke introduced me to a Zoe Hayes, who I tweeted to, asking if she knew Paddy and if he could get in touch. Zoe is Paddy's girlfriend and I found out that Paddy is now a successful playwright, working in Live Theatre in Newcastle, England. I found him on Facebook, sent him a message with a link to the exam story and went to bed.

To find out what happened next, you'll have to wait to a later chapter in the series, in one of the later volumes.

The Great Exam Heist had been and gone, for now. It was history.

And don't forget folks – 16th May every year is Paddy Campbell day!

* This chapter is dedicated to the genius that is, Paddy Campbell. Thanks mate, stay happy. You deserve it. Tonight and every night, you're a superstar.

Chapter 6
Where Were You While We Were Getting High?

Bangor and Belfast, NORTHERN IRELAND (1994 - 1996)
Cork, REPUBLIC OF IRELAND (August 1996)

"There's a bridge to the other side, don't take your eyes from the prize."- Dodgy.

So, Paddy had gone, but life had to go on. "The Great Exam Heist" occupied the rare position of being both a success and a failure. We succeeded in nicking the paper and passing the exams to get into the higher class.

Success!

But Paddy got expelled and I got suspended so it had also failed.

Failure!

"The Great Exam Heist" was a defining moment of my youth. It made and broke us and I was left to pick up the pieces. Being a teenager is meant to be the best time of your life. For me, it didn't always feel that. No, it never felt like that. I felt empty a lot, like something bigger and better was missing from my life. I'm not going to moan about it for chapters on end, as I try to be a positive happy go lucky guy, but anyone can get down. Sometimes in the aftermath of "The Great Exam Heist" I had these odd visions running through my brain. I'd close the door of my bedroom and listen to the Manic Street Preachers and become suicidal. I got angry a lot. I got depressed. With Paddy out of the picture, all that youthful vibrancy and enthusiasm had worn off completely.

All that was left was to go to school, play football and watch football.

Hardly a bad life, but I always wanted more. Northern Irish politics always gave me that extra interest in countries, geography and why there are wars everywhere. I still wanted the prestige that comes with an exam heist, I just didn't want to have to go through an actual heist again. Paddy, Scott and I were culprits. On with the fucking show lads, it's only a 3rd form history exam. Yes, seriously mate - it's only a fucking history exam paper, get over it. Speaking to a 14 year old Jonny Blair I'd say "Do you hear me mate? Get over it!"

"Heist: a theft from an institution which involves a large haul of loot" - The Dictionary.

I didn't share "The Great Exam Heist" story until the 20th anniversary of its occurrence –that day it just seemed the right thing to do. When the story went live on my travel blog, I knew nobody would read it. It wasn't related to travel, it was nothing to do with backpacking, it was my teenage story. I was writing for fun again and my inner passion. I didn't care about anything else. I had the story published and I was happy. Of course, the story was now on the internet, but I knew nobody would read it. I'd lose most of my readers but I didn't care.

I was wrong.

The story hit the 1,500 mark for views in one day. Yes, a twenty year old tale about two 14 year olds pinching an exam paper had gone wild. This was a first for my website. Yes, all those stories of working in Tasmanian farms, backpacking through Iraq and taking trains in North Korea were minor stories now. The Paddy Campbell story hit the jackpot of page views and I started writing some nostalgic stuff again about my teens, in the run up to this book. I realised that my whole life had been a spiral of odd events, ups and downs and some of them would be forgotten if I didn't get them written up or down soon.

I never told the exam story in person to my 10+ closest mates in the intervening years, nor indeed my best mate at present, not even in a conversation. Believe it or not, my best mate Rafał still doesn't know that story about the stolen exam (I write this in Warszawa, Poland).

Even though I love telling stories down the pub, I always skipped this one. I never told "The Great Exam Heist" story. However, in this chapter, let's pick things up from after 16th May 1994 as I tell a more selfish story of my teenage years, the 2 years that followed Paddy's dismissal. I'm condensing a lot of emotional shit into a single chapter by the way. A lot more happened, but I don't have time to write everything and you don't have time or patience to read everything.

"It may have worked but at what price?"
- Manic Street Preachers.

So yeah, Paddy had gone. He had been expelled for nicking the exam paper. I didn't know how they proved it or whether he actually put his hands up and admitted it. Nobody knew. Scott Callen and I had served our school suspensions and a string of Saturday detentions (neither of us ever admitted playing any part in the theft of the exam paper but they obviously saw us as allies to Paddy, without any concrete proof). And things had to carry on. And they did. But a void had been left behind. I was left empty.

"A mile empty inside" – Manic Street Preachers.

In fact, it still chills me to the bone to think that that one event catapulted my entire teenage years up in the air and to land on their head. For the better or worse is anyone's guess. But let's not dwell on the good or bad and focus on what came next for me. First though, with Paddy gone, it's weird to think that while he was my best mate for a while at school, I'd never been in a photograph with him, nor hung around outside school except for when we were in hospital together and went swimming after school or the day we photocopied the stolen goods in the library. The only class photo we had was from 1Y. Paddy joined in 2Y. Seriously, Paddy Campbell wasn't even in a photo with me – we'd never even met (first photo we have was in 2014!!)! It was as if the memory had been erased. None of that shit happened. There was no proof!

It was a bit like the story of Daniele Massaro, the Italian footballer (ironically a World Cup finalist in 1994 the same year of "The Great Exam Heist"). Massaro won the World Cup with Italy in 1982 aged 21, yet he didn't play a single match in that World Cup! Nor did he play a single match in ANY World Cup until June 1994. Twelve years after already being a gold medal winner, he finally made his World Cup debut, scoring against Mexico and later playing in the final. Something from that story resonated with me here. I still buzz off those crazy football facts. Massaro got a medal, disappeared and then returned for a final chunk of glory. Massaro however, was to be a scapegoat this time, as he missed a penalty in the penalty shoot-out for Italy against Brazil and lost the only World Cup Final he played in. Yet he earned both a winners and a losers medal in the World Cup.

But here, I had lost Paddy. We didn't have Facebook in those days. We didn't have mobile phones and we only saw each other in school really. Of course, I could have simply asked around, found out his parents' home phone number, found out where he lived, arranged to meet up and stay friends. But I never did that. It didn't feel like the right thing to do.

The truth is the next two years of my teenage life were tough for me (yeah right you will say - some people have been through serious illnesses, death, famine, losing family etc. - this was just a couple of kids stealing an exam, just a mate getting expelled, but still times were tough - adolescence is possibly the most important period of your life). I was suffering from depression, and yes it felt at that time, that it was own fault. Later in life I learned that depression wouldn't always be my own fault and sadly a notorious serial liar in my story would plunge me into a deeper depression, some years on.

Back to the 90s...I watched the 1994 World Cup and hung out with Peter Bell, who lived on the same street as me. Peter and I were good friends too and I of course confided in him with the entire Paddy Campbell story. He knew Paddy and I were good mates and he knew the whole story.

Then in the summer of 1994 I spent a fair bit of time in Belfast with my cousin Gary, playing football and computer games. I also had a week in Castlerock watching the football Milk Cup and a family holiday to London but much much more significantly, **Bournemouth**. That summer break in Bournemouth would have significant repercussions later on. Caught up in the here and now, I didn't know it then.

The absence of a school buddy as intelligent and hilarious as Paddy Campbell hit me hard. In the last week of June 1994, it came to choosing our subjects for the next 2 years of school – the GCSEs. By getting my 67% in History I was now above the 65% average over all subjects and I had scraped into the second highest ranked class, with the likes of Andrew Cowan, James Irwin, Robbie Milliken, Peter McIvor (Magoo), Simon Shaw (Shawzy) etc. I cheated my way there of course but I was in and the rest was, ironically *history*.

"Escape from our *history*, with nothing but memory"
- Nicky Wire.

History teacher Mr. Bonar came into our class one day and we were asked if we wanted to study history or geography or both for GCSE. It was an "H", a "G" or the famous "HG!" (my school buddies may be the only ones who actually find that bit funny). My mind had been made up; I was dropping history. I couldn't face the fact that I was still studying a subject I had cheated in. Also, for Paddy's sake, so I dropped history completely. Every time I had a history lesson I knew I'd just be thinking of Paddy and it was time to move on. Nobody would have been allowed to sit beside me. I'd have written a note on that chair and desk saying, "Paddy

Campbell's seat". Even though he was never going to be there to sit in it, it was still his seat. A bit like when Northern Irish MP Gerry Adams had a seat at Westminster yet he never sat in it. Except Paddy wasn't allowed to sit in it. Adams had a choice and chose not to.

September 1994 came round and I started 4th form at Bangor Grammar. Older, wiser and ready for my GCSEs. The original "Y" class at BGS had split up for good. We still met in the morning for form class and roll call but the magic had long since passed the class by. We were split into different classes for everything now and school life was boring. Paddy was like the guy who made school exciting, made it worth going to. Now, the highlights from school would be talking about football at break time, playing football at lunch time and believe it or not, actually doing some work. Shock horror. I got my head down and started studying, there was nothing else for it.

"I look at things now in a different light than I did before" - D: Ream, 1993.

However, one Autumn day in September 1994 I looked around the classroom and nobody present could replace Paddy. There must have been a tear in my eye. Sure, there were cool people about and I had new and previous friends, Peter McIvor (Magoo) sat beside me in most lessons and we played football together at weekends for 10th Bangor Boys Brigade. My Primary School buddies Scott Callen, Mark McCullough and Graham Irwin were all still around. Colin Walker and I were good mates. As was Michael Whitford. Tompo, Pamps and McKittrick all played football with me at lunchtime. There were no girls in the school though. Boys will be boys. It was a lads school and we all played football and messed around. It was the 1990s. That's what people did.

Bangor Grammar was a mostly Protestant and Unionist school too, so your usual sectarianism was ripe in this school, which admittedly was something to cling onto in the absence of Paddy. If they could see me now where I regularly attend Catholic Church in Poland, classing myself as a believer in God but with no preference of whether it's through Protestantism or Catholicism. Plus, I'm a Northern Irish Nationalist and not a British Unionist so I really didn't fit into such a school anyway.

There was an IRA ceasefire in 1994 though and Northern Ireland was almost as stable as it had been in my 14 years of life so far. But the truth of the matter was I hated the school more after Paddy's dismissal. I just hated it. At the time, I thought it was an over-bearing, authoritative and pretentious shithole. There was no get out clause. I was stuck here and I was just not that happy. My parents were forever supportive of everything though and I can't thank them enough for sticking by me all the way. But they didn't know how crap the school was – they saw it from the outside. I was in the inside and I knew it - a headmaster with an overarching ethos, I got detention for wearing a football badge, a real life child molester was a teacher there (Pogo), I was banned from playing football for a few days because I climbed on a roof to get a football. No shit Sherlock. If it had been a rugby ball, I'd have been a hero, as the Headmaster loved rugby. But climbing on a roof to get a football? You bad boy!

As I was in my mid-teens, deep down there was an unhappiness within. Listening to Nirvana or Manic Street Preachers and the birth of my brother Daniel were the sunshine in my rain. Daniel was born the same day that Kurt Cobain died. On the same day, an unknown rock band called Oasis played their first ever radio appearance. My brother Daniel was something in 1994 to keep me alive.

"I'm so happy cos today I found my friends. They're in my head" - Kurt Cobain.

After Paddy had gone, there was nothing too crazy happening in school. The rugby team got into the Northern Irish School's Cup Final in 1995 the following year and that was a major event. It says it all really. The place had hypocrisy embodied intill its brain from learning Latin the language of the Vatican City to not playing football in a town whose local team (Bangor FC) had been in European Competition three years out of the last 4.

The school thought it was cool but most of us didn't. A sentiment echoed by Northern Ireland football star Keith Gillespie who also attended the school in the 80s and 90s and wasn't allowed time off to represent Northern Ireland in youth internationals. The school had ludicrous rules - banning football, you weren't even allowed to eat in the school corridors, you had to write out lines as punishment. Yes - football was banned during games. Thankfully, Keith Gillespie also mentioned this in his book "How Not to Be A Football Millionaire". You had to choose either rugby or hockey and I hated both. But I got on with things.

1994 became 1995.

The year anniversary of Paddy's expulsion passed by the same week that Blackburn Rovers deservedly won the Premier League title. Paddy was a Blackburn fan - he'd have loved that and I thought of him the day I watched Tim Sherwood lift the trophy at Anfield in Liverpool. Well done, Blackburn, well done.

In 1995 I started writing for the Northern Ireland football fanzine 'Arconada...Armstrong!' Run by David Alcorn, this was my first writing job, I even helped sell the fanzines outside the stadium in Belfast, so things had changed.

1995 became 1996.

I still didn't really have a best buddy to confide in though, and I had been a surprisingly good student for those two years. And when the summer of 1996 came round, there was an air of change. It was GCSEs time, I worked hard on my exams and left school on a high. I'd milked all that I could from a school which I generally despised. Paddy Campbell's judgement in the early days had been spot on. He hated the school after a few months of attending it. They did him a favour - Paddy was a genius and he was too good for this school. I was still there.

"Where were you while we were getting high?"
- Noel Gallagher.

However. The mid-90s weren't the complete depressive disaster I've claimed. My youngest brother Daniel was born in April 1994 (yes, just before The Great Exam Heist) and I love him. I would stare into his cot thinking that was me 14 years ago. I was old enough to remember him crawling for the first time, talking, kicking a football. He was a breath of fresh air. I was never going to be the best brother to Marko, Cathy or Danny but I value the time when we do get together. Seeing Daniel grow up was a joy. He probably won't know the impact seeing him in his cot and singing silly songs with him as he blurted out words for the first time meant. I still remember the cuteness of his muttering "Noah Giker", Daniel's early understanding of how to pronounce Oasis songwriter Noel Gallagher's name.

Speaking of which, out of nowhere came a rock band that changed everything again for me. Oasis. Oasis had the tunes, the swagger, the attitude and the energy. I had something to relate to and I built up a collection of their singles and albums, spending my pocket money on their tapes and CDs.

My Dad played guitar and I picked it up and learned how to play 'Wonderwall'. Britpop was a crazy era of music and as Northern

Irish teenagers we got caught up in it. Colin Walker and I kept touch and we ended up going to an Oasis concert together with Keith Freel (from the year below us at school) in August 1996. It was down in Cork in the Republic of Ireland. It was a high. An all-time high. A great concert and I had become a massive Oasis fan in the absence of Paddy. They'd filled the void and life was great. The next day after Cork, I collected my GCSE results and got 6 As, 3 Bs and a C. That's 10 GCSEs. Five years of attending Bangor Grammar School and I'd done okay out of it. In fact, I'd done amazing – sorry 6 As?! It had been two years since "The Great Exam Heist" and I decided for whatever reason to hang around in the school and start my A-levels. As a 16 year old, I actually had nothing better to do.

"Aluminium tastes like fear" - Michael Stipe.

However, the Paddy Campbell day still lingered in my mind and while I started my A-levels, things could never return to the way they were and I lost any fulfilment in going to school any more. I simply didn't want to be there. I had got what I wanted from the school - I had 10 mega useful qualifications that could get me into any tech or college in the country, and even in other countries. My mind wasn't on A-levels at all and I often didn't turn up for lessons. In a crazy moment of madness, I would mirror Paddy's episode before my first year of A-levels were behind me, but I'll tell you the truth about that episode in Chapter 7. Yes, let's call this (Chapter 6) the "Part 2". We had "The Great Exam Heist" (Chapter 5) as the "Part 1", now some "Great Exam Results" were "Part 2", (though unchaptertitled) and in "The OXI one" (Chapter 7 coming up) will be the "Part 3". Now you learn, there's a third part to this story which suitably completes the hat-trick and closes the door on my Bangor Grammar Trilogy. Once and for all.

Good riddance.

Chapter 7
The OXI one

Bangor Grammar School, NORTHERN IRELAND (June 1997)

"Just because I'm sorry, doesn't mean I didn't enjoy it at the time" - Snow Patrol.

I am sorry about this story, but the story is true, that was me. Three years had now passed since "The Great Exam Heist" and I simply didn't want to be at Bangor Grammar School anymore. It was 1997. I'd been caught a few times bunking off school. Mitching. Skiving. Skipping. Not turning up. Missing lessons. On the beak. Studying for my A-levels was not all it cracked up to be. In truth it didn't even have a "crack up" to even attempt to be. In the absence of an Oasis album, I was listening to the Manic Street Preachers a lot again and decided it was time to become an "Education Terrorist", partly inspired by their debut album "Generation Terrorists". I wasn't just going to leave the school and walk away. I just had to make my point, leave a mark. Something had to be done about that school and its outrageously snobbish attitude. In many ways, I did it for Paddy. How dare they expel my best mate three years earlier. Teenage angst at the time was still in me and I got suspended from school for a string of minor incidents in between times. In the sixth form Common Room I graffiti-ed childish remarks slagging off the headmaster's obvious obesity. I wrote stuff like "Slug", "Fat Patton" and "Can I have another piece of chocolate cake?". I was a quiet lad at school apart from when I wanted to do something out of the ordinary, then I just went and did it and didn't care for the circumstances or the consequences. I played cards with Andy Corbett and listened to music to avoid putting up with our free periods, I did some excellent storytelling, poetry recitals and acting in our PSD (Personal Social Development) lessons, but life was so banal.

Colin Walker told me one day he hadn't revised for an exam the next period. I told him I'd get the exam cancelled by pushing the fire alarm. Colin, nor anybody else thought I would do it. It was like it was an excuse waiting for me to be able to act on something rebellious. I loved it. I pressed the button and we all had to evacuate because of a fire that never happened. Colin found it hilarious. Call it "good preparation". Setting off the fire alarm became almost a weekly "fire drill", my mates would give me the lesson they wanted to avoid most. 5 minutes in, I'd go to the toilet and set off the fire alarm. I was so blatant about it. The Headmaster called me in. "Why did you set off the fire alarm, Blair?" "I thought there was a fire. I thought I saw some smoke. I must have been wrong". They didn't buy it, but it was funny. Now, they know the truth. I set it off all those times. It was me. Thankfully, there was no fire.

"I'm a Firestarter, twisted Firestarter" – Keith Flint (RIP).

I wasn't actually a bad pupil though. I was just a bit confused and wanting to rebel against the school on my own. Looking back, I know I was right - the school was a stuck up, pretentious, wannabe conservative excuse of an institution. Opinions linger and this one never waned. Nobody else was going to rebel against it. Just take it like puppets on a string most of them. The irony being, I later became a conservative excuse myself and probably more right-wing than Bangor Grammar School ever was. My worldic judgements played a big part in that. I also became a professional teacher (the irony), but I had no interest in puppeting other people's strings or stringing other people's puppets. Put your hand in the box and see whatcha got.

"Isn't it ironic, don't you think?"
– Alanis "Mozzarella" Morrisette.

The third annual "Paddy Campbell day" came round and it was a Thursday. It was Thursday the 16ᵗʰ May ١٩٩٧ and with the three year mark now over, I made a plan to action. I was now ١٧, I had started my own Northern Ireland football fanzine called 'Here We Go…Again' (along with my mate Michael McClelland, who went to Sullivan Upper School in Holywood). I was aiming to work in media, become a writer (see where this is heading…?) and ready to say my farewells to this pretentious excrement exit. In the heat of teenage development, I had a crush on one of the teachers by now. That is ridiculous. Miss Anderson. Kathryn Anderson. She taught me German. A subject which would later come in mighty handy as I backpacked my way through Dresden, Osterweddingen, Leipzig and Hannover later on in life. I liked German back then, and I liked Miss Anderson. Katie, I called her. She was actually the only decent thing in the whole school and that grilled me. It boiled down to a teenage crush on a teacher now. But I knew I couldn't have her. You wanted this story to be that I kissed her behind a dilapidated blackboard. But I didn't and of course she wouldn't have had me. Not in a million years. I didn't have a million years but I was living in the moment and I had to act.

In the absence of Paddy, there was someone else who didn't like the school. Ryan Kerr. Often shortened to 'Rank'.

My classmate Ryan Kerr and I came up with a plan. We'd both get expelled on the same day, during the same lesson. We talked about it and we did it. I don't know if two pupils at Bangor Grammar School ever did that before, or since (with two separate incidents). Ryan wasn't even a close mate at all - we rarely spoke, we weren't mates at all, but we both shared our frustrations about the school. Similarly, to the friendship I had with Paddy, Ryan was an ally and we could rely on each other. For Ryan, he just wanted to get the f*ck out of the school. He wanted to join the army. There was no "karma" involved for him. I don't even remember what Ryan Kerr was doing during the time of "The Great Exam Heist", but I don't think he was involved. For me it was karma and revenge. I wanted my own back on what they did to Paddy, a hat-trick of years prior. I bided my time and waited until the 25th June ١٩٩٧. This was the day when it all kicked off. It was to be my final day at school in my entire life. That was the way I planned it; I knew it when I woke up that morning. This time, I went one step further than in ١٩٩٤ and planned the day›s proceedings to perfection. I didn›t have Paddy anymore so the best option was to do it alone.

There was no question. It was going to be the OXI one.

In 1997, Labour won the General Election, the big irony being it was Blair and Campbell, though not Jonny and Paddy. Tony Blair and Alastair Campbell. Tony Blair was the new Labour Prime Minister and Campbell was his Spindoctor or his PR and Marketing guy. They even released D: Ream's "Things Can Only Get Better" as their election song just to freak me out even more. If you read Chapter 5 on "The Great Exam Heist" you'll get the freakiness of that. It was all crazy. Oasis had just launched details of their forthcoming single "D'You Know What I mean?", Northern Ireland would have a new stand for home matches (the West Stand replacing the Spion Kop) and I was learning to drive. Life was changing and I wanted out of the school before I became an adult.

None of my friends at school understood my pain. I was a bit depressed actually. How dare they expel Paddy Campbell in 1994 and leave me to pick up the pieces for three years, even though in essence, they were right. Revenge is a dish best served cold and I wanted a storyline that people would remember. Everyone remembered Paddy, but they never knew the reasons for his dismissal. They didn't know the master plan we had in place stealing that exam paper. On this day, Wednesday 25th June I wanted to be remembered. I won't lie. It was all about me and my hatred for the school. I needed an audience, I needed a story, I craved to be centre of attention, if only for a split second. That was all I wanted. And needed. And all it took. I didn't want to look back. It was also the 15 year anniversary of "Arconada... Armstrong!", the night Northern Ireland bate Spain 1-0 in the World Cup. And I knew that. And I planned it for that day. It was the perfect time to act.

"Precious time is slipping away, but you're only king for a day" - Van Morrison.

During a German lesson, my classmate Ryan Kerr pulls out a feg and lights it. Blatant. Obvious. The teacher, Miss Anderson was lost for words. Well you would be. It was illegal to smoke in school. Ryan was making a point and saying his farewell. Well done mate. It was my trigger call to action too. At the same moment, I left the room to go to the toilet. Of course, I wasn't going to the toilet. I left my books and school bag in the classroom and I never studied in school again in my life. I'd love to know what the last sentence I wrote in my school books that day was. I'll never know that.

I was going to the school car park. If the only thing I actually enjoyed at school was staring at Miss Anderson during lessons, then it was time to call it quits. I decided I had to do something on Miss Anderson, then it would be a bigger impact. If even the thing I liked about the school was shit, then there was no way back. I'm sorry that it had to be Miss Anderson's car, I'm sorry you got caught up in it all. Miss Anderson - you might not even remember me. But on this particular day, you did remember me and that was all I wanted. It was her lesson and I knew the car park was an easy one to get to. I walked to the car park for staff cars where she had parked.

When I got to the car park, another lad was out there mitching off his lessons, having a feg. "Which car is Miss Anderson's?" I asked this ginger haired guy in the year below me.

"It's the OXI one" he said. It was a red or blue Fiesta with the registration starting with OXI. OXI. I was about to become an OXI moron. I don›t remember the full registration but it was the OXI one. To this day I also can›t remember if it was red or blue. I think it was a blue car. But the registration started with OXI. And it was a Ford Fiesta. That, I'll never forget.

I used the lid of a pen (always the writer) and let down all 4 of her car tyres so she couldn't go anywhere. It was the first time I had ever done that, but it was easy. A bell rang in between classes and knowing I hadn't come back from the toilet, my lesson was over and Miss Anderson raised suspicion. I got the audience I wanted now. I was shouting and there was a commotion. Out of nowhere, dozens of students and teachers started staring out to where I was in the staff car park. I was glad someone had alerted them. It may well have been the ginger haired guy that raised the alarm, but I wanted to be watched. I was on my own in the car park next to her car which now had 4 flat tyres. I was gazing up at my fellow pupils doing the fingers. Not to them, but to the school. I liked most of my peers.

Soon there were about 100 other people watching me (that could be an exaggeration but it felt like it or I wanted it to feel like it), some from the upstairs rooms near the Science corridor, a P.E. class came from the Clarke Hall. When the audience reached an acceptable peak, I lifted a large brick (more like a slab of concrete from the old school wall) which I found out of nowhere and I shouted "F*ck this school" before launching it at Katie's car. The back windscreen smashed and I sat down in front of the car in full view of the other pupils. And that was that.

It was all a blur. At that moment some were clapping, some were yelling but most were laughing at me. I don't remember much about it. I was sad. I was lonely. I was depressed. I was angry. I was also very immature and I thought it was hilarious. I don't know how many people saw it happen, but I had done what I wanted. A 6th form Prefect escorted me to the Headmaster's room and that was that.

Goodnight Bangor Grammar School. Tommy Patton's barmy army had been defeated. I classed it as a victory and moved on with my life. Next stop - a journalism course in Belfast City. Baby baby, I'm off to the Northern Irish capital and I'm heading on a journey around the world.

"Moving on up" - M.People.

<u>Reflections on chapters 5, 6 and 7 (the Bangor Grammar School trilogy):</u> As I recollect these events of the last three chapters, here in 2019, do I have any guilt? The truth is, I don't. It was teenage angst, they were good fun times and we did what we did and what we felt we had to do. I didn't like the school.

Am I sorry for what I did?

Yes, I'm sorry.

I'm sorry that we stole the exam paper.
I'm sorry that I set the fire alarms off and graffiti-ed the Headmaster's study.
I'm really sorry that I smashed Miss Anderson's car up. I'm genuinely sorry for all of that.

I was young, rebellious and I learned my lessons, life is a learning curve. I'm sorry. But apologies don't heal the truth and they never will. It was a long time ago and we all make mistakes. I made them; Paddy Campbell made them. Miss Anderson, sorry. I'm really sorry. I like the truth to be told. I like to be pure and honest. I didn't like the school. I did what I felt I had to do. At the time. But I was wrong.

"The good will out" – Embrace.

Chapter 8
The Good Friday Disagreement

Belvoir Park, Belfast, NORTHERN IRELAND (May 1998)

"Come eat tomatoes with me, sing me something new" – (Belfast's) Vicky Everitt.

After the crazy moment of madness on my last ever day of school, life had to move on for me, being the drama king that I was. I decided to study in Belfast, the Northern Irish capital city. It was a no brainer. Bangor in its disconnected splendour had taken me as far as it could and it was out to see the big world. Well, starting with Belfast. Hardly off on a backpacking adventure just yet. But I was 17, Northern Ireland was politically charged and Belfast was where it was all at. Belfast is a buzzing city and I embarked on a course in Media Techniques and Journalism at Belvoir Tech, in South Belfast. In this book, as well as using my own words and some Northern Irish spake and colloquialisms, I will use the word "Tech" to mean "Technical College".

I picked that course and that Tech because it was the most obscure thing on the menu.

None of my mates even knew there was a college in Belvoir, never mind a top class media qualification to be had. Of course, Belvoir Training Centre was merely just a massive wooden blue hut containing within itself a hat-trick of classrooms, a kitchen, a canteen and a radio studio. But it was perfect. I basically spent my days in a blue hut training to be a writer! Life was good again! Well it always had been hadn't it? The teenage rut was over and I was a 17 year old loving Belfast City.

"I get knocked down but I get up again" – Chumbawamba.

Aside from studying in Belfast, life was busy in 1997 - 1998 for me. I was back playing football for 10th Bangor Boys Brigade every Saturday, I was out drinking in the bars of Bangor on Saturday nights with new and old friends and I still ran the Northern Ireland football fanzine "Here We Go…Again" with my friend Michael McClelland.

As part of the journalism course, I took up radio DJ-ing. It was in the radio studio in Belvoir Park, where my tech buddy Keith Thompson coined the phrase "it's Jonny Blair on the air", a phrase which stuck and still comes up as a Facebook or real life greeting from time to time with friends who know me from my radio days. I was your old school wannabe student radio DJ - I was a total flop like Alan Partridge, I believed my own hype that my shows were good, I chose what songs I wanted, I got the odd cool person in to interview, I gave opinions and I told terrible jokes, I hated the technological changes as well. I used reel to reel and 8 tracks, with the odd vinyl, cassette and a few CDs. It wasn't all funny of course - but they were great times in the radio studio in South Belfast. I have one cassette tape of my 1997 Christmas Radio Show "Santa's Sack" and a documentary I recorded on the Good Friday Agreement, something I actually look back on with pride. That's the only thing that remains of my time at Belvoir. Sometimes I wonder if I dreamt the whole thing up. Even the building the tech was in no longer exists, nor do any records of Belvoir Tech online! But I made some good friends there, I grew up quite a bit, I became an adult fast in Belfast.

"The High Street never looked so low" - Paul Hewson.

The journey from 16 to 18 had been smoother than from 14 to 16. The rough and tough of Belfast always increases your confidence as a teenager. My new friends Jonny Kerr, Tommy Cunningham, Julie Cole, Keith Thompson and I all enjoyed a festive Christmas drink in the Monico Bar in Belfast around the same time and life as a 17 year old was pretty damn good. I had never looked back after life at Bangor Grammar School. I think about the way they treated Keith Gillespie (a top class footballer who played in the Champions League and was capped over 80 times for Northern Ireland). They wouldn't give Keith the time off school to play for his country, because the pretentious rear end departure point of a school loved rugby and hated football. They also tried to charge him money for his honours blazer. He was an international footballer! It kind of feels good that Keith slagged the school off in his autobiography "How Not to Be A Football Millionaire". I later shared a beer with Keith ("Keef") Gillespie on my 25th birthday in Warszawa in Poland in 2005, just after Northern Ireland had lost 1-0 but played well.

"Stand by me, nobody knows the way it's going to be"
- Noel Gallagher.

Back to the course in Belfast. All in all, the journalism course changed me as a person. When you're 17 you have this vibrancy that you will never have again. Living in Northern Ireland pumped such a vibrancy that little bit more. In 1997, the Drumcree protests reached a zenith and with politics a big part of my journalism course, I started reading up on it big time. I was still a member of the Boys Brigade and attended Ballycrochan Presbyterian Church. While officially a Protestant Church, my faith in God was always of my own irk. As I reflect on my days growing up in Northern Ireland, I know that I am much more Catholic than I am Protestant and I go to Catholic church now, usually to pray alone, and I mostly do that in Poland. But with the church and the BB, I loved that part of Northern Irish life at the time. Having given up history after "The Great Exam Heist", I would now sit with books in Belvoir Tech reading them and catching up on lost time. Northern Irish politics was my main interest now away from football (a sport which intertwined itself with Northern Irish politics so delightfully anyway).

"This happiness corrupt political shit"
- Manic Street Preachers.

Aside from the journalism and politics element, something else was on my mind. I had a crazy crush on a girl at tech to the point where seeing her smile would make my day. Since my childhood sweetheart days with Claire McKee, I didn't have too many major crushes on girls or any girlfriends or good friends that were female. I don't think smashing up teacher's cars or stealing exam papers were popular amongst the girls. I wasn't out actively seeking girlfriends anyway. I knew I was a fussy type with girls and back then a completely shy one. It took a lot for a girl to impress me, and it also was rare for a girl to like me. But this girl at Belvoir Tech kept me excited. Even though I couldn't have her. She was the one that opened the door for me on my first day in Belvoir as she worked on reception, as well as doing an NVQ in Business Administration. This was East Belfast girl Vicky Everitt (from Killowen Street) and to put it simply, she, was drop dead gorgeous.

"Take me in your arms again, leave me in my dreams again"
- Tim Wheeler.

Blonde hair, blue eyes, slim figure, bubbly, lively, chatty, fun. Her pristine hair flicked like a dream against a bombscare sky as we waited for the number 13 bus one night. There was a problem though. She had a boyfriend and of course she wasn't interested in me. Not in a million East Belfast years. But forget that - Vicky and

I always had quiet chats over a cup of tea. Vicky smoked Lambert and Butler (or on occasion Marlboro Light) cigarettes, and I used it as an excuse to chat to Vicky, smoking the odd cigarette (Sovereign or Benson & Hedges were what I chose to smoke) just to be in her company. I was too shy to tell her, every time I wanted to kiss her but always withdrew from any kind of flirting, remembering she had a boyfriend. I assumed she'd go mad at any advances I'd make and the boyfriend would come and hunt me down. He would have done. Although one time I did ask Vicky if she had blonde or brown 'pubies', and she giggled youthfully under the glow of her Marlboro Light (singular) as I grew effortlessly hard in my pants. Whoops. I really wanted Vicky. But this was a pipe dream. It was never ever to be. Better a pipe dream than a pipe bomb. Even sexbomb Vicky Everitt would agree with me in that one. When I looked at Vicky, I fantasised.

"I can see you and me doing things we shouldn't be. I can't seem to stop my imagination" – Louise.

Then, one day I got into tech in late December 1997 and Vicky was gone. She'd left for a good full time job and I never ever ever saw her again. Ever. That was it. I had one memory though - she gave me a Christmas Card which I kept and cherished. I admitted to a few others at tech that I fancied the pants off Vicky, after she had gone. I think the other lads fancied her but never made any effort to chat to her or show it. Sadly, they said she used to talk about how she'd love to go out with me too, when I wasn't in the room. Apparently. Turns out she rather liked me though I never heard it from Vicky herself, so it was merely hearsay. It was another "what could have been". Perhaps if anything had happened, I always thought, Vicky and I would have got it together, got married and life would have changed. Again. It wasn't to be. I wouldn't have backpacked the world and I wouldn't have had all that time to study politics. I doubt I'll ever see her again. Vicky, in the back of my mind was probably the first girl I had wanted since that childhood crush on Claire McKee. Girls like this are rare and they come and go into and out of our lives. I wonder what Vicky's doing now. I really really wonder and I'd love to see her face again.

All my crushes or friends were leaving my life. Claire had gone. Paddy had gone. Vicky had gone. None of them even said goodbye. There one minute; and gone the next. If Claire McKee was my childhood sweetheart, Vicky Everitt was my teenage sweetheart and I never got to date either of them. Nor even close. I should have stayed at the Heartbreak Hotel every night.

"On that damp and lonely Thursday, years ago..." – Pulp.

Crushes aside, Great Britain and Northern Ireland prepared to move into the 21st Century. I can't remember a more exciting time to be alive than when I was 17. Tony Blair was now the UK Prime Minister and one of his first jobs would be witnessing a handover of Hong Kong back to China. Oops. Prince Charlie of Wales was out in the Kong to pull down the Union Flag, it was a defeat for the Empire of course and coupled with the Drumcree stand-off in Northern Ireland, it had seemed Johnny Major got out at the right time. But Blair revelled and the UK had changed. Things seemed vibrant, ambitious and youthful under Tony Blair.

I had always sided with Conservatives and Ulster Unionists up to this point, but things were about to change in both regards. The Labour government concentrated on youth and Tony Blair's "New Deal" system in 1997 meant I now got paid to go to Tech. I would earn £57.10 per week and I'd spend some of that on buses (the number 13 from Belvoir Park) or a train back to Bangor and the rest on nights out and Oasis CDs. My Dad worked in Belfast every day though and usually I'd travel to Tech with him, he'd drop me at the top of the estate and I'd dander down the hill. It was a 9-5 thing for me. He'd either drop me in the city centre of Belfast and I'd get the bus up to Belvoir (that ever reliable number 13 bus which always cost £1.03), or he'd drop me at the top of the estate and I'd walk down to tech from there. My Granny and Granda, Mary and Sam lived in East Belfast's Cregagh Estate and I'd always call in to see them if I got away early. Granny always made sure there was a cup of tea on the table and a meal for me. Granda and I would watch the horses (and Countdown with Carol Vorderman) and we'd often have steak and kidney pie with spuds and peas as we tried to guess the conundrum. Granda was excellent at it. For dinner, Fray Bentos steak and kidney pies were Granda's favourite, he got me hooked on them. At the time, I didn't even know that Fray Bentos was merely a town in Uruguay!! I thought of Granda when I later toured the South American country. Life as a student at Belvoir gave me stability. Things were very routine back then, and consistent.

Granny and Granda were always so welcoming and excited to see me pop in after Tech and I loved it. They lived in the Cregagh Estate just round the corner from Dickie Best, George Best's Dad. I often kicked ball in the Cregagh when I was visiting them and I even stayed with my Granny for a few weeks at one point when my parents were moving houses and I was working in Knocknagoney in Belfast. I passed my driving test in January 1998 when I was at Belvoir Tech in a white Citroen – Mum's car. On exiting Granny and Granda's every night, Granny Blair always said to me "See you tomorrow. If God spares us". It was always "if God spares us" from Granny, a phrase which stuck and she was totally right. Our life could end at any moment. Maybe God will give us another day. Maybe he won't. That was my Granny's mentality. If God spares us. I'll never forget Granny's wisdom. She was profoundly right. If God spares us.

If God spares us. Copyright Granny Blair.

In local news, loyalist terrorist Billy Wright was killed in cold blood inside the Maze Prison in December 1997 and it was another of many turning points in the "Northern Ireland troubles". By April 1998, the four leading politicians had come up with the document known as "The Good Friday Agreement". John Hume of the SDLP, Gerry Adams of Sinn Fein, Ian Paisley of the DUP and David Trimble of the UUP. If I remember correctly, the four of them were on stage together for the first time in Belfast's Waterfront Hall. They also appeared on the front cover of a U2 single called "Please", where singer Bono prayed for peace. Despite liking a lot of U2's music, I didn't really like the way Bono saw himself as a guru who would or could change the world. In fact, I'd say he shouldn't get involved and let the politicians get on with it. Bono joined the politicians on stage in the Waterfront Hall in Belfast and together with Tony Blair and Mo Mowlam, they promoted "The Good Friday Agreement".

I'd no qualms with Van Morrison, Steve Lomas, Eddie Irvine, Fearghal Sharkey or Tim Wheeler doing that, but Bono? He's not even Northern Irish! In fact, call me a buck eejit, but the name Bono sounded more like a type of dog food to me, than a rock star with a fake interest in politics. I'm a hypocrite too though – I still bought and sang along to U2 records. Stick to Republic of Ireland politics, Bono!

It reminds me of an old joke my Uncle Jack used to tell me. Bono once said on stage "Every time I clap my hands, 1 child in Africa dies". Someone from the crowd shouts "well stop clapping your fucking hands then!".

On to "The Good Friday Agreement" even though I tried my best to keep this book unpolitical. I studied it from cover to cover. I was immersed in it. In reality, it was a difficult document to understand. I'd only just got into studying politics and tried my best to work the whole thing out. The main aim of the document was for peace in Northern Ireland with the understanding that terrorist prisoners would be released and Stormont would be re-opened to form a Northern Ireland parliament. It was also about the relationship between the Republic of Ireland's government and Northern Ireland, as well as the rest of the United Kingdom. There was of course a lot more to it than that, and it was a thick booklet with heavy reading, but it was eighteen years ago now (as I write this) and my memory is hazy. My parents and a lot of my friends voted in favour of it. But I didn't - at Tech, the guru was Dissident Ulster Unionist Jack Beattie. Jack was strongly against the agreement. In the space of one month, there would be a referendum and an election nationwide in Northern Ireland. I had just turned 18 and could vote in both elections. The whole country seemed to be buzzing and I enjoyed going down to the "tech local" the King's Head to chat to Jonny Kerr about "The Agreement". We also sometimes drank in the Centre Spot snooker club on the Castlereagh Road, which has just triggered another memory about a girl called Suzy Spence who went to Belvoir Tech and also to the Centre Spot.

In this agreement, the first vote was simply YES or NO. Do you agree with the agreement or not? I didn't. The fact that the DUP (Democratic Unionist Party) and my local MP (Member of Parliament) Robert McCartney already opposed it meant to me it was already "The Good Friday Disagreement". It meant terrorist prisoners would be released from prison. What did we do about it?

Well - I helped Jack Beattie out with a "No" campaign at the time. I had just turned 18 and was pasting posters and handing out leaflets for Vote No. Jack was the Mayor of Castlereagh at the time and a very well respected Ulster Unionist Councillor. However, Jack's decision to disagree with the agreement meant that he became closer to the UKUP party, run by Robert McCartney. The United Kingdom Unionist Party. This was the party that I myself sided with and voted for back in those days. Looking back, I'd never vote for them now. I'm a Northern Irish nationalist now. I am not a Unionist, an Irish Nationalist, a British Nationalist or even a UK Nationalist. I love my own country Northern Ireland and don't wish it to be part of any other countries. But, I met Bob McCartney walking through Bangor market one day and he chatted away to me. He was my MP when I turned 18 as he represented North Down - my constituency.

It came to the vote and there was a huge majority of Northern Irish residents who had voted in favour of the Agreement. The "no" campaign had failed. Next came the second election and the one that I got a bit more actively involved in. I went out around the streets of Ards Borough Council putting up election posters with Vote Jack Beattie on them. Jack missed out by a few hundred votes as it was stupidly done on Proportional Representation, which meant at the second and third counts, the transfer of votes, eventually knocked him out. In a first past the post voting system, Jack Beattie would have gained a seat in the new Northern Ireland Assembly and as a close friend of mine at the time, he certainly deserved it. Jack was a well-respected community man and he was eventually awarded an MBE from the Queen.

Without flinching an eyelid, I passed my journalism course with the highest grade possible and then I just wanted to earn money. The next 3 years of my life were the least exotic and the most mundane in my life. Nothing of note really happened and this book is meant to be more about my travels than my life pre-travel, so there's going to be a gap from 1998 - 2001 that's not really in this book. Everyone has a time of their life they like slightly less than the others, and for me those three years I didn't really gain anything. It was all a bit repetitive. I had about 5-6 different jobs in Bangor and Belfast and none of them stood out, inspired me or were ever going to change my life. I guess the only really telling job from that era was that I had my first bar job, working in McMillens Bar and Restaurant in Bangor, a skill that would later become essential on my backpacking journeys.

Oh, and in the madness of it all, I had turned 18. Childhood had been and gone…

Chapter 9
My Favourite Mistake

Gasworks, Belfast, NORTHERN IRELAND (April 2002)

"The worst joke ever" - Michael Stipe.

This backpacking journey was a slow burner as you can tell - we are nine chapters in and still I'm stuck in my home country fighting it out in dead end jobs! But I'm setting the scene here. I mentioned how the years 1998 - 2001 were unmemorable in my life. It was a stagnant period. Although I managed to travel to Spain, England and Canada, I was pretty much just working, partying and watching football. Life wasn't taking me anywhere, so I've neglected those three years completely in this book - something had to give and rather than bore you, we'll move on to late 2001 and more significantly early 2002.

The only real things of note in those three years were that I didn't miss a single Northern Ireland home football match, I had my first bar job (working in McMillens, thanks to my friend Darren Latimer), I tried my hand at being a postman (total failure after a doggy chased me down a driveway in rural Holywood) and I went to a load more Oasis, Manic Street Preachers, Ash and Radiohead gigs. I also appeared in a local version of Big Brother, called "Big Brother in Law" which was held in Bangor's All Ireland Club of the Year - The Boom Boom Room.

The story warps now to 2001, when I started working for the Halifax, which was then a Building Society and later became a bank as part of the Halifax Bank of Scotland. It's well known in the UK - the Halifax Bank. If you read Chapter 5 on "The Great Exam Heist", you will now find out that I never really learned my lesson from it. This story tops it and bottoms it all in one, and there will be a few more to come in the 'crazy shit cannon'.

So back to late 2001, I worked initially in Dundonald (Belfast, Northern Ireland) and that was mostly for training, but then we got moved to the main Gasworks call centre at the Ormeau Road in the centre of Belfast. It was a cool location and a decent wage. I wasn't looking for anything major at the time though, just another job really and definitely not one I saw myself staying in...just as well as life was going to take me on another path...

"I won't cry for yesterday, there's an ordinary world somehow I have to find" - Duran Duran.

The hours I used to work were from 8 a.m. to 4.30 p.m., Monday to Friday with the odd half day Saturday, which was fairly decent as I lived in Bangor at the time, and this avoided me rush hour traffic in the morning and also the afternoon. However, 'rush hour traffic' in Belfast and Bangor is nothing now, when I consider the amounts of travelling I have done since to proper busy cities like Jakarta, Chongqing, Sao Paulo and Tehran. But still in those days, it was a busy life and busy job and not a job I particularly wanted to do forever. At this point in my life, apart from the football writing I did, I know that I enjoyed the bar work most out of all the jobs I'd been in so far. But it didn't really pay well.

My job in the Halifax was a 'Savings Sales Advisor', which largely meant being on the phone and taking incoming calls on savings accounts, advising customers on accounts, giving out advice, interest rates and also booking appointments etc. I can't remember everything about the job, it was all rather a flurry of a non-event. There was certainly no gratification after another pointless and unwacaday 8 hour shift. While working there, I had also noticed Richard Henry worked a few floors below. I knew Richard well from supporting Northern Ireland and selling our "Here We Go... Again" fanzine next to him and Marty Lowry at Northern Ireland home matches.

Chats away from the desk were few and far between. There was no unique atmosphere and no real satisfaction, other than your pay cheque once a month. It was easily the most repetitive mundane day job I have ever had (and when you consider my work history all these years on - that's saying something). As I scratched my head each morning staring out at Belfast city (we were on the third/fourth floor with a view), I was dreaming of something bigger and better ahead. But you'd always have that bleep in your ear - a phone call came. And another one; I was busy talking nonsense about banking to people I had never, or would never meet. Phone calls were constant, all day long. What's more is I hate phones! And I especially hate talking on phones. If I don't see someone, I prefer to text them. To speak to them I prefer in person, or at worst, Skype.

"Bored of being bored" - Nicky Wire.

One of the positives was that I did have a few friends at work and I did bond well with my team, which included the easily fanciable Lisa Rodgers (a Carrickfergus lass) and top lad Chris Kruger (a South African). I became good friends with Chris. We were top mates - hanging out away from work, drinking down the pub, watching sport on TV, being typical lads - house parties, karaoke, overindulgence. Good times and at one point I was going to move in with Chris in East Belfast and then something happened one day...and that would all change.

This was to be just the normal sort of thing I do as comedy, which became slightly more tragic. It's only funny looking back! At the time, it was like something had ended. Actually, I love the story now and why not? It was years ago and influenced my route on this planet.

Onto the interesting interest rates story...in each group at work there was someone assigned to update the interest rates on ISAs and Guaranteed Reserve Accounts each week. They were updated on a chart in the office, on the computer system and on the website. It changed every week, there was a system and it was an extra responsibility of the people in that team to look after it. We earned no extra money for it, and it was a random order as to who was assigned to this task, week on week. One week it was my turn and I told Chris I would play a joke. It was April Fool's day and as an April Fool's Day joke, I decided it would be an easy wind up to put up the interest rates on one of the accounts that notoriously had low rates. This was just a joke. Bearing in mind of course that Northern Irish people are VERY aware of April Fools jokes and VERY unlikely to fall for them, especially since I was a bit of a joker.

On April Fool's Day 2002, I sent round a group e-mail to the rest of my team (as a total joke) to say what the new rates were but I doctored one of the rates. I made up a fake interest rate within the range of Halifax Accounts. I think it was for the Liquid Gold account. I don't know what really went through my head that morning, but I made the interest rates higher than they should have been for a bit of banter! Such comedy, I thought. And anyone who knows me, wouldn't exactly take it seriously. Nobody would believe it - it was April 1st, and by 12 noon I'd take the interest rates down, tell the team it was a joke and they would all find it funny. Surely.

Work was busy though, and I recall that particular day we didn't have a second's rest from phone calls. Because of this, everybody was work focused and in serious mode, and presumably had forgotten about April Fool's Day. Or more than likely, they actually thought that nobody would make an April Fool's Joke about interest rates. But I did. It was probably the most exciting thing in my time working there. The job was lacklustre and mundane at the best of times. We were even banned from looking up websites on our computers!

My manager had been on his day off on April Fool's Day (a dude called Eamon Somebody) and I headed out with Chris for after work drinks in Belfast. It was a good night by all accounts – we ate Biltong and drank Castle Lager, which Chris had got imported from South Africa. I stayed at his place in East Belfast as the day after was our scheduled day off that week. Chris and I were on the same team and we both loved the same music and beers, but it was back to work on April 3rd.

Straight into work the following morning after the day off and after an hour or so I'm called into the office. I had forgotten about April Fool's Day - it was now the 3rd of April and the joke was over. Unfortunately, the management never even thought the joke was funny, or that it was a joke, they believed it! Yes, that's right. They believed it. They believed me. Over 95% of staff working in the Halifax in Belfast believed my fake interest rates, quoted them to customers etc. Even though it was April Fool's Day none of them thought it could have just been an 'April Fool'. I was so surprised people believed them, as I had increased the self-confessed 'sh*t account' Liquid Gold (Halifax themselves admitted the account was crap). The Liquid Gold had an interest rate of 0.5% or something and I put it up a bit - when it hadn't moved in months. I thought that would be the clear alarm bell that my interest rates were fake. But they didn't suss it could be a wind up, a fake, a phoney, or a joke, and so I was in deep deep trouble.

"Suddenly I'm in too deep, to ever get out. I gave you my heart and soul to keep, don't give me your doubts" - Belinda Carlisle.

I was called to a management disciplinary meeting. The meeting started and ended within minutes; I didn't deny anything. I admitted the whole thing as my name was on the group e-mail and I was 'interest rates guy' that week. The outcome was inevitable.

I had lost my job.

Yes - I got sacked for making up fake interest rates on April Fool's Day 2002 in the Halifax in Belfast, Northern Ireland. Interest rates that the Halifax had to give to all customers in Belfast (and further afield actually) over the phone, who opened fixed rate accounts that day and who had maturing ISAs on that day only as long as they knew about the rates I quoted. At least until 12 noon, when I withdrew the joke, which was simply an April Fool!! It was only a joke, but it went too far.

People believed me and I was gone...soon I had closed all my Halifax accounts and I now hated the company. They are still the worst company I've ever worked for, and it was the most mundane job I've ever had! I'll never recommend banking with them, but I'm biased. Still, it's a real life story and not something I'll hide behind a curtain. I'll tell people about it. I made a mistake. I was wrong. They sacked me. I had to pick up the pieces. Again.

So, the first 22 years of my life were clearly about people "leaving my life". First Claire had gone. Then Paddy had gone. Then Vicky had gone and now Chris had gone. I knew life was telling me to get out of Northern Ireland. I loved my country, but wouldn't it be great if I could leave behind these crazy memories and start afresh in the bigger world?

What if people could now be 'joining my life' rather than 'leaving my life'?

Weirdly from here on in, my life was going to be like that.

I don't do lazy and I didn't linger on it before getting a new job. Within a week I was working for Grafton on a number of equally mundane jobs such as sorting envelopes and putting stickers on pieces of cardboard in an industrial estate. Within a month I was working in Steenson's Butchery in Bangor, happily loving that job I must say. Things had turned out for the best for me, post the fateful 'interest rates day'.

Oddly, sitting here on the east side of Hong Kong today writing this, having now passed the 100 country mark, I don't regret what I did at all. I'm not ashamed of it. I was wrong, I made a stupid mistake, perhaps they were all mistakes.

The exam theft, the smashed car window, the fake interest rates.

They were all mistakes. They were really stupid mistakes. But I made them. I was wrong.

But this Halifax "April Fool's Joke" was the worst mistake of the three, yet it was my favourite mistake. I did it, it was funny at the time, worked out bad for a few months, but in the end sowed my seeds for leaving Northern Ireland behind.

I never wanted to keep that job, I guess I could have easily just resigned quietly, but that wouldn't have made a story for "Backpacking Centurion" now, would it? Certainly not! This job at the Halifax, was my one and only banking job to date and I will never want a job in a bank again. It wasn't for me - I'm a business backpacker, a professional teacher and a travel writer now instead. Away from work, the way things happened with me, Chris Kruger and I kept touch for a few weeks (maybe months) then we just weren't friends anymore for some reason - I started plotting my path out of Northern Ireland, he was steady in a relationship and job focused. We drifted apart, my life really seemed to be a series of disasters up until this point. And as had happened with Paddy, I now lost Chris as a mate!

"Shed a tear cos I'm missing you, it's alright to cry"
- Guns n Roses.

So similarly, to the Paddy Campbell "The Great Exam Heist" story (Chapter 5), this one has a more emphatic ending. I became a backpacker, Chris a family man with his children. And I'm hoping to meet up with Chris again someday and laugh about all this.

"I tried so hard to get so far but in the end it doesn't really matter" - Linkin Park.

I've written about this 14 years on and for sure as hell closed the door on the story and on banking. If you ever get a job in a bank, please take it seriously. Unfortunately, that's what banks are all about.

For the record, some of my work mates in Belfast were Chris Kruger, Leandra Woolard, Leanne Cranston, Lindsay McCormick, Johnny McGreevy, Robert, Kathy, Lisa Rodgers, Stephen Hanna, Sylvia McConnell and Justin Kilcullen. Thanks for the memories. I haven't seen any of them since 2002.

Chapter 10
Don't Stop Living

Toronto, CANADA (August 2001)

"I might have been dreaming but I know I walked. On stepping stones. To Canada" – Jonny Blair.

My August 2001 trip to Canada changed things for me and after this trip I knew I wasn't going to spend my whole life living in Northern Ireland. However, chronological order doesn't apply here as I'm putting the chapter that datily happened before "My Favourite Mistake" (Chapter 9), after it. As it makes more sense to me. My cousin Alison from Belfast got married in 2001 in the city of Winnipeg in Canada. We were invited over for the wedding and my sister Cathy would be bridesmaid. I'd already been on a lads holiday that year in Spain and to a few concerts, so to be flying to Canada for the first time was magical. I was 21, older than most who go backpacking for the first time and besides, I was going with family so I still wasn't turning into a hardcore backpacker just yet. I roomed with my brother Marko as we toured Toronto, Niagara and then Winnipeg.

It was Toronto that inspired me and left a lasting impression.

As a sun sank over Toronto's skyline in August 2001, I made a deal with myself. The deal was that I would travel the world. Somehow over the next few years, I was slowly going to go wherever I wanted. All those teams in my Mexico 86 Panini Sticker album, they needed to be backpacked.

It was after a few days in Toronto that my sister Cathy and I went for a nonchalant mid-afternoon walk. The reason I had chosen that direction to walk in was because a girl that ran a Manic Street Preachers fanzine lived nearby. I had written to her a few times. It was on that walk to an area near Wellesley Street that I saw the most striking image from my journeys so far. A statement that changed my life forever. Completely and totally.

The message that I saw is one of the most vivid memories I've ever had. We stopped at a corner of a junction and there was a High School gaping down on us. I stared at some writing on a wall. It was teenage graffiti. It was a completely non-descript, grey concrete wall, with some red writing on it. It was just a one liner, and a message. It read in capital letters, complete with the grammatically correct apostrophe:

DON'T STOP LIVING

I stopped for a moment and thought that it was the most profound phrase I had ever heard or read. I got my travel notebook out of my bag and I wrote the words down immediately, though I wouldn't have needed to - I'd never forget them. In those days taking photos weren't a big thing – you'd get 24 photos on an exposure and have to use them wisely. I think I had 3 films on that trip – 24 photos on each. While part of me misses that lifestyle pre-digital era, on this day I wish I had photographed that graffiti on the wall. Graffiti that sent me a message to live my life by and change things again in an instant. The graffiti artist even bothered to put the apostrophe in. I admired the intelligence of that, knowing it was possibly some kind of rebel against a Toronto High School who had concocted this phrase.

In short, I pinched the phrase. "Don't Stop Living", became my phrase.

It kind of fitted my life's story and to see it on a High School wall hit the jackpot. To the unknown person who wrote that graffiti, thanks. In the unlikely event you are out there reading this, I'd love to hear from you and to know why you wrote that phrase there. I had no idea that the words would transpire into a 13 year long (and counting) travel blog and a phrase that some friends use to refer to me now. "Do you know Jonny? Which Jonny? Jonny from Don't Stop Living?" as if 'Don't Stop Living' is a 'thing' to be 'from'. But it is, it became that.

"Yes, I'm Jonny from 'Don't Stop Living' ".

I got back to our hotel, which was the Days Inn on Carlton Street - I wasn't much of a hostelling budget backpacker in those days. I was still buzzing by the phrase "Don't Stop Living". I remember I mentioned it to my brother Marko and he seemed slightly dis-interested in the fact that I was talking about a phrase I had seen on a wall. Different things inspire different people and I knew I had been influenced by the graffiti but that Marko wasn't convinced. There was no time to dwell. Marko and I headed out on the rip in Toronto for a few beers and had a good time (he was only 17 and used my mate Darren's passport to fake that he was 20, the legal drinking age there – another ridiculous story! We borrowed Darren's passport to take to Canada with us!). The next morning, we were off to Niagara and later we flew to Winnipeg for Alison's wedding.

The wedding and the entire Canada experience had been memorable. After a visit to the Forks Shopping Centre in the city of Winnipeg, I penned a poem, which I later put to guitar and wrote into a song. It's one of about a thousand poems and lyrics I have written down the years. The song is called "The Way It Isn't" and relates to the way the newspapers referred to Northern Ireland when I was younger. It's the only poem I have published in this volume of the collection:

The Way It Isn't

in my homeland forlorn
the sun shines down upon
a tattooed youth
his mind a microwave
of loss and feeling brave
in disrepute

my eyes bore into him
beneath a sky undimmed
by fear and callousness

i've worked out why my feet are cold
is that why i'm not getting old?
the winter air won't let me know
the summer breeze won't let me go
and i'm a faded mural

in bloodshot countryside
rain does its best to hide
un-needed graves
despite an empty hand
a balacalavad man is suspicious
another ambulance
can't take much more of this
pray it's a fire

i never got my fortune told
what that means i'll never know
the winter breeze won't let me know
the summer air won't let me go
and I'm a faded mural

another paper tells
it the way it isn't

we're front page news
and when we live in peace
I'll keep my memories
the nights of fear

I've worked out why my feet are cold
is that why I'm not getting old?
the winter air won't let me know
the summer breeze won't let me go
and I'm a faded mural

in my hometown forlorn
the sun shines down upon
a tattooed youth
we're front page news

I thought I'd put the poem in here and I want to release my other
1000+ poems someday. After the Canada trip, I knew I was going
to leave Northern Ireland. A few jobs later and I was back working
with the public in a local shop. While working in the local butchery
counter and salad bar in Steenson's Food Centre in Ballyholme in
Bangor, I plotted my path abroad. But the day of action came about
thanks to the 'foot and mouth crisis'. We had run out of meat due
to the crisis and there was no need for any butchery or counter staff
for a few days. I used one of those days to research a cheap way
for me to start a new life in England. I had no official A-Levels but
I had 10 GCSEs and that NVQ in Journalism. I was 22. Yes, I was
a really late starter!! When I called into the local Tech, they told
me I could do a morning course at Tech which would give me a
Foundation Studies qualification from Queen's University and
grant me access to any UK university that would take me. It was a
no brainer. The course had very little cost (I don't remember the
price, but it was probably about £100) and would change my life
forever. I shifted my working hours in the local shop to 2 – 8 p.m.
six days a week so I still got my full-time wage and in the

mornings I was enrolled on a full time course at Newtownards Tech, the town where I was born. Life had to go back a step for the meantime, in order to move forward a few more in the future. This job at Steenson's Food Centre was excellent though, and a huge thanks to Alma my manager and Trevor Steenson for allowing me to keep the same weekly hours at work, but shift the times.

I studied Irish history and politics yet again, as well as English Literature and Sociology. The course finished in May 2003 and if I passed, I would be moving to Bournemouth in September 2003.

Yes Bournemouth.

But why Bournemouth? Why the Cherries?

I had to choose six universities in the UK on my UCAS form at the time and I was so busy working to bother researching so I just chose the first six alphabetically that I liked on the form. I can't remember what they were but I think Brighton, Bristol, Bournemouth and Belfast (Queen's) were on the list. That's the way it happened – alphabetical order. I was too busy to go beyond B.

But deep down, I knew it was going to be Bournemouth. I had already visited the English seaside town in 1994 on a family holiday and thanks to Northern Irish striker Warren Feeney, I started to follow the local football team, AFC Bournemouth. The team also had three other significant links to Northern Irish football down the years – it was George Best's last club in English League football, Colin Clarke played for Bournemouth when he scored at the 1986 World Cup and for years Stevie Robinson had been a fan's favourite there. I watched AFC Bournemouth's results every week in the hope and knowledge that one day I'd be there and could watch them live. You can make your dreams reality.

I passed the course with aplomb and on a wet day in September 2003, Dad and I drove down to Rosslare and got the ferry to Fishguard and onwards to Bournemouth in Dorset. I had a house to stay in on arrival, at 256 Holdenhurst Road in Springbourne. I had a job within a week, working in a supermarket - Tesco. I had started a degree within a month and it was here in the seaside town of Bournemouth that my journey around the world really began. If you have met me since I left Northern Ireland, then it is highly possible that you met me in Bournemouth as my love affair with this particular town began in earnest and I met hundreds of people while based here.

Bournemouth was the beginning of a charming passion for travel and the town and its football team changed my life. #eddiehowesbarmyarmy

Chapter 11
The Lock-In

Bournemouth University, ENGLAND (December 2003 - February 2004, and beyond)

"My milkshake brings all the boys to the bar" – Kelis.

This chapter has to be split into parts, and while the journey began in December 2003, this odyssey is ongoing. It's still in progress, as a later chapter in an ensuing volume will testify. But we need to start where it began to get to the bottom of this. This was 'The Lock-In'. But what exactly was 'The Lock In'?

Part One - The Build up to 'The Lock-In' (November - December 2003)
I had only been living in England for two months. It was an advert up on the university wall in Bournemouth in November 2003. It just said, 'The Lock-In'. It stood out. I noticed it. It was like a

teaser. Something a bit crazy was about to happen and nobody knew quite what. I'll try my best to explain. Back in 2000 - 2003, reality TV shows like Big Brother and Survivor were all the rage in the UK. People watched them on TV all the time and they were popular. I loved them too at the time, probably because these were normal everyday people getting their moment of fame on TV. I always felt that everyone in life deserves to be in the limelight at some point. All of us.

"Everyone will be famous for 15 minutes" - Andy Warhol.

It used to annoy me a bit how celebrities piss away their money while getting overpaid for essentially "what they do". With many exceptions of course. I've lots of time for the likes of Noel Gallagher, David Healy, James Hayter, David Beckham, The Queen, Madonna etc. I like their personalities and they all work hard, in my eyes. But generally, some people have crept up into the money without any real talent or reason other than good PR and marketing. Reality TV changed that - anyone can be famous. When faced with that old question "would you rather be rich, powerful or famous?" I always used logic to say "famous". On the understanding that if you are famous, you will probably be okay for money and will likely have some power over something. If you have the money, you may not have the fame. Like a bank executive or a doctor. He's rich, but unless he does a scandal or some major groundbreaking discovery, he's not that famous. If you have power you may not have the money, like the Pope.

What was 'The Lock In' exactly?

'The Lock-In' was a mini spoof of Big Brother at Bournemouth University. It was a reality TV show and at the time was advertised as the UK's first ever online 24 hour televised reality show based in a university. That was never proved and often a doubted fact but we went along with it.

With 'The Lock-In', I wanted the limelight and just the fun of it all. So, going back to that advert, it read something like "12 students, 1 house, 1 winner". The Lock-In. As long as it was free to enter, I was in for it and I wanted to win it.

Part Two - First Round of Auditions for The Lock-In (December 2003)

Hundreds of people turned up in D2, one of the Bournemouth University bars for the first round of auditions. Many people in the University knew what 'The Lock-In' was, it had been publicised on posters, in Nerve magazine, in adverts, by e-mail, on Nerve Radio. There was some kind of a buzz with it. My flatmates at the time, Steve Compton, Claire Curtis and Hannah Thompson didn't want to enter nor did any of my other good friends - Austin Sheppard, Dan Stead, Leigh Brimicombe, Australian Emma, Claire Jennings, Abi Clark and Denise. For the record, at the time I had yet to meet the famous 'Millwall Neil' AKA Neil Macey, who will feature more and more in my adventure, later. I actually first met Neil the night I came out of 'The Lock-In'. Yes, this was another moment of fate on the journey. And he didn't even vote for me.

"Danni's on my course mate, I voted for 'er"
– Millwall Neil (2004).

Nonchalantly, on a Monday night in December 2003 I went to the auditions. We were put into groups of 10 if I recall and out of each group, they would pick 4 people. Then they'd whittle it down to 2 from each group. By the end of the night there were between 24 -30 of us left in, a diary entry I wrote at the time mentions 24, so we'll go with that. I made it through each round and had passed the first stage of auditions. It came easily for me. The reason was I was passionate. I wanted into that Lock-In. I put effort, desire and passion into it. Yes, it's only a gameshow and a bit of fun. But at the time it felt like the right thing to do. Those who got knocked out were cool people too - they just didn't want it enough. They just didn't show that inner passion. Am I making a big deal about what is essentially just a University Reality TV Show Experiment? Yes, I am, but what's a big deal to me may not be a big deal to you. I was buoyant.

I have a slight confession to make here too, the Lock-In was organised by the Student's Union and the Vice President was a lady called Natalie Johnson. She joins a list in this book that Vicky Everitt and Claire McKee once graced: I fancied her. Quite a lot. She actually came over to the table when I got through and asked me if I got through to the next stage. I told her I did and she gave me a big hug and a bit of excitement. Natalie said she was hoping I'd get through. Excuse me - hoping I would get through?? I didn't even know that she knew who I was, so I was pretty happy about that! She had heard my infamous university radio show and that's how she had heard of me. Natalie is still one of the coolest girls I've met in life that also carries personality off with her looks. A damn good package and probably an extra incentive for me to crack the next round of this 'gameshow', which brings us to the second round of auditions.

Part Three - Second Round of Auditions (December 2003)
We were down to just 24 of us for the second round of auditions. The second round would take place on a Wednesday in mid-December which would be a full day out at a secret location for the Nerve Media team to kick out 12 of us and leave just 12 to contest in 'The Lock In'. I was up for it big time, buzzing, I didn't drink alcohol the night before, up early with a breakfast and a morning coffee and I headed to the Student's Union at Bournemouth University. I was pretty happy to be in the last 24 but I was convinced I would make it onto the show. I was eager, passionate, determined and unusually lively. We were whisked away in the University minibus to this secret location, which turned out to be Southbourne for a day of fun overlooking the beach. It was an

all-day session in The Commodore Hotel in Southbourne where the judges decided who would enter the 'house.' And fun it was, from improvised comedy sketches to quotes from Alan Partridge to seeing the size of Sarah's and Sophie's breasts (albeit from the outside) to meeting Nottingham Forest's number one punk, we had a great day. I added the spice of Northern Ireland to some dour English people's lives that day, and this group of 24 would be whittled down to 12 by the day's end. There was a Welsh person and a Scottish person in the final 24 but apart from them I was the only non-Englishman and I thrived on it. I simply had to be one of the 12. Defeat was unacceptable. This was my dream. Move over Beethoven.

By the end of the day, we were all sat round a table and we were put into twos when the verdict had been made. In each group of two, there was one who made it and one who didn't. It was dramatic. We also found out that out of the 24 of us, actually only 10 would make it into the house, so 4 were kicked out early including a guy that stood out called Tarik, who was a Portsmouth FC fan. So basically, from the 24 they had decided on their final 10 but to make things nervy they separated us into groups of two, knowing that one from each of the two was in and one wasn't. The guy that I was "up against" was Tommy Payne, a top English lad from Birmingham. He was funny, popular and down to earth and we were the last two to be decided. We already knew which 9 of the others had made it and which of the other 24 hadn't. Now it was down to Tom and I. I knew Tom was a popular lad and I liked him, so I now assumed I wasn't making it.

"Best when under pressure, with seconds left I show up" – Usher.

"It's Jonny" came the shout from the Student's Union crew and I was overjoyed, relieved and pumped. This might sound over the top as it was really just a university game show but I felt sorry for

Tom though, and knowing he liked football, we swapped numbers and I invited him for drinks and also to watch the Cherries (AFC Bournemouth). Tom and I met up quite a few times after the event and had some wild lads' nights. Now that the final 10 had been sorted, we would be screened on University TV and in the Old Firestation Nightclub over the next few weeks before the voting would start. Yes, not all 10 of us were going into 'The Lock In'. It was still to be determined by public vote and only 6 out of the 10 would go in. Most of us assumed this to be some kind of trick and that the first 6 would go in, later to be joined by the losing 4. But alas it was time to get excited about the campaign and get people voting for me. It was like a fun election with zero politics.

Part Four - The Campaign and the Voting (December 2003 - January 2004)

I enlisted upon my good mate 'Dandy / Dancing Andy' (Andrew Stokes) as my Campaign Manager, then the fun would commence. There were only going to be SIX places in 'The Lock In House', out of the ten of us, it was done by text vote. I did a few things as part of my campaign. Firstly Steve, Andy and I made hundreds (and I mean hundreds) of VOTE JONNY Posters, each had a different slogan on them. We plastered these all over the university, especially in places that couldn't be reached and places where other guys wouldn't remove them. We even stuck them in the girls' toilets, behind the doors. At which point my friend Rebecca Taylor said, "Jonny this is fucking ridiculous, I cannot even take a piss without seeing your face!" That's what I wanted. Hold on, I was studying Public Relations wasn't I? All publicity is good publicity. Allegedly.

I also did a lot of promotion on Nerve Radio (both my normal show and on FM). Buzzed to the hilt, one day I did a speech in Dylan's Bar in front of loads of people telling them why I should be in there. I added a mix of politics and randomness. I was 23 but

I was still harping on about Northern Ireland and Oasis quotes like I was 17 again. Then Andy and I dressed in suits and stood outside the student's union handing out leaflets on VOTE JONNY. We also wore 'VOTE JONNY' T-Shirts which said 'Which came first? The bacon or the egg' or 'marzipan sunk the Titanic' or 'Grimsby Town don't even play in the town of Grimsby'. Even if nobody got the jokes, we were laughing at ourselves! I was really influenced by the Northern Irish elections of 1998 when we did this, but also by TV shows The Office and I'm Alan Partridge. When someone asked me why they should vote for me, I said "Jurassic Park" to them and that has ever since been another catchphrase I used, in addition to "Don't Stop Living". Classic. Stuck up twats found it completely unfunny but each and every morning I woke up I thought of more and more ways to get votes and wind people up. We stuck condoms on some of the "Vote Jonny" signs. While females weren't exactly warming to me, we had done something - people were aware of 'The Lock-In' now and if pushed for a vote, they'd remember my posters and my campaign first before anyone else's and they'd "Vote Jonny". We knew it.

During the voting campaign I didn't take much notice of the others, my 'rivals', as this was a competition. I concentrated on my own campaign and getting in there. It was a pretty exciting time. I even got chased out of the university one night for putting up VOTE JONNY posters in buildings that were banned after midnight. It was all a laugh and if anyone around thought we were taking things too seriously, *the truth is we weren't, we were just young people having a laugh*. That's all it was. On the outside, life was changing too. During the campaign I met a local girl called Emma Halstead on a night out in the Litten Tree Pub in Bournemouth. She had just got back from a round the world jaunt to Australia and New Zealand for a year and was spilling stories at me. Emma and I started going out together in January 2004 and for once I took the role of listener and let her tell me her story. I wouldn't say we were in love but I was fond of Emma. My friends didn't like her, they saw her as too boring for me. But Emma wasn't – her stories of backpacking through Australia were more exciting than their tales. Emma was adventurous when it came to sex too. One night Emma and I were lying in bed naked together when her friend walked in to give her a lift home. I whipped off the sheets to show her friend we were both naked! Some girls would go mad at that, but Emma didn't. It was funny. I'll get back to Emma after this chapter.

Also, during the campaign, I had been holding a "Vote Jonny" demonstration right outside the Students Union shop and a rival for 'The Lock-In', Lee Adams, came up and asked to borrow 20 pence off me to buy a Mars Bar (or something). I gave it to him but kind of frowned at the time, thinking that's my good deed done for the day, I should get onto the gameshow for a gesture like that. I didn't know the significance of lending Lee Adams 20 pence until later. Just for now, I was his enemy. I treated it as the competition it was and no two ways about it, I wanted the votes to get into the house. By the way, Lee features in many more chapters of this book to come, and became one of my best friends in life, ever…known to many as "Lock In Lee".

Part Five - The Results of the Voting (February 2004)
One Friday night, the 6th February 2004 was the night where a big crowd gathered in Dylan's Bar at Bournemouth University to hear the results of the voting. I seem to remember it coincided with either Comic Relief or Children in Need or some kind of charity night in the Students Union. The place was as packed as I ever seen it. I spoke briefly to my rival Lee Adams at the bar again as we ordered pints, but we were enemies to get into the house. Another contestant, Danni wished me good luck too. Beers were cheaper and some of the proceeds were donated to charity. During

the night, the votes would be announced and one by one the 6 winners would enter the house. I was confident and buoyant.

I turned up with my mates in Dylans Bar at Bournemouth University for the big voting results night. That night though, my girlfriend Emma wasn't there. I didn't invite her. She knew I was going in for this University thing, but she was older than me by a year and she had just finished a year abroad backpacking in Australia. I didn't want her to have the pressure of being there, seeing me all happy and nervous at the same time and then when I got voted in, she would feel awkward talking to my friends. I'd only started going out with Emma about a week or two before that, so she wished me luck and off I went with my friends. I turned my phone off and gave it to Austin to mind if (make it 'when') I got into the house.

We played games in the bar, 'The Lock-In' organisers included a few free beers for us. I got pissed up and soon we were up on stage (all 10 of us, awaiting the vote!). I was getting nervous that I wouldn't be selected as the vote continued. One by one the names were called out of the successful entrants and I hadn't been called yet. Up first was Danni (who replaced my coursemate Laura Inston), the lively Sophie was up next. Then Paul and Lee got called and there were only now two places left. Those four had all already left the stage with their bags and had now entered the house. I was left with Rebekah, Alex, Dave, Elliott and Reeder on stage. I totally expected Reeder to get into the house as he worked in the Student's Union and was a popular guy and I knew they would want 3 girls and 3 guys so I thought I was out. I had failed. But no, I obviously had worked hard enough on my campaign and had more contacts than I thought as I was called next! I was ecstatic. I said a quick goodbye to my mates before the extremely hot Natalie Johnson (who I would spookily meet again later while doing PR for Apple in London Town...) whisked me up a lift to the

Student Union Centre and into the Custom Built House, which would be my home for the next 3 days! This was THE LOCK-IN! I was the only non-English person in the house, and in being so was also the only Northern Irish person. This victory was up for grabs, but the fact that I was in the house was enough for me. Let's get the party started.

Part Six – 'The Lock In' Day 1 (6th February 2004)
I'm writing this over ten years down the line and my memory is hazy but being in 'The Lock-In' was a turn of fate for me. It changed my belief in myself in many ways. I was a more confident man after this. I didn't want to be an "also ran" ever again. I liked winning, I liked success and popularity and from this moment on, I was a much more self-confident and self-assured person. 'The Lock-In' was a turning point in my life for that reason but also because of someone I met through 'The Lock-In', a person who you will read a lot more about. My mate, drinking companion, former 'The Lock-In' housemate, backpacking buddy and all round hilarious guy, Mr. "Lock-In" Lee Adams.

The first night in the house we just got to know each other. We had a few beers, some chatting etc. It was totally like Big Brother. An announcement would come out of the speaker "This is the Lock-In. Would Jonny please come to the diary room?" You'd go in and talk about life in the house, your fellow housemates and "The Lock-In" voice would act as "Big Brother" to us.

Inside the house there were games to play, there was no contact with the outside world and it was a fun place to be. We had six mattresses on the floor each with a condom on them, we picked our beds for the night. The three girls were Alex, Sophie and Danni. The three blokes were Lee, Paul and me. Lee and I hit it off early on, as good mates and since we had both brought in beers and weren't girly lads, we shared stories of beer drinking and football.

The other lad Paul had more feminine traits to him, but I had got on well with too. He just seemed like a barrel of laughs, always laughing and joking. At least at the time.

With the girls, I fancied Danni and she knew it. She confessed in the Diary Room she felt awkward about having me around her. There was no escape in the house. We had a few tasks to complete in order to earn food and drink.

There was a fridge in the kitchen. There was a shower and a toilet. We weren't sure if there were cameras in the shower and toilet or not. Lee and I both went in and tried to investigate them. The three guys all admitted to waving our willies about in there just to see if we heard a laugh from somewhere. Though later Lee and I reckoned Paul was lying a lot of the time. He was the one who was "playing up to the cameras" and pretending to be all nice to everyone. When we got out into the real outside world, the only two people I kept touch with were Danni and Lee. Significantly Lee.

On the first night it was hard to get to sleep. The chat kept us all up as we all shared stories about our individual lives. I must admit I loved being the only non-English one in the group. I buzz off that sort of shit.

Part Seven – 'The Lock-In' Day 2 (7th February 2004)

The second day was the main event. We were awoken early for some keep fit. A lady from the outside world came in and got us to do press ups and sit ups. The reward was a Subway breakfast and a cup of tea each. Alcohol had been banned for the daytime and that came as no surprise, given the previous night's antics.

It was also eviction day and 'The Lock-In' staff had kept things quiet for us. We assumed one of us would be leaving and it was all done by public vote. Action in the house was being streamed on the internet 24/7 as well as in the Student's Union Bars during their opening times. My flatmates had come to the bar to watch it, but admitted they got bored! I think it was because there was no narrator. They didn't really know what we were up to. Inside 'The Lock-In', we were never bored.

We were called to the Diary Room to give two nominations for eviction. I voted out Lee and Alex, which looking back is ridiculous as Lee is one of my best mates now. The weird thing is that in that environment, I felt that I was closer to Paul, but it was a gameshow – he played the game. This friendship with Paul was a red herring. Paul was in it to win it, becoming the game player, he was the 'Nasty Nick' of 'The Lock-In' but in retrospect not as loveable.

Alex and Sophie were voted out first, leaving four of us in there. Girls received more eviction votes than guys. Whether that is the power of the woman voting out other women, or the ladies wanting us three handsome hunks to stay in, who are you or me to say…

Part Eight – 'The Lock-In' Day 3 (8th February 2004)

My memory is opaque again. I think we did our own Olympics on the third morning inside the custom built house. There was also pillow fighting, which I lost extravagantly in. I always hated the idea of pillow fighting.

Lee and I took it in turns to go to the Diary Room and ask for the football results. I asked for the Glentoran and AFC Bournemouth scores from the day before, but the rules were that we couldn't know the results from anything in the outside world. I remember being particularly frustrated by that, almost akin to my time in the Netherlands in 1991 when I couldn't discover the Northern Ireland v. Faroe Islands result.

However, The Lock-In at one point told me Glentoran had lost 3-1 at home to Dungannon Swifts. I didn't quite believe it to be the real result though. It turned out to be a hoax. When I got out I found out that we had won 1-0! They had lied!

When Lee was denied the Nottingham Forest result yet again, we then asked the Lock-In for a football quiz as surely they wouldn't turn that one down. We told them we were having football withdrawals.

"Can we have a football quiz please?"
– Lee Adams and Jonny Blair.

It was just something to pass the time as we headed into the final leg of finding out the winner of the gameshow.

The girls and Paul didn't like the idea of a football quiz. They just weren't into it. So basically, it was just designed for Lee and I! But the others perked up when they found out if we got more than 70% correct, we would all get a treat. During the quiz, the clinching question was one of these two (and Lee and I often debate which question it actually was):

"Who played in England's 5-1 win against Germany and 2-2 draw with Greece in 2001 and never played for England again?" or

"Who is the only player to have scored in the Premier League for five different teams?"

The answer, of course at the time, was Nicky Barmby. We both got it right and won the quiz and the reward for our housemates, which was pizza and good wine, I think. But the football player 'Nicky Barmby' would become a codeword and was the start of a crazy barmby army life involving myself and Lock In Lee.

A few hours later and as darkness arrived, we were about to find out who would win 'The Lock-In'. Danni was voted out next so she came fourth, but Lee, Paul and I were now left to battle it out. Three lads made it to the top three! Why were people voting the girls out first? We couldn't work that one out. In the end I liked all my 'The Lock-In' housemates except for Paul.

As the final 30 minutes in 'The Lock-In' drew to a close, Paul, Lee and I were battling for the title of winner.

I was next though. No silver or gold for me. But a nice bronze. I came third. I was pretty damn happy to have made it until the last 30 minutes in the house. We then awaited the winner as I joined my mates in the bar.

I was up on stage dancing around with my Northern Ireland flag and made a speech about how good it was in the house. The bar, Dylan's was packed and I was glad of the freedom again, seeing my friends and we were drinking pints and playing pool.

Paul was out next – he came second. Lee Adams was the winner! Lock-In Lee won it! I spoke to Lee and Paul briefly after 'The Lock In' but we all headed back to our own groups of friends and nobody really knew what was happening. The whole experience had been draining, confusing and life-changing.

Part Nine – 'The Lock-In' Aftermath

The next few days were all a daze. It was a lifechanging headfuck! I couldn't get back to my normal life. My head still thought I was inside 'The Lock-In'! I stayed the first night at Austin and Jody's flat but I kept waking up in the middle of the night asking if I could use the toilet! In 'The Lock-In', we had to ask permission to urinate or poo. It was crazy. It had messed with our heads. The only thing that could help me was talking to someone else who was in 'The Lock-In', and going through the same emotions.

By complete coincidence, I received a text message out of the blue from an unknown number. It said, in two words only, "Nicky Barmby". It had to be Lee Adams and it was. I had written my number on a piece of paper for him in Dylan's Bar that night as neither of us had our phones of course – those were the days. So naturally, after the "Nicky Barmby" text message, I met up with Lee for a pint and neither of us could stop laughing. I congratulated him on winning and I turned up for his photoshoot for the local paper, the Daily Echo. We were also invited to a Bournemouth University TV chat show type thing and I got a part in a radio play of some description for B1rst – another University Based Radio Show. We were being invited to random events including an all you can drink night in a new nightclub. In truth though, 'The Lock-In' was messing with our heads, it had been weird being locked away from civilisation even for just 3 days. I sook professional help with a psychiatrist for a few sessions. I couldn't fathom what was going on!

As I type this up, some eleven years on, from my flat overlooking Yau Tong in Hong Kong, I raise a sneaky smile. 'The Lock-In' changed my life and it could be the single most amazing thing I feel I have done in life so far. So, thanks for voting for me, thanks to the organisers for picking me and hopefully I will see a proper video of it someday, as in truth the book remained open and we never got to see a decent video of it. The friendship I have with Lock In Lee is now is one of the best friendships I've ever had and likely will ever have. Lee and I have been on some truly crazy adventures since 'The Lock-In' and he is the only one I have kept proper touch with. There will be more to come from Lee Adams and I in later chapters of this book, on my blogs and forevermore.

Chapter 12
The Night I Sacked My Flatmate

Bournemouth, ENGLAND, February 2004

"Let's do windmills with our willies" - Jody Casey, 2004.

When I first moved to England, I loved the sheer diversity of the whole shebang. Nights on the town, able to talk away to everyone without ever being scared of people or wary of their reactions. I couldn't have done that in Northern Ireland. The whole Protestant - Catholic thing would rear its head in my home country more often than I wanted it to and English friends of mine didn't really know about that. But living in England changed things for me in that life became smoother with less baggage. I loved getting in on the messing around lark with my mates without a care in the world. My lifestyle in England began in 2003 in the charming seaside town of Bournemouth on Dorset's south coast.

A few funny things had happened in the early weeks of January 2004. I'd 'pulled' the same girl twice without her remembering me from the first time - Hannah from New Milton. On the first night, we'd been in the Opera House in Boscombe and her mate Laura came up to me and started chatting. Then she said her mate had her nipple pierced so I asked to see it. She said, "she won't show you it - I haven't even seen it". I bet her a drink that I'd get her to show me her pierced nipple. A few minutes later and I sauntered back with this Hannah girl, "show Laura your right boob" I said. She did. I then asked for a gin and tonic from Laura. Hannah, being the recipient. That wasn't the tactic but it was part of the plan. These moments were typical of nights out in the early days living in Bournemouth.

But my flatmate Steve at the time used to take the piss out of me. We were good mates for the most part but every now and then he'd say something about some girl I fancied and indeed mocked my double pulling of Hannah that time. It was all in good spirit though and I liked Steve, but I did want to wind him up. Then a chance came through.

One night, Steve and I were sat in the lounge and he says to me "Jonny at work the boss is always checking my till and it's down". Steve worked in the local Co-Op in Springbourne while at the same time I was working in Tesco in Branksome.

We were both students as well as flatmates and shared all these things with each other over a beer in the flat. He supported Chelsea and England. I was Bournemouth, Glentoran and Northern Ireland. There was always a bit of banter between us.

So, on hearing the Co-Op story I thought of a way to wind Steve up. He needed shutting up at some point as he was always boasting about getting the best girls, having the biggest c*ck and Chelsea winning everything in sight. I never actually saw his c*ck, but Claire that lived with us saw both mine and Steve's so I guess she could judge that one (she slept with Steve and she came into the kitchen at 4 a.m. once when I was drunk and naked looking for cheese on toast and she was sober on her way to the toilet so she'd got a glimpse of both her flatmate's willies!). Anyhow, it was time for a prank.

Next morning I'm at university and I draft up a fake letter on Co-Op printed paper using the university computers (didn't have nor want a laptop in those pre- "Don't Stop Living" days). The letter was addressed to Steven Compton, my innocent flatmate and read something like this.

Dear Steven,

Thank you for your work at the Co-Op store in Springbourne, Bournemouth recently. However due to a number of discrepancies in the till counts following your shifts, we have no option other than to dismiss you from the post.

We will be in touch with the payment for your final week's wages and a P45 will be forwarded in due course. Should you wish to appeal, please do not hesitate to contact the manager Dawn or myself at head office for the south of England based Co-Op stores.

Yours sincerely,

Peter Taylor

Co-Op South of England Regional Manager

And with that, I showed it to my mate Austin who laughed his tits off but said "he won't fall for that – it's signed off by the England football manager!". Yes, at the time, it was Peter Taylor. I put the page in an envelope, stuck a first class stamp on it and posted it immediately. I posted it to my own flat as I knew Steve would be in in the morning and would open the mail first. The next night or two I wasn't around. I stayed at Emma's for a night and spent the other night at Austin's. Emma was my English girlfriend at the time and the first non-Northern Irish girl I'd ever been with. Sexually, romantically, well in any real way bar a few snogs with English girls in Magaluf notably Hoddeson babe Catherine Taylor. Another place, another time, honeypants.

I came home on the Friday after university to find Steve sitting on the sofa not so happy. "What's up mate?" I asked him.

"Been sacked" came the genuine reply. He had fallen for it left hook and sinker.

"Oh yeah? What was it? Those dodgy till readings, you didn't actually steal money did you?" (I knew he wouldn't have done, but it went along with the whole belief he had that the letter was legitimate).

"Yeah apparently. They think I did."

"Appeal it."

He wasn't happy and I went back to my room, got my guitar out and played some Oasis. I was trying not to laugh at the whole thing. Steve then told Hannah and Claire - our other flatmates that he'd been sacked. The type of character that Steve was, he wouldn't phone his work up or call in and I knew it - he was too proud. I went out to the kitchen to make my dinner and asked Hannah, Claire and Steve if they were going out that night or if they wanted to join me and a few others (Dancing Andy, Australian Emma, my girlfriend Emma, Abbi, Dan and Austin). Claire and Hannah were up for it and this felt good as I knew that Steve was down in the dumps from the news and wouldn't go out. My fake posted letter had worked. We were going to the Showbar.

I told Steve he should come out for a few drinks - would be fun. Eventually he said yes and I told him I had some good news to tell down the pub. We got the bar and I could still see he was down. Austin was pissing his pants as nobody ever wound Steve up - an untouchable type of bloke always in a good mood.

Hey Steve - take a shot mate as I bought him a cheap Corky Cherry shot (or something that cost about £1) and after that I said - you're not sacked, I wrote that letter! At the start he didn't actually know whether as a mate I was just trying to make him feel better or not. But he took it in good heart and actually shook my hand and said "well-played, good joke". He was back working in the Co-Op the next day in his normal shift!! It was just the crazy type of things we were doing to each other at university. This is one story from a plethora within that era. For the protection of some, many such stories will remain untold. Meet me down the pub for an onslaught of them.

Steve didn't get exact revenge for that moment but something really weird happened the following week which at the time I called it karma for my wind up. I had stayed the night at Emma's or at Austin's instead of sleeping in my room and had locked the door of my room as I always did. I'm still like that – I trust no-one. When I returned the next day there was a massive dent in my door. I wondered if Steve had actually got drunk and wanted to come in and get me, though it later transpired that Steve had accidentally broken my door and we would need to fix it to get the deposit back. His Dad and him came down and fixed it in the end and we got the deposit back, while ironically, Steve moved out in June and my mate Austin moved in.

It had been a funny experience and the only time I got one over Steve. Thanks for taking it so well mate. As I write this, AFC Bournemouth have quite recently dicked Chelsea 3-0 at Stamford Bridge and 4-0 at Dean Court. Nice moments those, Steve!

While I did three chapters on my youth in some kind of trilogy, these three chapters are somehow a short trilogy of events from my first year of life in Bournemouth. "The Lock-In" (Chapter 11), "The Night I Sacked My Flatmate" (Chapter 12) and "For Your Arms Only" (Chapter 13) are just three of many stories that made the cut from this time of my life. I could have written so much more, and even these are not the best stories. I'll perhaps keep the others for another time. Before I report on "For Your Arms Only", I'll just write a bit more about the things that were happening at the time in my life.

With Bournemouth, I had landed on my feet. I had swapped a Northern Irish "B" seaside town for and English one. It was a simple move – B to B, Bangor to Bournemouth, beach to beach.

Within a few months of life in this seaside town, I was already a massive AFC Bournemouth fan. I didn't miss a single Cherries home match during my first two years living in Bournemouth as long as I was in England at the time of the match. I loved it. I got to meet Warren Feeney twice and Saturdays were spent at Dean Court and out with the lads. In February 2004 I was there on Pancake Night to watch the Cherries thrash Wrexham 6-0. We were 3-0 up and coasting, then James Hayter came on as a sub. "Oooh Jamie Hayter!" came the chants from the North Stand as we danced in the February Air. Three nil up, on the edge of the play-offs and it was Pancake Night (Shrove Tuesday). Hayter then scores a hat-trick in the space of 2 minutes and 20 seconds. Right before our eyes in front of the North Stand. It was simply unbelievable. We had all witnessed a piece of football history and we knew it was fast but didn't know it was a UK record until we got to the pub afterwards – the ever vibrant Dolphin Pub – our local at the time, which is now shut. In those days, no smart phones or Wi-Fi – the news that Hayter beat the record was shown on the pub's television.

I was going out with Emma around the same time and we got on well, never argued and enjoyed ourselves. But we broke up and it was all my fault. I don't regret it of course, as life happens. But the lads and I were sat in the Dolphin Pub in Springbourne planning my 24th birthday night on a night that the Cherries had lost 2-1 at home to Blackpool and probably blown our play-off chances. I decided I just didn't want a girlfriend. I phoned Emma and told her I had to finish with her. There was no genuine reason. I just wanted to be single, footloose and fancy free. It was to turn out to be quite a summer for the ladies as I flirted my way with a Danish girl, two Germans and sank my sausage with Denise, my brief flatmate who was back in town only for an exam re-sit. I wasn't looking for any long term relationships, that was all. It was a shame that Emma got caught up in it all as she was truly a lovely girl and I remember her well by her audacious blow-jobs, her easy going ways and of course her backpacking stories from Australia which later played a huge part in my own life of travel. She inspired me for sure. She'd forget my name, I'd remember hers.

Emma and I were single now and we never met each other again in life. I had now become best friends with Neil Macey ('The Famous Millwall Neil') and Jody Casey. Both of whom I would live with that Summer, and Jody for a further two years. Neil and I had some crazy nights out in London and on a day when Bournemouth were away, I went to watch his team Millwall in South Bermondsey. Way on down south, South London Town…

Jody, Steve and I stood outside our flat at 2 a.m. once with three beers and Jody yells "let's do windmills with our willies". We pulled our pants down and we flicked our willies round like windmills to any cars and cyclists that went past. Stuff like this is immature but somehow hilarious. They were some of the best times of my life with the lads on our nights out in sunny sunny Bournemouth.

I had completely forgotten about my life in Northern Ireland and I knew I wasn't going back. I had clearly left that all behind now. With my feet firmly on the ground and everything going well, it was time for my 24th birthday…

Chapter 13
For Your Arms Only

'For Your Eyes Only' stripclub, Bournemouth, ENGLAND (30th March 2004)

"I'm not cracking up; I'm just getting older" – Noel Gallagher.

I was only turning 24. Hardly a major landstone in life. But still it was the lads' lads on those nights and we got about 10 of us together with about 4 of the girls to come out and celebrate my birthday. It was just meant to be a pub crawl in Bournemouth culminating in a strip club. I'm not really into stripclubs incidentally, but it was just an idea we came up with at the time for my birthday. I had just split up with my girlfriend a week before, perhaps that had influenced this decision. Emma Halstead. I don't know why we chose a stripclub though. Emma had done nothing wrong and was a great girl, but my lifestyle was a bit topsy-turvy back then and I'm not sure she suited it so as mentioned in Chapter 12, I phoned her in front of my mates and "dumped her". It wasn't really that harsh. I think she should have come out that night but she was working the next day and she wasn't a big football fan. Bournemouth had played Blackpool at home that night and after the match I phoned her from the Dolphin Pub and ditched her. Emma - I hope that's what happened and no bad feelings but at the time things weren't right.

So, the following week was my birthday and we headed to the Dolphin. I declared it as a "Silly Hats Night" and everyone had to wear a hat. I don't like generic shit - turning up for birthdays and nights out as if it's just another day in the week. Make an effort to stand out, wear a hat, we will remember those nights. I had a sneaky pint in Dylans Bar at the University with Dandy (Dancing Andy had now become 'Dandy') at 3 p.m. But 6 p.m. hit and I joined Steve, Neil and Austin in the Dolphin. The lads were good - they bought my beers and we headed to Inferno next and then to the Gander in the Green which is where everyone was. Another beer in the Slug and Lettuce, then the Litten Tree, then Bar Fruit and so on and so forth. It was a decent pub crawl.

I always wanted to be the big man. One of the lads. I didn't like being the un-noticed one. I hated it. So, as it was my birthday, I told Austin I'd always have two drinks in front of me for the duration of the night, even if there was one sip in each. In other words, before I'd finish one, I'd have the next one ordered or lined up. So, as the night progressed, I kept this up and at by the end of the night, we got to a strip club called "For Your Eyes Only". I decided to take two beers to the top of the stairs and walk down singing the James Bond song "For Your Eyes Only". Halfway down I collapsed, landed badly on my arm on the floor, keeping one beer in one hand, and the other was confined to the floor. As I ventured inside again I thought nothing of it. The guys ordered a girl to dance for me. I took my pants off, showed her my erection in secret (which was frowned up in 2004) had a quick laugh and we drank up and left the club.

The thing is, I left 'For Your Eyes Only' strip club with a broken arm.

From that fall down the stairs, but I didn't know it at the time, I had broken my arm. Caught in the moment and intoxicated I had no way of knowing – pain was numbed.

On the way home, I asked Neil if he wanted to just crash at ours for the night and he agreed. We had beer and cider in the fridge, Neil was a good mate and all was good. On the way home though, there was a poster for an Adult Shop that I wanted. I told Neil for a laugh "we should take the poster down. I'm drunk enough to do it. Let's do it!" And we did. I ripped the poster off and fell down to the ground. I landed on my arm. That was twice I had landed on my arm now on the same evening. I was fucked.

I couldn't get back up but in those days as a new 24 year old you don't think of it like that. I carried on. We went back to mine, had a beer and I went to sleep. No idea what time it was. My arm had already been broken in the stripclub, or was it cracked on the street

trying to nick a stupid poster. It was carnage and I didn't have
the answer.

Next morning I woke up in agony and told my flat mate Steve
"think I've broken my arm". I told him this as he was leaving the
house anyway to head to University. I was supposed to study
something that day and work later that night but I knew something
was up. Emma and I had split so I couldn't ever have texted her
and asked for help - as much as I wanted her back that time. Neil
was in studying and wasn't my best mate just yet so I texted
Austin. Austin was round within 30 minutes of my text message.
Bear in mind Austin had seen me sober, drunk and at my best and
worst the previous year or so. He knew something was up. He
booked us a taxi straight to Littledown Hospital and they
confirmed the arm break. "He's broke it in three places" they said
to Austin. Austin, as hungover as me said "Oh right mate yeah"
cool as a fucking cucumber and we headed to Jody's bar at
Littledown - the Harvester - to tell him the news. Jody was Austin's
flat mate and we would be all moving in together from the first
week of July anyway. In the meantime, with my broken arm,
Austin said I was staying back at theirs that night which had a new
arrival. And a change. The world was coming to me.

We sat watching the Office, it was now Easter and some of my
friends had left Bournemouth for Easter, but one new friend had
arrived. Charlotte Seres. A French girl studying at Bournemouth
for only a few months. Charlotte had an instant feel good vibe.
"I've always wanted to meet someone French" I said to her as I
danced around the living room" in Ricky Gervais style.

"Show me how the English do it" she said.

"I can't, Charlotte. I'm Northern Irish", I mumbled.

Scarlet Charlotte I nicknamed her and she had some wild nights out with Lee and I before she headed back to France. She once texted me:

"Waking up next to you was better than waking up alone without my hat" – Scarlet Charlotte.

So, in the heat of this crazy night, I now had my broken arm and was on Incapacity Benefit from my job in Tesco. But the worst consequence was that I was about to fail my first year at university, entirely because of the arm incident. Yes, I failed. I had to repeat most of my tail end of year coursework for the University. It was my right arm that was broken and the worst thing for me was that I couldn't write and I couldn't type. I once tried to narrate an assignment to Austin, but he'd have been too much of a saint to write my article for me. It was all my fault of course and I take responsibility for my actions. It wasn't all good. I won't pretend to be James Bond in a strip club again and I won't deface or steal road signs or shop posters ever again. I didn't mean any harm, but some kind of karma had worked on me. I had to repeat my first year of university and I was almost back to the drawing board in terms of work and academic stuff. I hated not being able to write, and I tried hard with my left hand, but it just wasn't the same.

However, looking back, breaking my arm was a blessing in disguise. You know how one instance changes your life forever? If I hadn't broken my arm, I'd have passed my first year and I might have gone working full-time in Tesco that summer which would have been ridiculous given what was around the corner for me. But a certain job called 'Best Break' would never have happened, ironic completely that the word 'break' was used in my job location to follow.

If I had never broken my arm, I stand by the fact that I would never EVER have applied for a job which involved arm strength, which was my first task with a newly recovered arm in May - scooping up ice cream. I had got a job at a fast food and ice cream shop next to Bournemouth Pier, called 'Best Break'! As I served my first ice cream in my new job, I never pondered, as I don't BUT my life had changed. I was global. I turned around to look at my 5 new friends at work - from China, Poland, Colombia, Guinea and New Zealand. There were 5 continents there and I told them I'll get out and see the world and so will they. I have no doubt they did. I worked for Bournemouth Borough Council in their seafront huts in the summer months.

By breaking my arm and not passing the first year of the degree, it also influenced every little event of my life from there on in. The people I met in London in 2006 while working for Bite – if I hadn't broken my arm, I'd have probably moved to London in 2005. I may not have gone backpacking in 2007. Really, really this arm break was a blessing in disguise. Like many of my taints and mistakes in life, I felt this one was good in the long run. It was just another step on my journey.

So, within two months of the arm break I was now working in three jobs at the same time and had my three best mates as my flatmates – Austin, Neil and Jody. We also had 'Total Mike' living with us for a spell (a Welsh Phillipino lad who worked in Walkabout) and our friend Denise stayed for a few nights to do a University re-sit as well. For one night only, Denise was my 'summer sunshine' back in 2004. But nobody needs to know.

"I'll kiss you, but nobody needs to know" – The Corrs.

The Summer of 2004 was amazing. I worked every day in some capacity. Either on Bournemouth beach for the local council in 'Best Break' (cheeseburger joints and ice cream huts) or by night I was the barman in the Heathlands Hotel in East Cliff. That bar job itself was ironic enough as it was the hotel I stayed in back in 1994 when I was in Bournemouth with my family as a teenager! Here I was exactly ten years later working in the bar there!

Once a week only I still worked in Tesco in Branksome on the tills. I had 3 jobs and was able to have a busy social life whilst also keeping all three jobs. My life was busy, hectic and complete. Financially I was good - now with three jobs, recovered from my broken arm and top mates with Neil – who was always there for a pint after work as he worked in town too. We had the craziest summer ever. It was a lad's flat but we had girls in and out all the time and Millwall Neil's mate John Johnson would come down on occasional weekends to party, even though he knew we were all at work. Neil worked right next to me too! I worked in the ice cream huts, most notably the apt 'Best Break' by Bournemouth Pier and Neil worked in Jumpin' Jaks nightclub.

I don't want to go on about this period of my life too much as I cover it often on my blog and over-reminisce, but it really was the best time ever. We played football with work some nights – there would be 30 of us playing a massive match at Pokesdown, Littledown or a park somewhere near Charminster. It used to be the UK v. the Rest of the World. Bournemouth is one of the most popular places in the world for learning English in the Summer. My workmates hailed from over 30 different countries and I met Julio Felipe, my Colombian friend, the Polish crowd, the Spanish, Angolans and Libyans. It was international class. After work, everyone I worked with was always up for a beer or to hang out. We'd go down the pub and we'd know everyone in there. It was finish work, head to the pub and see who is in there. The cheap Wetherspoons, the Moon in the Square was the after work local. There was no Facebook, Twitter or any Smart Phone bullshit. It was "go to the pub, know everyone in there, have fun, go to bed, wake up for work again". Life was brilliant in Bournemouth in 2004-2005. Everyone that was there remembers that forever.

In short, breaking my arm, getting the job selling ice cream and moving in with my best mates was the best time of my life in Summer 2004. Long before I became a long term lunatic backpacker. It was the people I met from around the world in Bournemouth that summer that inspired me to travel more and more.

During 2004, I also travelled back to Belfast for the Northern Ireland matches, most significantly in March when David Healy scored against Norway at Windsor Park, ending a run of over TWO years without a goal. Yes, Northern Ireland hadn't scored in 1,298 minutes of football, and I had been there in the stadium for ALL the home matches of that spell. Things got better towards the end of the year and I travelled to Cardiff in Wales, where we went 2-0 up and ended up drawing 2-2. A Stuart Elliott last minute goal also grabbed us a 3-3 draw at home to Austria and I booked my flights to Germany for March 2005 to go to the Poland away match, via Berlin. Just before that, there was also the small matter of the England away match at Old Trafford. In the intervening months, a lady called Lauren somehow came into my life…

Chapter 14
Lauren

Jumpin' Jaks Nightclub, Bournemouth, ENGLAND
(November 2004)

"I could never be the right kind of girl for you, I could never be your woman"- White Town.

This is not a chapter about a Cameroon footballer. There was a more important Lauren than that in my life. I wasn't ever actively seeking a relationship at the time. It was late 2004. The most important things in my life were watching football (Northern Ireland and AFC Bournemouth), hanging out with my mates, working (I had multiple jobs at the time - barman at a hotel, ice cream seller in summer and cashier in Tesco a few weeknights) and studying (I was still doing a degree at Bournemouth University don't forget). When I say, don't forget, I almost did.

Then one night in November 2004, I was down Jumpin' Jaks nightclub with my mates to meet ITV celebrity Timmy Wallet. Yes, a hero of mine and him from "Wacaday" fame. He was doing a show, a repeat of Wacaday, singing and signing autographs at Jumpin' Jaks – it's a bit of a singles nightclub down by Bournemouth Pier. I used to love it down there. By the end of the night, all my mates were still up dancing away, it was about 2 a.m. I hung around and sat down next to some girls. The one on my right was a pretty, smiley and slim English girl. We got talking. Her name is Lauren and I liked her instantly.

"I have a boyfriend you know" she mumbles to me as I chat. "I'm only chatting, when did I mention anything about boyfriends or girlfriends?" She laughed and we had a drink together and a good chat. She seemed like my type of girl. She was local, attractive, hard-working and a barrel of laughs. We swapped numbers and left it at that.

I did text Lauren a few times in the run up to Christmas but I was busy with work and also trying to date another English girl, Charlotte Marsh. She was a pretty Dover girl with a fanciable demeanour and nice boobies. Outrageously, Charlotte once texted me asking me to be her "f*ck buddy", before passing notes of a sexual orientation while I was working on the tills in Tesco. It was a bit mad and though we enjoyed a raunchy kiss outside her flat one night, nothing actually worked out and there was no sausage sinking or sizzling. This Charlotte kind of stood me up and got moody with me a few times and while that fizzled out, my God's coincidence, Lauren became single.

A text in January 2005 confirmed that Lauren and I would finally go out for a drink so I took her to the cheapest bar in town, the Wetherspoons. We met at the fire in the square and I penned a poem for her with a line "with the moon in the square and the balloon in the air and the fire that never goes out". It's quintessentially Bournemouthic.

I did wonder if maybe Lauren's boyfriend was still with her. But he wasn't - he was completely out of the picture and well we had a good night chatting and drinking. It got to about 11 p.m. and she asked how we would get home. I was still pretty cheap in those days so a taxi wasn't a realistic option. Luckily my flat mate Dan was out driving with Claire and they could give us a lift back - Lauren all the way to her flat.

When Lauren left the car, I kissed her on the cheek only and said "bye. See you soon". I hoped she'd want to see me again. When we drove off I said to Dan and Claire "I like that girl. She's got style". That night I thought of Lauren as I slept and she texted to say it was cool to meet the following night again. We started dating instantly. It was so fast – we had snogged within 24 hours. I invited her down the student club to meet 2 of my mates and just hang out. That night we went back to mine after a few drinks and we slept together. I gave her a lift home and we met up again the following night. Three nights in a row we were together. It was the first time I'd done that with a girl in a long time. There must have been something good about Lauren.

Lauren was a really really fun, happy girl to be around. She came out with my friends, she liked my sense of humour, I loved her company. She looked good. We went to the pub, we went to the cinema, we went to her cosy local pub (in the countryside). I went to see her horse, Mossip which was her love. My love had always been football. In March 2005, Lauren accompanied me to the student awards for Nerve at the swanky Durley Hall Hotel and we were sure as hell dressed up for the occasion. Lauren was stunning. She looked fantastic that night. My 25th birthday was coming up though and wanderlust mixed with football was in the air. I decided to go on a 10 day trip with my mates from different periods of my life to celebrate my 25th. I would be in Poland for my birthday this time, and I had learnt my lesson and moved on from the previous year's 'For Your Arms Only' incident. Lauren was busy working and the trip was pre-arranged so off I went on holiday.

I headed to London first for a couple of nights, then north to Manchester to watch Northern Ireland play England. Then we flew to Berlin before getting a train across the border into Poland, for another football match. I would be in Warszawa on my 25th birthday and we stayed in a swanky 5 star hotel. Well, back in those days it was about the same price as a 2 star hotel in England, Warszawa was so cheap and my first trip to Poland certainly sowed the seeds on my love for the country. From my bedroom in Warszawa, I phoned Lauren on the night of my 25th and we had a good chat - she even said I could get a stripper on my birthday if I wanted. I admit it now, we actually did end up in a stripclub on that evening!! For the second year in a row and never since on my birthday. But in 2005, I wasn't carrying bottles of beer down steps this time, or trying to be the big man. Our short time in the stripclub consisted of two Northern Irish football internationals walking in, only to find the place full of us – the Northern Ireland fans, now known as the GAWA (Green and White Army). Lauren was fine with it and I told her all about it when I got back. She found it funny and liked it.

Lauren and I met up a few more times in April 2005 but then it just fizzled out, too. We never once argued, we were quite a cool little couple and my mates all approved of Lauren. After a night at the cinema in Poole, we then decided to split, amicably. We both got on with things. Lauren later went on a trip to Amsterdam with my mate Millwall Neil and his ex-girlfriend Jenny Daniels.

Things ended and I never fathomed why, I wasn't in love with Lauren, nor her with me (I presume) but we had fun and we were a cool couple. I met Lauren once again only in life and that was in the Malt and Hops bar in Southbourne in April 2007. I was back in town for a night having relocated to London and we agreed to go for a drink. It was cool and my mate Scott Gordon commented "why is she your **ex**-girlfriend? Didn't you make a mistake?" Scott was right - Lauren was a great "catch" at the time.

According to my mate Millwall Neil, I once phoned Lauren on a bus back to London when I was drunk and said some rude things to her. I have no recollection if they were true or not, or why I would have done that. We had nothing bad together and I always thought we ended things on a good note. I haven't seen Lauren since 2007 which is a shame as she was a top top girl. I doubt our paths will ever cross again and to top things off, Jumpin' Jaks nightclub where we first met and used to party, doesn't exist anymore. Claire was gone. Paddy was gone. Vicky was gone. Emma was gone. Lauren was gone.

I'll never forget our short few months together and the times we shared. Thanks be to Lauren.

Chapter 15
The Seventy Quid Taxi

London, ENGLAND (February 2005)

"You're a slave to money then you die" - Richard Ashcroft.

For the second year in a row I was in London for the Big Brother Auditions. By this time Lock-In Lee had relocated to Birmingham and was struggling for money so he couldn't make it. Millwall Neil wasn't interested and neither were my friends Austin or Jody. Or anybody else I knew. Nobody in my circle of friends wanted to join me to audition for Big Brother. However, one man always interested in it was John Johnson, so a swift call and John and I agreed to meet at London Bridge and head to the auditions together. John Johnson may not have been mentioned in the first 14 chapters, but he has certainly featured on my travel blogs and was a huge part of my story in England and further afield. John attended two Northern Ireland away matches with me too, despite being an Englishman!

London, February 2005 it was. Millwall were at home that day and "Millwall Neil" was heading on the bus from Bournemouth so I arranged to stay at Neil's, head out to the Big Brother auditions and meet up with Neil after the match. We both booked a mega cheap £2 Megabus return and the whole weekend would probably only cost us about £20 if we were sensible. If.

We got to the Big Brother auditions, and John had brought Hazel along. It was my first time to meet Hazel Gordon. A girl who would come in and out of my life a few times over the next 4 years. We said bye to Neil and headed for a drink in London Bridge then travelled over to Excel Centre on the London DLR for the auditions. We had a few cans of lager and cider on the way, we did our auditions and got on with it. It turned into a heavy night, so the £20 budget option was probably blown by around 6 p.m. We met Neil and watched the football down the pub. Millwall had drawn 1-1 with Leeds, and Bournemouth had won 3-0 away to Swindon Town so we were all buzzing. We hit up a cheap pub in Lessy's Q (Leicester Square) which was then called The Bat and Ball. Pints were £1.50 – we heard it was the cheapest pub in Central London at the time - and in those days Neil and I would drink beers like tap water. There were still four of us and we managed to get into the Hippodrome in London, a swanky nightclub. A few hours in there and we were all worse for wear. I headed outside on my own at one point and ended up in a bar in Soho where I fell asleep. I woke up some time later and didn't know where I was. I must have been texting Neil when I fell asleep as my mobile phone was now gone. I had lost my mobile phone or it had been stolen and in those days I was a fairly crap backpacker. I couldn't have found my way back to Neil's flat, or John's flat or Hazel's flat at 3 a.m. I really was in no state either and in fact I don't think I had been to John's house ever before on public transport, I'd only ever gone there with John. My phone was a cheap one so I wasn't bothered. My jacket had been stolen or lost too - again a cheap one – I didn't care! It was a cold winter morning in London town though. I was down and out and this was a low.

But I knew John's address. I had £70 left in my wallet, some of which was John's and I knew I owed him it. So, in my drunken state and also without a phone and a coat, I decided it would be an easy option to just get a taxi from Central London to John's house. Can't be more than £20 I thought. Even that sounds crazy money as a bus there in those days would have been about £2-3! Then, I got in a Black London taxi, must have mumbled John's address to the driver and fallen asleep. He left me right to John's door, which was in Dartford in Kent. Not even in London. The bill for the taxi - £70!! I had the money to the exact amount and was glad to be there and not alarmed as I was still drunk so I paid up, got out of the taxi and rang John's doorbell.

No answer.

I knocked and knocked.

No answer.

It was 5 a.m. I had spent £70 getting here. I could have flown to Italy, Croatia, Germany, many destinations in Europe for £70! With Ryanair I could have had a £70 return! And yet I spent it on a taxi to John's and I couldn't get in! John clearly wasn't here. Next thing you know, I lay down in his front garden, covered myself in tree leaves and fell asleep. I was really cold! At this point my bag was still at Neil's and I had a Megabus ticket to head back to Bournemouth that day, but it was in the bag in Neil's. On me all I had was my wallet. My phone and coat had gone. My house keys and other stuff were all safely in Neil's, with my backpack. I didn't even know Neil or John's phone numbers or have a piece of paper with them written on it.

I woke up in John's garden at sunrise and was absolutely freezing. It was so cold. My balls were peas and my willy was a nail. I had messed things up big time and I now just needed to get back to London so I walked around and finally found a train station - Slade Green - where luckily there was no barrier and no attendants. The £70 I spent on the taxi was all I had. Now I had zero cash. At 7 a.m. I got on the first train I could back to Charing Cross. Yes, Charing Cross. Just round the corner from Lessy's Q where the madness all began. It would have been better just to have stayed there and saved the £70!!

£70 for a taxi to Dartford, slept in a garden with tree leaves then a free train back. I thought to myself I could have just stayed in the Casino and gambled away £Υ· and at least been inside in central London and been warm. It was a major error yet again. What a waste of money.

The next day when I realised I had just blown £70 on a taxi I decided I could easily get that money back so I hatched a plan. My plan was simple. I was aged 24 and I calculated that all the money in my life I had wasted on taxis, including this one, was colossal. Since that day I decided I would NEVER get a taxi again unless it hit one of my new found criteria. Since then, the only reasons that I have got a taxi have been:

1. Someone else offered and was paying for it.
2. Peer pressure (a lot of my Northern Irish football mates tend to take taxis instead of using local transport).
3. Danger or risk of attack (for example in Iraq and Venezuela).
4. Health (if I was ill and needed to see a doctor ASAP).
5. If it was the ONLY way to get from A to B.

If you have followed my travel adventures you will know I hate taxis. I normally refuse to get them, it wasn't just this one incident but this one was the catalyst that changed it.

I now walk as much as I can, I love using local buses and trains, I am public transport loyal. I find them much better experience seeing larger groups of real life people than being stuck in a taxi with one person who only wants your money (most of the time). People standing next to you on a bus don't want your money. They are fellow travellers and passengers.

Since that £70 taxi day, I reckon I have saved over £2000 in the last 10 years that I would previously have spent on taxis, or that other people would have spent on taxis given the same situation. It was a lesson and a big mistake to pay £70 for that taxi that night. But I paid it, I made a mistake. At the time I was gutted, but it changed me. I needed to have made that mistake to realise how horrendous taxis and their drivers are. It was proof I was becoming a cheapskate backpacker.

Some good examples since this event are that I spent 1 and a half years in Australia and took only two taxis. So few that they are both memorable:

1. I got a taxi in Devonport, Tasmania from the pub to our hostel because 3 of my mates didn't want to walk the 3 kilometres at midnight.
2. I got a taxi from Parramatta to Sydney because my boss paid for it - for a function.

Amazing really.

I also spent around 4 years living in Hong Kong and got less than 10 taxis, so the £70 taxi was later a learning curve to never do that again. During 2005 I actually paid a lot less for flights from Poland, Austria, England and Northern Ireland than this 45 minute taxi ride. Crazy.

Even though I had wasted £70 on a taxi that night, and lost my phone and coat, it made me wiser. I learned from that mistake and would never ever waste money in that way again.

Chapter 16
Barfgate

Berlin, GERMANY (March 2005)

"Where it began, I can't begin to knowing" - Neil Diamond.

I was 24. Old enough to know my way around Europe. Young enough to stay out drinking until 6 a.m. and still get up for breakfast at 8 a.m. and make my cross border train to Poland from Germany before noon. Easy peasy. In those days.

We were staying in the former capital of East Germany - East Berlin in the classic Aldea Hotel. A hotel that offered all the glimpses of communism - grey, drab and prisonesque and this was my first visit to Germany. It had been a lads lads lads trip and my friends Gavin and Michael McClelland booked the hotel and I roomed with them. I had a girlfriend at the time, the lovely Lauren who was back in Bournemouth England laughing at my drunken atrocities by the day on text or e-mail. We ended up in downtown Berlin. A quick city tour in the daytime, some Bratwurst and a sing song with some of my best friends from the last couple of years since I left Northern Ireland and the previous double decades when I'd lived there. Michael and Gavin McClelland were here on this trip with me of course, but I hadn't really seen them much in the last few years, with me living away from Northern Ireland and wanting more and more travel all the time. They were two of my best mates from childhood. By now though, we had drifted apart a bit mainly due to geographic separation, having been big time friends back in the 1990s (we even ran a football fanzine together until just a year before this adventure). There were the English based Northern Ireland lads that I knew (or was getting to know) - Nolers, Owen Millar, John Hart, Toddy and Rob Gray. The banter was cracking down the pubs of Berlin. We were all big Northern Ireland football fans onroute to Poland. I'd never been to Poland before.

There were a few new lads on the block as far as my journeys had been concerned - Ian "Skin" McKinney was there - I had first met Skin in Belfast in 2004 the night that David Healy scored against Norway (we had a pint and cigar for that one - any Northern Ireland fan will know why a cigar was needed). You could smoke in the kop in those days, as you could in bars. Dave Watson was there and was now secretary of the Bangor Northern Ireland Supporters Club. I was introduced to Tim and Charley Beattie, Roan, Wendy, Andrew and Colin. Then there was a young lad. Boisterous, enthusiastic and Northern Ireland through and through. It was Dean Nutt from Londonderry. An Institute fan.

Dean was young - only 17 and must have been loving his first big trip on his own around Europe (well Germany and Poland). I was

24 and most of the other lads were the same age as me, give or take a year up or down. So, when the beers kept flowing in those days, you'd have been hard pushed to get me back to the hotel or hostel early. When the bar was open, I'd be there with a beer. Dean and I were the late night drinkers of the team. The majority of the lads called it a night around 3 a.m. But Dean and I found "a wee bar" still serving. In fact - it was a bar with hookers in it, though we didn't indulge of course, we just drank the night away and chatted shit about Glentoran, Institute and Northern Ireland. The bar was pretty close to our hotel and neither of us will remember getting home but one thing was for sure. We had a morning border train booked to Poland the same day - before noon. I think it was a 10 a.m. departure from Berlin.

I must have got back to the hotel where I roomed with Gavin and Michael, at around 6 a.m. and they were fast asleep. Dean was in the same hotel in another room. I packed quickly, then grabbed an hour of sleep (something I couldn't do now as I write this book a decade on) and up for breakfast downstairs in the hotel. As ridiculous as it sounds, I had eaten my breakfast, worked out the U-Bahn route to the train station and was sitting packed and ready in reception about half an hour earlier than the lads. Dean was one of the last to materialise and he looked in a bad way to be honest. A few of us asked him if he was alright. Being a 17 year old Maiden City boy, of course he was - I don't think he'd had his breakfast though (but I can't be sure). Tea, water and a full on German breakfast had sorted me out to the point where I wanted to get on the Berlin to Warsaw train with a huge carryout of German beer and a ghetto blaster (in 2005 I was still tied to the 80s, my friends). I was pumped and it would also be my last 24 hours as a 24 year old.

All set, the lads rocked up to reception and we headed around 8.30 a.m. to the U-Bahn. The U-Bahn from round the corner would take us all the way to the main station in Berlin where our train direct to Warszawa Centralna would leave from. Easy stuff for a crowd of hungover Northern Irish lads. There were about 10 of us, soon to be joined by about 20 others on what was dubbed as the "party train", a niche which repeated itself regularly on my European Norn Iron supporting jaunts.

So, we hopped on the U-Bahn, some of us bought tickets, some of us 'chanced it'. I remember that Dean and I decided to 'chance it' since we had been the last two out, we stuck together and would back each other up. Mike and I were dressed in Northern Ireland shirts and looking particularly foreign and it also looked like we weren't on our way to work. I quickly looked around and it appeared that apart from our group, everyone was on their way to work. Dressed in suits, carrying briefcases. Normal day for these local Berlin residents. I glanced back over at Dean while Dave and Gavin asked me what time we stayed up till. I said we got home at 6 a.m. - just Dean and I and we ended up in a dodgy club but didn't do anything crazy - just sang a bit, drank some beer and flew the Northern Ireland flag. That much was true and I felt fine.

Dean was looking rough at this particular point. Then something happens. Let me just tell you the scenario before I launch into it. The train was PACKED with German businessmen and women - We all had massive bags with us - backpacks, suitcases, day packs etc. Some were on the floor of the train, some were not. Most of us didn't have a seat. It was rush hour. But Dean looked wrecked still so we let him sit down in the middle seat on the left of one of the doors as you enter a carriage. It was the only seat available, the rest of us stood. Dean didn't look well.

On a packed U-Bahn, on Easter Tuesday morning in Berlin in March 2005, with hundreds of Germans on our train all heading back to work for the first time since Easter, Dean opened his mouth and barfed everywhere. Everywhere. Upwards, downwards, sidewards, in front, below, beyond, behind. Beneath between betwixt. It was an explosion. I mean graphic stuff, it was horrible puke, you could smell it everywhere. German business types ran for cover. I lifted my bag up so it didn't get covered in pure spew from Dean. It wasn't just one big barf, more followed. There was a river of sick running through the entire U Bahn carriage. It happened so fast and everyone knew it was Dean. We all saw it - the locals knew it - sick was everywhere. We had backpacked to Brandenburg Gate the previous night, now we were witnessing the legendary "barfgate". Dean's barf was running through the carriages like an endless river - you could even spot schoolkids dancing past the continual line of lager fuelled puke, with women in high heels dodging their way past trickles of orange, red and white pure barf material while organising business meetings on their vintage mobile phones. To be honest, my shoes got partly covered in sick, but mostly I was doing two things:

1. Laughing my fucking head off. It was hilarious.
2. Hoping Dean was OK. He was only 17. I knew he'd be fine somehow.

It happened so fast and all of us had to bundle our stuff off at the next station and make a mad dash to ensure we didn't miss the train to Poland. There was another quick bit of crazy confusion. Mike had booked our train tickets but for the wrong day, so we had to make sure we could get them changed over as well!! A sort of mistake that has typified my travel lifestyle the last decade or so. You buzz off mistakes as they give you that extra rush of adrenalin. In the end we had time to spare on the exact platform as our train from Berlin to Warszawa pulled up, a train which has become known as the original party train when I speak with my mates about it. I had time to buy a 4 pack of Becks. I wasn't particularly cultured at drinking beer in those days, I grabbed the first 4 pack I saw. Right now, as an older man, I'd have been searching for a cappuccino or some craft beer!

A quality picture moment then occurred. Dean had seemingly recovered from "barfgate" and was spotted next to the ice cream stand buying an ice cream. As you do - you've just barfed gallons on a packed U-Bahn and you opt for a Cornetto!! That was Dean and that was Nutts.

The weird thing is that, once we boarded the train, I didn't see Dean again until we arrived in Warszawa and saw him in a bar that night. He was on the train for sure, but he wasn't up partying, singing and drinking with the rest of us. He was probably sleeping it off. Fair play to him. That's what I call entertainment and crazy moments.

We've all had our bad nights and this was Dean Nutt's moment of fame. I for one will never ever forget my exit from Germany that day thanks to Dean. Keep er lit, Deano!

We sauntered across the border to Poland and the following day would be my 25th birthday. It had been a bit Nutts. I've barely seen Dean since.

Our time in Warszawa watching Northern Ireland and enjoying my first glimpses of this city would have telling repercussions later on in my life. I really didn't know it then. There is no way that on the 29th March 2005, I expected that one day I would or even could live in Warszawa. No way. It's a funny world.

Chapter 17
The Original Monopoly Pub Crawl

Old Kent Road, London, ENGLAND (April 2005)

"Nice day for a white wedding" – Billy Idol.

The madness of Poland and Germany had died down, I had settled back into life in Bournemouth, finishing the first year of my degree (finally) and working back on the seafront selling ice creams. However, I had booked yet another trip to London, by way of a Manic Street Preachers gig on a Monday night in Hammersmith in late April. I had four days off work and headed to London on the Friday night to stay with John Johnson to make a weekend of it.

Neil and Jody were down in Bournemouth for the weekend but I planned a day out on the Saturday. The original idea was to have a Saturday down the pub watching the football scores come in. At the time Bournemouth were certs to make the play-offs to gain promotion for the Championship. I had been to every home match while living in England and a few aways. Plus, every weekend I had been in London, we had won our away matches that day, it was a lucky omen for the season. There was Wrexham, Walsall and Swindon. On this particular day we were due to play away at Chesterfield, knowing that winning all our remaining games would guarantee a play-off place (either 5th or 6th in the third tier – League One). With two home matches against relegation candidates coming up, it seemed certain.

So, I arrived in London on the Friday night and left my bags at John's flat before John decided we should head to The Venue (a rock club near the Millwall stadium) for a nice easy night. There was an Oasis tribute act on in The Venue in New Cross and we could watch that. We got there around 9.07 p.m., we sang away to Oasis and partied. The plan was to head back to John's around midnight or 1 a.m. on the night bus to Dartford. However, Hazel had joined us late on and there were now three of us.

At around 2 a.m. I asked John what time The Venue closes and he said "6 a.m. geeza". Then a crazy plan was hatched. We realised that The Venue was in fact on the Old Kent Road (or at least on the New Kent Road or within the area!). Significantly, the Old Kent Road is the first square of the Monopoly Board, the original Monopoly Board. I remembered my friends Andrew McGill and Dave Paine from Bournemouth University had once done the Monopoly Pub Crawl and written about it for the Nerve University Magazine. The idea had stuck in my head and I'd always wanted to do it. Now, we were on square one and had the chance. Even if it was 2 a.m.

With all of us off for the weekend and planning a football day on the Saturday, somehow nobody was tired come 4 a.m. As we sat relaxing in The Venue, John, Hazel and I decided we were on square one of the Monopoly Pub Crawl and that could do the full pub crawl that day. Or at least see how far we could get. We were all in our twenties, all so young. It just happened naturally. This was the start of a crazy day, looking back it was lunacy personified. Nothing was planned. This chapter does its best to encapsulate everything that my insane journey was all about.

Of course, in those days there was none of this "smartphone" nonsense. There was no checking Google Maps, no Facebooking selfies and certainly no hashtagging on Instagram. We left the venue at 6 a.m. when it shut and we headed for Leicester Square. It was in a coffee shop that I asked for a pen and paper and between us we wrote down every square of the Monopoly Board - there are 41 in total, as we counted "Just Visiting" and here they are:

1. Go
2. Old Kent Road
3. Marylebone Station
4. Income Tax
5. Super Tax
6. In Jail
7. Just Visiting
8. Free Parking
9. Go To Jail
10. Chance (Chancery Lane)
11. Community Chest (Dare)
12. Park Lane
13. Mayfair
14. Pentonville Road
15. Whitechapel Road
16. Northumberland Avenue
17. Bond Street
18. Leicester Square
19. Trafalgar Square
20. Euston Road
21. Vine Street
22. Marlborough Street
23. Pall Mall
24. Oxford Street
25. Regent Street
26. Bow Street
27. Kings Cross - St. Pancras
28. Picadilly
29. Liverpool Street Station
30. Fenchurch Street Station
31. Community Chest (Dare)
32. Chance (Chancery Lane)
33. Waterworks
34. Electric Company

35. Coventry Street
36. Whitehall
37. Strand
38. The Angel Islington
39. Fleet Street
40. Chance (Chancery Lane)
41. Community Chest (Dare)

We phoned our mate James Condron to tell him that we were in town doing the Monopoly Pub Crawl. At the time I had no idea how legendary the weekend would turn out to be, but James knew he wanted to join in and he got there into the Moon Under Water at Lesi's Q as quickly as he could. James ran back to a few streets / pubs he had missed to catch up with us. From there we plotted our way through each square on the Monopoly Board on a crazy mission. We got pieces of paper and I wrote down each square of the Monopoly Board, the pub or bar on that square that we visited and the time we visited it. Alcohol didn't seem to affect us, nor did sleep deprivation.

We were in the Jeremy Bentham Pub at Euston (on about square 27) when I found out that the Cherries had beaten Chesterfield 3-2 away. It was a mixture of a text message from my mate Dean Nutt (of Barfgate fame) who said, "get in" and the Sky Sports newsfeed that alerted us to this! For the fourth time that season, AFC Bournemouth had won an away match while I was in London, even though I wasn't physically at those games! And I was only in London 4 times that season! It was a crazy fact! The day progressed and we ticked off squares thick and fast. Then, John got stuck in the London Underground at Angel (he was slightly intoxicated) and he called it a day, but Hazel, James and I continued the pub crawl long into the night. By 4 a.m. we still had 6 squares to go and we were knackered. We had stayed up for 2 nights in a row, without any drugs. OK, well alcohol and one coffee. Only one coffee!

We grabbed some more coffee but the tiredness had condemned us to bed, so James, Hazel and I went back to Hazel's place to sleep and then woke up again around 10 a.m. I could do that easily when I was 25. I couldn't do that now. Hazel was busy on the Sunday looking after her two kids, Lauren and Kian but James and I decided to head back into Central London to finish the pub crawl! We had only 6 squares left to complete and they were: Mayfair, Vine Street, Regent Street, Traffy's Q / Trafalgar Square (which was odd given we had been nearby so often the previous day but never had a drink there to "tick it off"), Coventry Street and Picadilly ("pick a dildo", "pick a willy").

James and I finished the six of them very quickly and easily by mid-afternoon. This meant in 36 hours or so we had visited and ticked off all 41 squares of the Monopoly Board. With squares like 'Chance' and 'Community Chest' we either did dares or used logic to call it. 'Free Parking' was getting a free beer in a promotion in one of the bars. 'Just Visiting' meant we walked through one door of a pub and straight out the other door. It was a truly crazy weekend and I remember how we had DOUBLE bloody Mary cocktails in the last bar, the Chandos at Trafalgar Square to celebrate.

This is an epic pub crawl, probably the best I have ever done and I have often thought about organising it as a business and taking tourists round the circuit. The problem is it is dear, involves alcohol and may cause problems in a group as some drink fast, some drink slow and some can't really handle their drink or they get bored to keep going to all squares after a while. For this one weekend in April 2005, James and I had cracked it. We killed it. We were winners.

On a side note and to close the chapter off, for James's birthday in 2015 – 10 years on, I decided to organise the EXACT same pub crawl for him. But he had lost the enthusiasm for it and quit early. Neil and I ended up finishing the pub crawl second time of asking, by default on the second day, using our "passes" to drink tea and orange juice in a few of the squares. I have certainly mellowed since those crazy days in 2005 but it's an amazing memory of a weekend that epitomises what I love about a life of pure adventure. Monopoly Pub Crawl? Been there done that, 41 squares in 36 hours! If you fancy a crazy challenge and a barrel of laughs, try doing this one in London!

Chapter 18
Travel Blogging Chilled The Radio Star

Belvoir Tech in Belfast, NORTHERN IRELAND (1997 - 1998)
Nerve Radio, Bournemouth University, ENGLAND (2003 - 2008)

"What's the frequency Kenneth is your Benzedrine?" – R.E.M.

As mentioned in Chapter 8, an old friend of mine from Belfast, Keith Thompson, first coined the phrase "Jonny Blair on the air" when I was a student at Belvoir Tech in Belfast back in 1997. I didn't keep touch with Keith sadly, but he started a bit of a craze for me when I took my voice to the student radio waves in Belfast's fair city. Originally, I used to spend hours in the radio room at Belvoir Tech recording radio shows around the time of the Good Friday Agreement (1998) as well as a 1997 'Christmas Special', featuring contributions from my old tech buddies Jonny Kerr, Tommy Cunningham, Brian Finlay, Julie Cole, Suzie Spence, Keith Thompson and my own favourite 'pin up girl' Vicky Everitt. Vicky was my radio newsreader and I couldn't ever take my eyes off her lips as she spoke into the microphone opposite me. Those were good times. I'd learnt how to record radio shows during that journalism course and I loved it. It was a release. If I have nobody to talk to, I will talk to a microphone on radio. If I have no microphone, I will write. I always need some kind of output for my thoughts. I could sit on my own in a room with CDs, LPs and cassette tapes and play my favourite songs, record soundbites, talk rubbish and experiment. I was only 17-18 back in those days but the buzz of it all was unreal at the time. That radio studio in Belvoir, I made it my own and loved it. As I recorded my final show in 1998, I remember closing with the Eagles song "Tequila Sunrise" and that was that. Another career option shelved, but all in a happy way. I had been using the fake radio station name "Radio Belvoir" with the catch-line "Jonny Blair on the air".

However, time passed me by and when I left the radio studio in Belvoir in September 1998, I never returned. The studio was knocked down a year or so later and my radio "career" was dead and buried. I didn't even miss it. I was too busy to miss it. You'd never hear the infamous "Jonny Blair on the air" catch-line again. Or would you?

Arrival in Bournemouth in 2003 changed all that. With the option to DJ on Bournemouth University's "Nerve Radio", I auditioned, got in and took the opportunity with both hands and one bake. "Jonny Blair on the air" was back on the airwaves and into the ears of students in Dorset. I created my own brand of radio and was broadcasting on the internet at http://nervemedia.org.uk/. I did some joint shows with Hannah Thompson (my flatmate), Tom Clarke and Australian Emma Broomhall from my course, but the passion to be solo in that room was too strong to resist. I wanted to be alone in there. There was no money involved of course - for me it was the release, the prestige, the passion. I was a volunteer. I buzzed off it.

From 2003 - 2008 I spent five years DJ-ing on Nerve Radio. I am sure that I did more shows on the station than anyone else in that period of time (a fact which can no doubt be confirmed by Jason

Hawkins, the former editor of Nerve). I possibly even broke the record for the most amount of solo radio shows ever at the University. I couldn't possibly count them but sometimes I did 5 shows a week when most students did one. I did the radio for 6 years, I'd even go in on summer and Christmas holidays and play songs to nobody. I'd talk when nobody listened. It was a buzz and a passion. I met a ton of absolutely cool people through that including Tom Clarke, Abbi Love, Neil Lancefield and Chris Latchem (who has since gone onto BBC Radio 5 fame). I still catch up with Tom, a Plymouth Argyle fan, when I am back in Bournemouth.

I also acted in a play on B1rst Radio - the other University station on the campus. I saw myself as something similar to Alan Partridge, a flop who faked that he thought he was something bigger. A completely failed and wannabe comedian on the air waves. My stuff just wasn't funny unless you knew me. You have to laugh at your own jokes in life. But that was the point - I never took myself too seriously nor did I want to be a good radio DJ. I was always myself, people listened and occasionally, people laughed. It was like I was still down the pub with my mates lost in conversation about the Cherries, David Healy or a packet of Hobnobs. I recorded over 50 FM radio shows, which meant my workmates, flatmates and even people in cars could listen in. I used to get them all to tune in and force them to listen, often against their own will. I also did over 300 radio shows that were not on FM, just for listening online or on the campus. As I say, it was probably a record as I never met another student who lasted 6 years, or did anywhere even close to 100 shows.

In May 2005 my radio highlight was that I was allowed to take over from Radio One DJ Colin Murray in the DJ box in Jumpin Jacks Nightclub by Bournemouth Pier for a few songs. I had just recorded a Comic Relief Special with Nerve which was a naked show for charity and one that was broadcast on Comic Relief Day on a crazy day at the Students Union in Bournemouth.

About a month later, I went down to Jumpin Jaks where Colin Murray (a popular Belfast DJ and media personality) was DJ-ing. I introduced myself to Colin by way of dancing in front of the DJ Box waving a Northern Ireland scarf. He came over for a chat and had remembered my e-mail to him before, asking to meet up. Colin is a great lad and we chatted about football and crazy nights out before he said I could get in the DJ box and DJ with him for a while. Was he serious? Damn right. There I was DJ-ing with Colin Murray. It was all a bit surreal really as just before that, he had handed myself and my mates (Steve, Austin and Jody I believe) all these free drinks vouchers. He told me just to speak to the bar staff and say we were with Colin, according to Colin Murray, with your Northern Irish accent, they'll not even ask. "We're with Colin" I said when I ordered at the bar. And sure enough, with an accent like mine, there was no questioning it. I got a shout out on BBC Radio One the next day from Colin himself and met Colin again at the University Summer Ball near Hurn Airport the following month. We were all so full of energy in those days. It was a bit crazy. In June 2016 at the Northern Ireland v. Wales match in Paris, I met Colin Murray again by chance outside the stadium and we had a brief chat where he remembered the night in Bournemouth! In short, I have met Colin Murray three times and each was a blast!

The whole radio and TV thing at University in Bournemouth reached a few lunatic zeniths at the time. We were all zany students, the lot of us, Lock-In Lee, Millwall Neil, Jody, we were legends in our own lunchtimes and we were fooling nobody but ourselves, but we had fun! After The Lock-In in 2004, I won two awards at the Nerve Media Awards. I scooped two more in 2005 and got an invite to the NASTAs in Loughborough. The NASTAs are the National Student TV Awards, held annually in a random

University in the UK. Around our table representing Bournemouth that weekend were Sandra, Eric, Rachael, Paul, Jason and Alex. Alex and I went up to pick up one of the awards at this crazy function. The function was all paid for by the Student's Union – the food and the drink! I was fuelled on wine and champagne and was handed the microphone on stage in front of hundreds of people. I grabbed it like a lunatic still down the pub with my mates, "I'm glad I came up to collect this one [award], as the rest of you are all spunking off monkeys in the corridor, up the f*cking Bournemouth", I said, as Alex in front of me gave a calmer speech and picked up the 'dong' for Nerve with decorum. Two days before the event I had been celebrating my 25th birthday in Warszawa in Poland. Yep, same week as Chapter 16's "Barfgate". The whole series of events that emanated from my decision to go on the radio was a crazy high and really made me happy.

A few friends expected me to make a career out of radio (Austin particularly kept saying – "Jonny you are made to be a radio DJ"), but I didn't want to be bound to a radio studio or station. Austin still insists I should have been on radio all my life – he insists I was in a league of my own and a born radio presenter. But I'm not. I didn't want to adhere to rules and have to change. "Jonny Blair on the Air" only worked because I was myself, I was talking about Northern Ireland, Bournemouth, my mates down the pub and telling stories such as my mate <u>John Johnson doing a wee wee then drinking it</u> or <u>the night he got an erection and fucked an inflatable donkey in my front room</u> the same day that Bournemouth drew 2-2 with Bristol City. I told all those stories live on air, without the profanities. If anyone had bothered to listen they'd have known about the night we did willy windmills. I remember asking our manager, Jason Hawkins if I could say "willy" on air and he said "no swearing". Then I did a football quiz where the answer to a question was "Willie Johnstone", so I knew I could mention that word on air! Or there was a wacky challenge on radio one day

- Jody and I picked Song 2 by Blur as it was less than 2 minutes long. The deal was, we had to press play on the song, go downstairs to the bar, order and pay for a pint, down it in the bar and run back upstairs (entering the code for the door) and back into the seat before the song was over. It was a mega challenge and we both succeeded. We had the song due to end and go into dead air afterwards, which was a huge incentive to complete the challenge. The things we did were funny at the time. Mine (and Jody's radio shows) were like a mini fucking radio travel blog of my life down the pub with my mates. I was basically just telling people what I did at the weekend with my friends and adding some music to it. But it had ran its course. It was over and I did shed a tear this time.

In May 2008 I recorded my last ever radio show on Nerve at Bournemouth University. I have a copy of that show somewhere on a mini-disc but I have no recollection of it, or what the last ever song was. I will have to check someday as I really want to know what the last song I played on Nerve was. It will have some personal meaning to me and I wouldn't be surprised if it was also "Tequila Sunrise", which was the last song I played on Radio Belvoir back in 1998.

Radio was just a bit of fun along the way really. If anyone wants to hear my voice on the radio again, who knows, maybe I will do it again one day. Appearing on BBC Radio Ulster's drive time show in 2013 and a special Travel show on Hong Kong Radio 3 in 2015 and even on Polish radio in Poznań in 2017 have been my radio highlights since the Nerve Radio days. I was also contacted by radio in Belfast quite a few times during my story. The most recent radio appearance was in the city of Poznań in Poland where I discussed my journey around the world and its ups and downs. With radio, I was hiding in a room behind a microphone. You couldn't see me. These days I'm telling my travel stories through my website and unless you subscribe to my YouTube channel you won't hear my voice. But you'll see me. On Instagram, Twitter, Facebook, Travel Blogs. I showed my face. I won't shy away.

I've done a bunch of travel Podcasts now and I'm proud of them and the fact that working on Nerve and Radio Belvoir gave me the confidence and passion to do these things in life.

To my Radio Belvoir and Nerve Radio buddies - good times my friends, good times. Travel blogging, in this case chilled a radio star. The word is inevitable debatable. Can I have a cheeseburger with a blueberry muffinhead please? That was a song by an artist. This one is the fourth track on the current album. Are you guys on Micebase? Jonny Blair – tomato sauce on Radio Nerve. Jurassic Park.

A listener to me on radio - "What's this Jurassic Park thing all about?"

Me – "It's a f**king film about dinosaurs!"

Nobody got it, nobody gets it, nobody will get it. Enough said. I'm a travel blogger, a writer, a global whackpacker, I'm not a radio DJ! TK Rantie, baby! Jurassic Park.

Luckily, travel blogging killed this radio star.

Chapter 19
The Best Rock'n'Roll Band You Never Heard Of

Bournemouth, Poole, Southampton & London, ENGLAND (2005 - 2006)

"I can't belong here; alone inside of you..." - Ben Paulley, 2005.

I'm kind of linking this story in well here from the radio chapter – it's a double bill on music as I report on another career I could and should have had. We should have been monumentally famous and I should have been rich. Andy Kaufman in the wrestling match. Yeah yeah yeah yeah (thanks to Michael Stipe).

The era of music I grew up listening to was monikered "Britpop". British Popular music. I loved Oasis and that's the sort of music that makes me tick. I love it. Guys with proper tunes, genuine enthusiasm, guitars, decent melodies, lyrics that are a bit off the wall, catchy choruses etc. "Wonderwall" and "Girls and Boys" had been and gone and in the year 2005 I was still a Britpop kid. New bands did nothing for me and in fact I still went to see Oasis, Manic Street Preachers and The Bluetones all in 2005. What I didn't know was that the venue The Bluetones played at (Mr. Kyps in Poole) would soon be the venue where I would be **managing** a rock band at a proper gig in front of hundreds. Yes, I managed a rock band, and to me, they were the best rock band in the world. On the planet. I mean it. There is no bias here. We were the best.

So, the story begins.

In 2005 I was working as a supervisor for Bournemouth Borough Council for the second summer in a row on their 'Seafront Services' section. This basically meant I was selling ice cream. I met some amazing people through that job, including Warszawians Rafał Kowalczyk and Artur Gorecki, plus that's where I met the genius of Ben Paulley. This young man will strike you as being a modest genius, without even stretching either word to any fabricated extent. While selling cheeseburgers by the beach, Ben and I used to joke around with customers, staff and even sink the odd pint on a 15 minute tea break just so we could be arsed to work – Harbour Lights was the bar of choice. (Kind of). Ben made it known that he was in a local rock band called 'The Waves'. I was already intrigued.

On boring days at work, we would have football and music quizzes. He'd play air guitar as I smashed a slice of fake cheese 'intill an over-priced cheeseburger'. I just wanted to hear 'The Waves'. It just sounded like the name of a band that gave a fuck and could do an audience over on stage. Plus, my mate Ben was lead guitarist and songwriter. Soon, I'd be attending a 'The Waves' gig.

My first 'The Waves' gig was August 2005 in Mr. Smith's, Bournemouth. The band had been around for a lot longer than that. The crowd I hung out with in those days included Charlie Messenger, Jody Casey and Gary King. 'Millwall Neil' had moved to London in May or June 2005. Charlie and Gary were English lads from work with the identical loves to me: music, football, beer, ladies (in any particular order depending on circumstances really). Of course, we had varying tastes within those loves, but one thing we established was that 'The Waves' were the best band we'd seen since Oasis. That first 'The Waves' gig was to be the first of many as I became obsessed with their music. By coincidence, my family were also visiting me at the time of this 'The Waves' gig and so my Dad came to the gig too - amazing! My Dad and I had a beer together and watched 'The Waves'! My Dad's first and only 'The Waves' gig was my first of many 'The Waves' gigs.

The band was fronted by the excellent James Corbin, who was backed up by Ben Paulley on lead guitar, Andy Galliers on bass and Ryan Glover on drums. Ryan had already sampled some fame, having been a session drummer for Kasabian and also comes from a family of drummers. The band meant business, they had the tunes and were great lads to hang out with. I went to every gig they did since the Mr. Smith's one. I didn't miss a gig. I'd change my work shifts and schedules just to be there. I was taking photos, making videos and just really chilling and enjoying the music. I was like a groupie, that became a roadie, that became their PR guy, that became their manager. I have three of the early gigs on video somewhere, which I treasure and will have to get onto DVD somehow or put on YouTube to encapsulate how good the band actually were. I was 25 at the time, I knew they were a good band. I knew they were the best band in the world, that you never heard of.

The song which immediately stood out for me was 'Something to Shout About', it rocked along in some kind of youthful fighting spirit which was basically in my opinion the band saying, "we're here, come and give us a listen". It knocked every other chart song in 2005 into oblivion, vocally, musicly, lyrically and the overall message. I'd be caught two years later in New Zealand singing the line "Fools walk the heavens that I'd never seen, maybe that's what we need" on a bus to fellow tourists who agreed it was a top tune. It deserved to be heard. I love that song.

Then there was the dreamy 'Lonely Cloud', which Ben always described as "that's our Champagne Supernova", and for the most part it was, a "lighters in the air" moment, which graced the setlist only when the scene was right. Other songs would come and go in the sets and I loved all the songs. I totally fell in love with a 'The Waves' song called 'Kaleidoscopes', a gem which Radiohead, Manic Street Preachers and Embrace would gladly add to their back catalogues.

But they can't.

It's a 'The Waves' song and what a song. Based largely on a relationship break up, James sings "I can't belong here alone inside of you", before realising "every night kaleidoscopes are spinning in my head, and I don't know if I can go on, with you, by my side". Superb poetry in motion sang eloquently over a mellowing guitar and ensuing sombre drum beat. 'The Waves' weren't just any band.

Nobody could knock them.

They were the best rock band in the world.

I never openly said I would be their manager; it just sort of happened. I wanted the best for the band. I wanted them to be recognised for what they were. I started doing fliers for gigs and handing out demo CDs at gigs, as well as building up some music and media contacts and starting a mailing list. Andy and Ben had set up an official website and a MySpace page. It could have been something. It should have been something. Every gig we played a good gig. We rocked the place. Every gig was impeccable. I could find no faults, even when asked by Ben what we could do better. I was convinced they were the next Oasis. I told him don't do anything better, you're the best band in the world. I think the band didn't actually think I was serious, but I was. I was serious. I started off as a fan, became a groupie, a roadie and eventually I was the band manager in early 2006.

I loved it all and thought not only was the band this good, they were my mates. I wanted to get them a record deal. I put my heart and soul into it for a good few months. I had DJ-ed with Colin Murray so I sent him a CD. I "MySpaced" Radio 1 DJs Edith Bowman and Chris Moyles countless times. I was the band manager and PR guy. At each gig I would look all around the room hoping, just hoping some record company boss was there sipping a double whiskey thinking "these guys are the best. 6 album deal lads. What's the singer's name again?"

But it never happened. We spent hours and hours on gigs and rehearsals. We'd rehearse in a brick wall studio under a bridge somewhere in Southampton. We'd spent lots of time, effort and money on the band.

If my job as manager of the band was to get 'The Waves' a record deal, I failed miserably. We had a lot of fun on the way though. Looking back, I had two jobs, a university course, a radio show, a football supporters club to run as well as a busy social life, so it was a hard task to bung it all in. I did the best I could. I loved it and I loved 'The Waves'.

We did some random gigs and enjoyed ourselves. One particular night (after being at Brentford to watch Cherries win 2-0), we played a low key bar in London's Baker Street, rocking the socks off a place with less than 20 people there! It was one of the best gigs ever! We banged out immense acoustic sessions in Klute and The Portman to mixed audiences in a never ending myriad of busy pubs. We turned up at a Comedy Club in Westbourne for a jam in front of older folk, and we did a dancingly good Good Friday gig in Hammersmith (probably our best ever gig) to a packed crowd in the English capital. It was 'The Waves' finest hour. I handed out CDs and fliers after the gig, expecting us to get that 6 album deal...

We even did a gig in support of AFC Bournemouth in the club's dark days when people were putting money into buckets. I still have a ticket and video for 'The Waves' AFC Bournemouth gig, which took place at Mr. Kyps. AFC Bournemouth, you might have read, is my football club of choice, we later succumbed into receivership before living the Premier League dream by 2015. A fairytale of its own.

'The Waves' gigs were wide and varied. We changed the set list a lot as well. I wouldn't really have any input into that sort of thing, just let the band get on with it. I often requested 'Something to shout about' but it didn't always make the competitive set list. One thing that I always tried to get was loads of mates and loads of people to come to the gigs. This often didn't work with people's busy lives and sometimes I'd drive myself down to a gig, stay sober (against my usual attitude) and do my PR for the band. I was mostly sober at gigs, perhaps that was the problem! We also built up rapports with other local venues and bands, with Southampton Joiners becoming a regular haunt. I still love that venue.

I honestly believe and stand by my claim that 'The Waves' were the best band in the world. I told a slight lie though, Oasis first, 'The Waves' second...

I sent about 50 CDs to record labels and venues all over London, each with signed A4 pages from Jonny Blair (Band Manager). The band thought they were the best thing ever and so did I. I expected the band to win 2 Brit Awards, appear on Top of the Pops and for myself and all the band members to become millionaires within a year. Aged in my mid-twenties at the time, we were all so young, enthusiastic and vibrant. We rocked an Easter Friday gig in 2006 in West Kensington, where there were rumours a dude wanted to meet us and sign the band. I spoke to everyone in the venue trying to flog CDs, hoping we would be signed, I scoured the bar clinking beers with everyone in search of the record label attendee.

I never met the industry rep.

We never got signed.

We continued to play gigs in Bournemouth, Poole and Southampton the next few months. Another band who supported us got signed at a gig in the Southampton Joiners. They were shit. I can't even remember their name. You won't either. Neither will Ben Paulley, lead singer of 'The Waves'.

"Jimmy quit; Jody got married" – Bryan Adams.

Then in June 2006, there were a few band disagreements and Ryan, Ben, James, Andy and myself all went our separate ways in life. I got a job up London, Ben later released an excellent solo album called 'Multiples' (which Ryan drummed on) and I hope Andy and James are out there with some fond memories. Apart from a chance meeting with Ryan Glover at an Ash gig in Southampton in 2007, I haven't seen any of the band since sadly. True story. The Waves never became the biggest band in the world and I was never that millionaire, but they were nice dreams and good times. Thanks for the memories guys.

To quote James Corbin, **"we're walking through walls, fighting our cause, changing the scores and I feel nothing but love..."**

Key Songs - Fighter, Looking Like A Liar, Kaleidoscopes, Surrender, Something To Shout About.

the waves - gigography:
saturday 21/5/05 club destiny, bournemouth
wednesday 25/5/05 jongleur's, southampton
wednesday 1/6/05 the talking heads, southampton
tuesday 14/6/05 mr. smiths, bournemouth
sunday 19/6/05 the wedgewood rooms, portsmouth
wednesday 27/7/05 the joiners, southampton
sunday 14/8/05 mr. smiths, bournemouth
thursday 1/9/05 o'neill's bar, bournemouth
thursday 15/9/05 lennon's, southampton
saturday 29/10/05 the playrooms, baker street, london
thursday 22/12/05 the opera house, boscombe
monday 9/1/06 the joiners, southampton
sunday 19/2/06 mr. kyps, parkstone, poole (AFC Bournemouth Festival)
good friday 14/4/06 the orange rooms/west one four, west kensington, london
wednesday 19/4/06 klute, bournemouth (acoustic set)
thursday 27/4/06 the bullet bar, london
friday 28/4/06 the joiners, southampton (Jar Music Group Showcase)

friday 12/5/06 the nexus, southampton

saturday 20/5/06 the opera house, boscombe

thursday 25/5/06 planet sounds, southampton (Bunker Showcase)

tuesday 30/05/06 centre stage, westbourne, bournemouth

thursday 15/6/06 the green rooms, portman hotel, boscombe

monday 19/6/06 the joiners, southampton

(there was a gig in Bar Fruit just after this but only Ben and James turned up so it wasn't a 'The Waves' gig and there were probably a few other gigs that I've left out or forgotten)

Websites that we had:

http://www.myspace.com/thewavesmusic

http://www.thewaves.co.uk

CDs available:

the waves EP 2006 (1. Looking Like A Liar/2. The Tom Song)

"Fools walk the heavens that I've never seen. Maybe that's what we need" – James Corbin.

Chapter 20
The Isle of ~~Wight~~ Green

Cowes, Isle of Wight, ENGLAND (November 2006)

"There's painters in the Painter's Arms" – Tim Beattie.

The first three years away from Northern Ireland were probably the craziest three. I was still young, I was mostly single, I had a regular group of friends, life was good. There was less nomadery. I even stayed in the same flat/room for at least 12 months a time (except the time Jody and I shared a tiny room in Lansdowne, Bournemouth for 2 months and the dingy bedsit I had in Shepherd's Bush in London when I first moved to the English capital). But with all things in life, you'll reach a peak. A high point of elation, one from which, you will never improve on. For love, nor want.

For the South of England Northern Ireland Supporters Club, this zenith happened in the town of Cowes on the Isle of Wight in November 2006, linked us all the way back to Chapter 3's "Arconada...Armstrong!" adventures and ensured that for once, some of us had left behind a crazy legacy on England's south coast. You see, it was all everybody's fault. The South of England Northern Ireland Supporters Club was born on the post-barfgate party train between Berlin and Warsaw in Spring 2005, launched officially in Weymouth, England in December 2005 and continued to prosper. The club, was born in Poland (or Germany), launched in England and dedicated to Northern Ireland.

"Come what may, we're unstoppable cos we know just what we are" – Noel Gallagher.

It all reached a very very surreal peak when I led the troops of the South of England Northern Ireland Supporters Club all the way to the Isle of Wight in the first year of my chairmanship of the club. It may just sound like we just fancied a party on the island, but the story of the trip will forever live long in the memory of those privileged enough to attend that weekend. We thought, at the time it would always be like this for the club in only its 11th month in official status, but little did we know of the perils in Oxford, Weston Super Mare and Gillingham to follow the next year and later the club's decline. So why the fuck did the South of England Northern Ireland Supporters Club hold a meeting on the Isle of Wight in November 2006??

We cast our minds back to a busy Southampton airport and my pint of Carling in December 2005. As a south of England based resident, I often enjoyed trips back to Northern Ireland to visit family and friends. On this particular morning I was with my flatmate and former workbuddy Jody Casey for a very early flight, where I would show my mates Jody, Neil Macey and James Condron my home patch of Bangor and Belfast in Northern Ireland. It was also the weekend of George Best's funeral so I'd be back in Northern Ireland to pay my last respects to a sporting hero of mine. And there, like a gift of fate from the heavens was an Alex Higgins... No, not the snooker player Alex Higgins, but a man with a beard and a George Best T-Shirt who was in front of me as I went to the departure lounge to board the flight from Southampton to Belfast City Airport (now unironically and beautifully named "The George Best Airport"). Alex was queueing for the flight as well, but who was this man? He looked like a cool figure of a guy, and then, he started talking to me.

On speaking to him, it became obvious that he was a massive George Best fan. Doing a fellow human a favour was always something I enjoyed, and this morning I thought - I'll tell Alex where George Best grew up, as my Granny still lived round the corner from Dickie Best's house in Burren Way in the Cregagh Estate in East Belfast. In fact, I'll tell Alex his exact house. My Granny lived at Drumragh End, only a school and a square to play football on separated my Granny's flat from the place George Best grew up, Burren Way. Alex said that he had never been to Northern Ireland and was only going to pay his respects to his legend, idol and hero, George Best. I was enthused and impressed and popped him my mobile phone number and e-mail address, saying "I'm the chairman of the South of England Northern Ireland Supporters Club. Come along anytime, and join us for a drink. You're always welcome. The boys would love it". I also asked where he was from and what his link to Northern Ireland was. It turned out he was from the Isle of Wight, and dated a lady from Helen's Bay (one of Northern Ireland's posher haunts). A story was building itself here, a chance meeting at an airport and fate had leant my life and others a bonus hand. If that chance meeting hadn't happened, neither would the meeting on the Isle of Wight, or indeed this chapter of the book. Jurassic Park.

Before I launch into the whole Isle of Wight meeting, there was also the sublime moment in an East Belfast pub later on the same day that I met Alex Higgins. At the airport in Southampton after we swapped numbers I had invited Alex to the Crown Bar in Belfast for a pint, as me and my mates were going there. I expected him not to remember, or even visit. But me and my mates were only in the Crown for about 40 minutes (quick pint) and there he was – Alex Higgins, he turned up! Then later that day we were in an East Belfast pub (of which I bizarrely forget the name) and we happened to glance at Sky Sports News and there was Alex Higgins who we had met that very morning, being interviewed on his thoughts on George Best, directly from the Cregagh Estate and George Best's house! Even I had influenced the media on that occasion, and if you can't work out why, read again! I had given Alex Dickie Best's address and he went there to pay his respects and ends up on TV that night. Amazing! So Alex then joined our supporters club, bought a Northern Ireland shirt and turned up at every meeting, including playing for the South of England NISC in their first ever public football appearance (a Mainland NISCs 5 a sides in Manchester), until the thought and possibility came up... why don't we have a meeting on the Isle of Wight? The answer was a straight yes and I took pride in making the first steps in what became a historic day for the club. Suddenly we had members wishing to attend the most random of meetings on the Isle of Wight. To this day it remains the first and only Northern Ireland Supporters Club 'mate-in' on thon Isle of Wight. At the time, I had never even been to the Isle of Wight. A magical island which would later play an even bigger part in my journeys.

Availability for committee members to attend an Isle of Wight meeting was checked and we finally agreed on the date: Saturday

4th November 2006. I was working in PR in London at the time and saw the opportunity to gain some publicity for the club. It would be along the lines of changing the name of the island for the day. No longer was this the Isle of Wight, we were nutcases and we were changing it to the Isle of Green. The publicity on this stretched from simple comments on the 'Our Wee Country' Northern Ireland fans forum to a preview article on The Isle of Wight Beacon ("All that's good on the island") to the Ireland's Saturday Night (The Pink, The Ulster - a publication that has sadly ceased to be). The scene was set, the meeting place of The Painters Arms in Cowes was announced and suddenly we were on the brink of madness, hardly for the first time in my life. The South of England Northern Ireland Supporters Club were heading to the Isle of Wight for a historic meeting and were front page news (at least for a day). Everyone who was there, will have their own story of the weekend, here's mine.

"You're only king for a day" – Van Morrison.

The weekend began for me on the Friday night. I finished work in Bite Communications after a busy week and Owen Millar (club secretary) got a bus/train down to visit me from his new abode in Manchester. I arrived at the Shakespeare Pub in Victoria, where a cultured Owen Millar bought me a pint as we wasted shit loads of money on "the millionaire machine". We drank quite a lot and later on the train home to my place in Dartford, Owen played Live Forever on an acoustic guitar owned by the fit lead singer of a band called "The Veez". Yes, it had started already - the SOENISC chairman and secretary were on a train pretending to be Oasis. I love spontaneity in life and this was to be one. The next morning we would be up early and head for a train, then a tube, then a train in order to get to Southsea, by Portsmouth, where we would get a "Party Hovercraft" to Ryde on the Isle of Wight. My now housemate John Johnson joined us for the trip, as he is nuts, despite being a cockney London lad, he has a soft spot for Northern Ireland. He twice went to Northern Ireland matches with me (and we won them both, un-Sherlock excremented!).

The train on the way from Waterloo - Southsea (Portsmouth Harbour) was where we met Scotland fan Ed Broussard, who was one of Tim Beattie's mates (Tim being club treasurer of the SOENISC) and was joining us for the day for the craic! It was sure to be a mad one. I opened a tin of beer on the train and we had begun the drinking fest already. I also opened my party bag which contained many and numerous green items which would assist in our changing of the colour of the island from Wight to Green for the day. These random items included a green sieve, a green and white "Santa Stop Here" sign (one month too early), green sunglasses, green feather dusters, green wigs, green hats and many other things which you wouldn't believe a supporter's club chairman would bring to a meeting. For something to be unbelievable, you have to make people believe it. Really. No really.

"You are who you make people believe you are"
– Malachi Murray.

After some random chat and beer on the Waterloo - Southsea train, we alighted and headed in search of the Hovercraft Terminal. The walk turned out to be longer than we thought, but soon we had paid about £14 each for a return on the Hovercraft, getting the obligatory photo of our supporters club fleg by the method of transport, and then cranking open another tin of beer as we cruised the waves cleverly on route to the island. I had never been to the Isle of Wight before and we enjoyed the views as we neared Ryde. On exiting at Ryde, the place was shrouded in November sunshine, and we were destined for Cowes. There is only one train system on the Isle of Wight and I think this covers the Ryde - Shanklin route, therefore not even passing through Cowes, or indeed the capital of the Island, which is Newport. So, there was Owen, me, Ed and

John with beer on the Isle of Green and we were looking to get to Cowes. This sort of travel was certainly off the wall stuff and just feels like part of my backpacking adventures, despite the fact I lived in England at the time. After the £70 taxi fiasco (in Chapter 15), a taxi is normally my last ever resort as a means of transport, but divided between 4 it was a gift at less than £15, so we got a photo by the railway track and bridge, and boarded a taxi (my fifth different mode of transport for the day). The taxi left us at the picturesque East Cowes, where a narrow river met the land, in what looked like scenery out of a film, or even somewhere like a down market Venice. The taxi driver said you can get a chain ferry to West Cowes, which is where the Painters Arms pub was. Soon we boarded a lovely party chain ferry on route to Cross Street. It was all very surreal as there was us four dressed in green, attracting attention, my green shiny wig dazzling in the morning wind against a backdrop of organic fishermen and word slurring whackoholics.

On the chain ferry we met some Cowes residents who actually get the (free) chain ferry every day going to work. What an interesting lifestyle. We also got in touch with some of the fellow SOE NISC members to see how they were getting on (we all took different routes, some via Southampton, Lymington and Portsmouth) and whether the meeting time of 11.58 am would be achieved. We dandered through the quiet streets of Cowes until at the bottom of a hill the black signage of "The Painters Arms" brushed up at us in our green tops. We were the first four people to arrive. The pub had just opened and we perched ourselves down on seats and started putting flegs up and turning the pub green, I remember saying to the bar lady, Mez Blackwell, "Did anyone tell you that there were a load of Northern Irish lads coming to the pub today?" She knew about it, not just through Alex Higgins, but the full swing publicity campaign had alerted the locals of our presence. It felt like a party atmosphere in the town. Soon Richboy (Richard Ingram) had arrived in usual green attire and me and the Rich started the kitty for the drinks, which would actually last us almost all day in the end. It was going to be a long one, and I remember pacing myself a wee bit at the start.

Within 30 minutes we had been joined by special guest and author, Shaun Schofield (who wrote the book "There's Always One" on following Northern Ireland). I had invited Shaun to the meeting, and was really impressed and surprised that he made it. I mean holding a Northern Ireland Supporters Club meeting on the largest island in England was hardly sensible was it? Also, on Shaun's Red Funnel ferry was Scott Gordon (Club Charity President), journalist Marshall Gillespie and his son Calum. What a fantastic turnout already. Scott had arrived via a sign reading TOKOGAWA where a mandatory photo was taken, as GAWA in our case stands for 'Green and White Army'. Just as it looked like the pub couldn't get any greener in walked the host himself Mr. Alex "Isle of Wight Army" Higgins with his girlfriend Beverley (from Helen's Bay, Northern Ireland), and then in came Tim Beattie with his English mate Leggo (sporting a 1997 vintage Norn Iron tap for the day). That wasn't the full turnout however as there was Nat and another lad (2 of Owen's mates), plus Carlo Bell (an English/Italian wannabe Northern Ireland fan who looks like Gareth Southgate!) so the turnout on the island was incredible for a club who hadn't even been in existence for a year. We all got our beers and chilled out for a bit before starting the official meeting, with members participation.

Random items of the day had been provided mainly by me and Scott, who had constructed his own A4 pages with the words "Isle of Green" and "Our Wee Island" on them, including photos of the Isle of Wight. Richboy and I attached these to the door of the pub and on the nearby streets till lampposts, to alert any locals and we would have happily welcomed anyone to our meeting. The craic was fantastic and soon I began to chair the meeting, standing up wearing a Viking Helmet (not sure where it came from - Denmark perhaps, where I had visited the previous month) without a care in the world. I sided to Alex, who introduced the island to us with heart-warming aplomb and then to Shaun Schofield who gave a riveting edge of the seat speech about his book, of which he sold many copies that day, and all to a good cause. It's a fabulous book - in fact, Shaun has two books now – There's Always One, and Albania to America (with Belfast in Between). I wrote a chapter for the latter book.

The speeches and the meeting all ran as smoothly and with as much comedy as ever and some group photos were then taken while Richboy and I continued to put posters up on the streets, electionic. The Painters Arms pub itself was tiny, dingy and dark. Just the perfect place really for our wee meeting. Soon the locals were flocking into the pub, and strangely none of them complained one bit about our green-ness, mad-ness or alcohol intake!! We were the talk of the town. I also asked Mez the barmaid if it was OK to put our CD on, which was a special NI compilation. This was great for the banter and we ordered more and more beer while the first live football match of the day came on. Mez provided us with a raffle (where I won some brown candles...!) and free hotdogs. Where would you get this sort of welcome? We had started singing already, and even did a song of tribute to Mez, "Stand up if you all love Mez", the memories of this chant came back a few years later when I heard of Mez's unfortunate death from cancer. A sad sad world we live in, and a brilliant lady who made us feel so welcome that day, as eejitiotic as we were.

Owen was mad keen to watch the Manchester United match at 3 p.m. and as The Painters Arms didn't show it, and we were in danger of spending the entire day in one pub, we decided to move on from The Painters Arms, but promised to pop back later, before the night of clubbing. Tim Beattie at this point, pointed out that there were actual Painters in the Painters Arms, which inspired a new chant of "There's Painters in the Painters arms, Painters Arms, Painters Arms" to the tune of that song about "Klingons on the starboard bow". In a boating town, in a pub named after artists, we were certainly keeping things afloat, drawing people in and making an impression. As we dandered down the main street we found a pub whose name I forget but it was stationed on the cobble stoned high street on a corner near The Fountain Hotel (where some of us would stay that night). The day had started with some comparison contests, including everytime we saw someone with a beard, we would line them up beside Alex Higgins (our member with a beard) and then I would ask the entire club to vote on who has a better beard. To add to the lunacy of this, the vote was always fixed, Alex's beard was always voted the worst, much to the delight of Howard (pronounced Hard) in the pub, who we sang "Howard has a better beard..." to. Soon the song changed to "We've drunk them out of Fosters!" as Tim Beattie announced the keg change required to maintain our club's alcohol requirements. There were about 12 of us, though by mid-afternoon some had left the island due to other commitments. Shaun Schofield, Marshall and Calum were away after having contributed to what was already becoming an incredible day out. In that pub, where we drank them out of Foster's, Richboy and I noticed a group of girls wearing green so we sang "stand up if you're wearing green!" at them until they stood up and gasped in disbelief at our range of singing poems. Soon though a group of England "fans" in the pub thought they would wind us up...cue unworked and listen...

Following an impressive SOENISC chant of "We're Not Brazil, We're Northern Ireland", these England fans all stood up to attention and started singing "God Save The Queen" thinking for some bizarre reason that this would wind us up, or shut us up. These guys were uneducated though and they were obviously completely oblivious to the fact that this song was ALSO our national anthem, maybe they were unaware of the two countries and the divide on the island of Ireland? Whatever inspired them to sing that, we'll never know, they expected the fact that they were singing "God Save The Queen" to wind us up and that we would get offended! But of course, as soon as they started singing it, all of us stood up and joined in as loudly as we could, mostly louder than the English themselves! This was a classic 'had to be there moment' as we made them look totally bewildered, confused and tongue-sunk! Once we had finished the anthem that they had started, we all launched into a "Same National Anthem, we've got the same National Anthem" tune, which was the funniest period of chanting I've ever heard in my life. Ask anyone who was there in that wee pub that day. We had amused the entire pub, and got English people on the patriotic Isle of Wight confused over their identity and in awe of a bunch of cultured and beer loving Northern Irish guys. "Thanks for having us in for a pint, we are the South of England NISC" I said to one of them as we exited the pub and dandered for a quick look at the harbour, where a sun glanced over yachts none of us could afford, nor crave.

The next pub I remember, was The Waterside and it had great views. We drank and ate in there, getting a window seat and table and putting our fleg up over the harbour. By this point Beverley Perrett (Alex's girlfriend) had joined us and we were chilling out away from the madness of the previous two pubs. At this stage some of us checked into our accommodation for the night and in mine, John's, Owen's and Richboy's case we booked ours, with The Fountain Hotel being chosen. I almost forgot a genius moment however, before all of this and before we left the Painters Arms pub for the first time, a man looking like Colin Murray (Belfast Radio One DJ and self-confessed Northern Irish lunatic) walked in. The chants at this point somewhat took him aback, unaware of the party nature of the SOE NISC, we sang "One Colin Murray", "Colin Murray; On the Isle of Wight", "Colin give us a song" and

"Are you Colin Murray in disguise?" His name was Ed and he ended up joining in with us the rest of the day. A top man, any person could have taken offence to the singing if they were shallower minded, but he loved it!

About an hour later everyone was quite refreshed and ready for what Tim Beattie referred to as "second wind". Then a bunch of sailor types (girls and boys) walked in and the girls swarmed around Richboy and I for some reason. I tried to chat one of them up, she was Nicki from Kent. "I live in Kent too" said I as she asked to borrow my hats and scarves for photos which her mates took, including one where she squeezed my genitalia, probably an unknown story to the others that were in the pub at the time. "Did you like that?" She said nonchalantly "I always wanted to squeeze an Irish willy", I was quite startled, and also actually pleased, it was a chat up line (and squeeze) I enjoyed, but she should have said Northern Irish. She disappeared into the night with her mates soon after, one of which was a posh spoilt schoolboy, who stole my "Santa Stop Here" sign and whose retort to "We're Not Ireland, We're Northern Ireland" was "we own you". I often wondered what inspired Nicki to do that ball squeeze to me, and indeed why it all happened in the blink of an eye and indeed why our paths crossed for two minutes and we'll never meet again. Noel Gallagher hit the nail on the pint of beer when he said, "you don't get; you won't get; what you need; life is a strange thing". I rather liked Nicki. Another romance went abegging.

Tim and Leggo had begun a wee conversation over by the window and I could see a cheeky school kid grin on Beattie's face, as he walked over to me and said, "wait till ye hear this yousens". It had to be something good or I wouldn't have listened, he goes "see that couple on that table over there having a romantic meal?" "Aye I said", Tim continued "let's sing them a song..." Getting my digital camera on video mode and forming a line, the members of the SOE

NISC were informed of the chant due to begin, and soon I started filming as we circled round and round and round their table (a young couple enjoying a romantic meal by the harbour) singing "Propose in a minute, he's gonna propose in a minute..." It was true comedy and the embarrassment on the lad's face was met by a teasing smile from his other half as we left our empty pint glasses with aplomb and departed our third pub of the day. It was all going very fast...

Another walk by the harbour and Scott found a more traditional wee pub called The Union Inn. We popped in there and got our own wee table at the back, where there were some adverts for Irish Whiskey and hospitable friendly locals. At this point we were all chilling though a few more chants were started in there, as my housemate John started going a bit mental and chatting away to my supporter's club mates. This wee pub hit the spot. "What's the occasion?" asked the landlord to me as I sipped on my lager. "Life" was my abrupt and obvious reply.

At this point Owen's islander mate Nat had arrived and was wearing a green Halifax Town shirt. For the entire day the Isle of Wight was blatantly the Isle of Green. Everyone was actually a bit tired and weary so as a Tim Beattie 'third wind', we decided it was essential to liven up spirits and those regulars in The Painters Arms by walking back into the pub where it all began. The pub was packed at this point and my CD stole the Dukebox show. We didn't even care that we had to pay to put our own songs on by now as my CD was now included in their paying Dukebox! It was worth it as Tim Beattie stood by the Dukebox, we sang "You're paying for your own music!" at him. Soon the laughs were on me as my self-recorded songs such as "Northern Ireland South of England Army" blurted out on a Saturday night in a local pub in Cowes. Bemused locals looked so confused as Richboy stated "that's Jonny singing on the toilet". I didn't actually sing them on the toilet, for the record. It was on a free iPod recording device I picked up in England at a PR event but it was me singing intill it.

More and more comedy continued in here including the first ever Isle of Wight SOE NISC "Gay Disco". We all took our tops off and danced around the pub like maniacs. The flegs were up again and some locals chatted to us as we explained all about ourselves and drank yet more local brew, or indeed Fosters – no idea why this bog-standard Australian beer was a feature of the day. I did sample one local ale that day, the rest was your usual lager shite. More songs continued on the Dukebox, and some strange chants had developed during the day. One lad in a previous pub had said "do you want to see my testicles?" for some odd reason, and we hit back with a "we don't want to see your testicles", so as Alex Higgins and Beverley got cosy on the seats we sang this to Alex, a recording of which survives on a video on my YouTube channel. A video of us singing our new-ish song "Swing Low Sweet Northern Ireland, who's gonna carry me home?" also appears on video. Earlier that day Shaun Schofield, while doing the speech on his book, said "I have been to many Northern Ireland matches and supporter's club meetings, but this supporters club are by far the craziest Northern Ireland Supporters Club I've ever seen". Great words from a great man, and we were living up to this expectation.

Alex Higgins had prepared a nightclub for us, across the way, which would stay open till 2 a.m. and he had booked the upstairs and a DJ, with karaoke and everything. In fact, I don't think we have ever thanked Alex enough for his organisation of the day. From meeting in the Painters Arms to the karaoke, everything was as good as it could have been, it ran like clockwork or a smooth slice of peanut butter on toasted Kingsmill. So, we spent a bit more time in the Painters Arms before heading to the nightclub. Before we left the Painters Arms we said our thankyous and goodbyes to everyone in there, and even laughed at Scott Gordon who had ordered a HALF pint of Lager "What the fucking hell is that?" we sang at him!! Full pint loyal, we were.

The club was £2 entry or something and we had the whole upstairs to entertain ourselves in. The bar was downstairs but we could take all the drink upstairs, and there was karaoke ready to go, a DJ to play any requests, a pool table and plenty of space for the flegs to go up. We soon filled the dancefloor and Owen Millar and myself made a total hash and shambles of some UK chart classics. "I butchered Lucky Man" revealed Owen after his poor attempt to sing like Richard Ashcroft for four minutes in a Cowes nightclub. "I only sing Common People cos I want to be one" said Jonny Blair after a woeful performance of the Pulp classic in the club. And these two guys were the club's chairman and secretary!! To add to the comedy, both videos were recorded and are now on YouTube for your un-amusement. Just check out the laughs we both get from the lively Cowes audience. That's why we're not pop stars. As we continued to dominate proceedings in the wee club, we filled the dancefloor with green and the DJ played whatever hits we wanted. It even culminated with me joining Tim Beattie for an embarrassing duet of Take That's "Back For Good". Despite my closeness to Tim, I hope never to have his lipstick marks still on my coffee cup. Before this we had Owen's mate Carlo on vocals singing "Don't You Want Me Baby?" We all agreed that Carlo's performance was indeed the best of the night, at least he could sing a bit. A few songs later and we were doing a "gay disco" in the club. The "Gay Disco" was basically a thing we did at the time whereby male members of the supporter's club would take their tops off, swing them in the air and dance around each other. What was crazy was that other blokes joined in. It was ridiculous just how many non - SOENISC members actually got their kit off for the "Gay Disco". A shocking amount of testosterone was on view for those Cowes ladies lurking nearby. Even Ed "Colin Murray" Gladdis got his top off. I think this was probably the beginning of the end for the "Gay Disco" within SOENISC, it really wasn't healthy or cool anymore. Soon we noticed that the host himself Alex IOW Army Higgins had called it a night as he had overdosed on the old booze like the rest of us.

At this point, Owen, Richboy and I headed back to the Fountain Hotel up and down hilly back streets, at one point Tim will recall me streaking down a hill for no reason whatsoever other than drunken idiocy. Richboy and I had pre-ordered a beer but it was all locked up and we had lost our final chance of alcohol before sleep allowed our weary eyes and heads to recover once again. It took a while...

At breakfast the next morning we all had a fry and a lovely cup of tea. Key quote came from Owen Millar, who when looking at my photos professed, "that picture is a total disgrace!!" It was a photy of the "Gay Disco" and as Owen remarked "only about 3 people in that are actually SOENISC members!". If we needed proof that we had turned the island a metaphorical green for the day, that was probably it. The day will never ever be forgotten, we appeared in the Ireland's Saturday Night and on the Isle Of Wight Beacon the following week, and had made some impression on the locals.

A few years after the meeting, Mez Blackwell the barmaid, lost her fight with cancer and Ed "Colin Murray" Gladdis fittingly placed a Northern Ireland scarf by the pub with the tribute to a wonderful lady. These are just the memories, and those who were there will remember the day that the South of England Northern Ireland Supporters Club re-named the island "THE ISLE OF GREEN". I don't even remember (or need to remember) the journey home...

Chapter 21
Biting the Apple

Bite Communications, Ravenscourt Park, London, ENGLAND (2006 – 2007)

"The winner takes it all, the loser is standing small" – Abba.

I knew I would live in London at some point in my life and I always wanted to. I had toyed with the idea so many times having visited the city around 30 – 40 times before I eventually moved there in 2006. When I look back on my year working in London, the memories are really good, but I know I was working too hard and it wasn't all fun and games in work. But I lived out a childhood dream. I lived in London.

Through doing a degree in Public Relations in Bournemouth, I accepted the option to take a year out from the course to work in the industry as most people did. During that year I decided on living in London, I'd always wanted and needed to live in the UK's capital city. I never felt as British or Irish as I did Northern Irish, but London had a big appeal to me. A job opportunity came up as a PR Accounts Assistant with a company called Bite Communications. Their UK office was in Hammersmith, so I headed up to London in my car early morning from Bournemouth for the interview. This interview, like many single moment events and decisions, would also change my life and my destiny. I have no doubt, it changed my destiny for the better. No doubt.

The interview was with Robin Wilson and Karen Hardinge, two PR directors with a wealth of experience in the field. Bite Communications are a top notch PR company, they're really good. They have offices in China, UK, USA and Sweden. Their London base was at Ravenscourt Park, Hammersmith. The company employs people based on their interviews and their personality, rather than your qualifications and other generic bull-excrement. I loved this, but I didn't expect to get the job of course. I was a novice PR guy – I had my radio shows, I was chairman of the football supporter's club but I was a glorified ice cream seller at best and I could pour a decent pint of Guinness. I could talk you through the Northern Ireland football team's last 26 years of results and goalscorers, but doing PR for a multi-national company? Hmm, not sure. Yet. But life is full of surprises.

During the interview I mentioned that on my radio show I have "themed shows", like for example I have a "Thirsty Thursdays". Karen and Robin liked this comment and noted that at Bite, every Thursday they also have a "Thirsty Thursdays", a night out for a few drinks with workmates. The interview discussed Apple Inc. ; the massive company co-founded and chaired by Steve Jobs. If I was successful and got the job, I would be doing the UK PR for Apple. I perked up when I heard that. I always liked a bit of glamour and I wanted a challenge. No part of me thought it was a job too big for me, not overaud by it but aware that this company was huge. It's a selfish dog-eat-dog business in the world of PR and people will definitely bite a piece of your donut to make sure you don't have it all. I scoffed my morning donut on the way up to London. Nobody was having a bite on this particular day. The interview ended and I returned to selling ice cream, by 2 p.m. that afternoon. I was sat reading a newspaper serving whippys by Bournemouth pier in the sunshine ready for a night out with Zoe Oakley (my friend from the Tesco Branksome job).

I was working in an ice cream hut by Boscombe beach the next day and I got a phone call from Kat Fletcher at Bite Communications. I had got the job and was due to start on the 1st July 2006. I was so delighted to be moving to London, where my best mate Neil lived, where I was going to be working for a big company with career opportunities and it was a break from selling ice cream on Bournemouth beach. I'd decided to make a good go of it and gave up my Cherries season ticket for the next season, deciding I'd just pop down to the odd home match and get to all the London aways.

I celebrated getting the job by announcing a farewell party in Bournemouth and booking a trip to Copenhagen in Denmark for October 2006. I found a cheap (and quite lousy) bedsit in Shepherd's Bush (Shepi B) and I moved in two days before the job began. It was a lot more dramatic than that – the final month in Bournemouth had a few more twists and turns and was busy. As well as managing the band 'The Waves' (see Chapter 19), working in both Tesco and down by the beach, I was out and about the town all the time. Not a second to spare. I went to a Girls Aloud gig with Zoe Oakley from work. I also dated a pretty English–Iranian girl called Fariba Allayarzadeh. I held a South of England Supporters Club meeting with style in Bournemouth. My brother Marko spent about 10 days with me and I got him a job by the beach, which he later declined. My Dad came over for a Bob Dylan concert in the BIC and the 2006 World Cup started. I then met a local girl on a bus, Katrina and we decided to go out for a while, albeit I was about to move to London. When I got to London, I didn't take long to adapt to the city I already knew well. Neil was less than an hour away on the tube at Greenford and I was round the corner from QPR's football stadium and had a new local pub, The Greens. It was the time of my life in many ways. I loved it. I felt I had made it now I was living in London.

But, workwise, my first two months working in Bite Communications were pretty tough. I loved living in London, my weekends off, my mates and the nightlife. But I hated the whole PR front thing and I found the job a bit stressful and tricky to get my head round. It felt to me like I wasn't being myself. I was quiet and shy in work and I barely even spoke up to the managers if I didn't like something. I felt a bit unwanted but it was my own doing. It was totally my fault. I hadn't settled into the job well. I probably didn't mess around enough. I was probably too serious. I'd sip my tea or coffee, compile client reports, make phone calls, send e-mails and attend events. But I was always too serious and cautious. That is just not me being me. But there's a logic behind everything and times would change. When I look back on it, I compare it to a footballer settling in at a new club.

My colleague Andrea Littler once said to me "we knew you were good for the job Jonny, we stuck with you, you worked hard and we knew eventually you'd be a good PR person". It touched my Bangorian heart.

However, in those first two months, I was realistically a small town boy living the fast paced city dream. I was invited to exclusive Apple events, I got to meet the UK and Europe equivalents of Steve Jobs and I got the inside gossip on all the upcoming Apple products. I was attending conferences with top industry professionals, exchanging business cards and I met people like Edith Bowman, Jonathan Ive and Rory Cellan Jones. I was out on "Thirsty Thursdays" with my workmates having a laugh and a drink away from my office desk. I found it tough to understand phone systems, Apple Macs, e-mails. At one point I was a PR assistant for Apple doing my work on a PC because my Mac kept crashing (no excrement Sherlock!!). Life had also become routine again. It was the 9 a.m. – 6 p.m. "rat race" malarkey, what nightmares are made of. On and off the tubes all the time. I knew I could crack this PR thing and be good at it, but sod that for a game of toy soldiers. One day I called my manager Jonathan Hopkins aside and told him I was quitting. That was it. I'd been in the job about two and a half months. It just wasn't for me. I had tried and failed. It was September 2006 and I wanted something new again.

I'd done my two months in London, I'd given a busy office job a crack, but I felt I was happier on Bournemouth beach selling ice cream, or in a Bournemouth hotel serving pints. In fact, back then, I was scraping £1000 a month at Bite. Yet the ice cream job and hotel job together would bring me in £300 a week if I got the hours, so £1,200 a month. The hours weren't much different once you factored in the time spent on the tube reading the Metro or the London Lite. I wasn't in it for the money clearly in that case, more for the experience of living and working in London. Though the job did have some perks – I got some iPod materials, invites to events with free food and drink and I got some benefits within the company. However, I didn't want to start at the bottom of a PR company's pyramid, aspiring to "one day" reach the top of a PR company's pyramid or God forbid my own pyramid. I had no intention or respect for that lifestyle – in every gathering, a scapegoat falls to climb. You can just cut out the shit and head straight to the top. Norman Whiteside went from the Shankill Road to the Manchester United first team to a World Cup quarter final. Open the door, see the mountain.

But during that chat with my line manager Jonathan Hopkins, when I said I was quitting, he asked me to think about it and get back to him. What he really meant was "don't quit, stick with it, we actually like you". To this day, I don't think I ever got back to him as I didn't need to. I had a pint of Guinness in the Boadicea Pub at Charing Cross after work that night and I'd made up my mind by the time I got on the train back to Slade Green (where I lived at the time, with John Johnson). I wasn't quitting. I forgot the fact I even wanted to quit and I was all over it. I was staying in Bite Communications and I would work as hard as I could for them.

The next day I was in my job for Bite again earlier than usual, and I had changed my mind. I was a new man. I was loving it. I started talking to my workmates, becoming part of the team and I started working on some other brands like Sonos and Iomega. I still hated talking on the phone though, not just the Halifax story from Chapter 9 ("My Favourite Mistake"), but the chasing journalists on the phone. The phoning people you don't know to ask them to review a product or to invite them to a launch of something ridiculously mediocre. Like why the fuck would anyone in their right mind travel 200 kilometres to an event they have no interest in, when all they get in return is a free coffee and about 20 business cards? Forget longevity, we live for today. This is our time and our moment. Not tomorrow. The world of Public Relations, well it's a glammed up pile of shit sometimes and I saw through it. But it wasn't my fault that it's a glammed up pile of shit. It wasn't my manager's or my director's fault. It was just life. Sometimes life is a pile of shit. But it was only a job. After work, I'd be down the pub. In August I still went to two Cherries matches, in September I still went to two Northern Ireland matches and in October I went to four matches (two of each). I was back to my best and I had the pleasure and business sides of my life sussed and well separated. 6 p.m. - walk out the door of work. Wetherspoons cheap beer and a feed by 7 p.m. Jurassic Park.

Looking back at it, I can cut my time at Bite Communications into two parts – the first part was July and August 2006 when I wasn't happy in work and wanted to quit. The second part was from September 2006 – June 2007 when I loved my life in London and buzzed off working at Bite. Life in London as a Public Relations person is challenging, rewarding, fast paced and self-fulfilling. I kept striving to be better and better at it and sadly a few times I fell into the trap of staying in work beyond 6 p.m. I hated that. We're not paid extra for over-time. It's our lives here, nobody else's. I'm not spending more time than I should in a job. And don't tell me any bull excrement about getting rewarded for it. I'll have my 6.03 p.m. pint of Guinness please, and you should too. The best PR workers leave on time. Because they've done all they needed to do in that timeframe. If you haven't, then it wasn't important enough to do. Nail on the pint.

My travels didn't cease though and I still made some slow progress to becoming the backpacking centurion that this book is named after. During this year of working for Bite Communications, I also travelled to Switzerland, Northern Ireland, Denmark and Liechtenstein. With each trip and each new country I was visiting, I kept realising something was missing. I wasn't seeing Asia, Africa, Middle East, Antarctica, Oceania, South America, North America. I was having to do small trips because there would be an end to my travels – I would have to go back into Bite to work. Monday morning time again or at most I'd have a week off work.

I excelled on the Sonos PR account and got to meet Thomas Meyer, the CEO of Sonos at a business lunch. I had a month left on my contract at Bite in May 2007 and my manager knew I had to return to Bournemouth University to finish my degree at some point anyway. I had forgotten all about that in fact – pieces of paper with qualifications were secondary to me. I've always been a better worker than I have a student. But my time was coming to an end at Bite and I had to make new plans.

On the same day that Jonathan Hopkins came to ask me if I'd stay for 2-3 more months to work on the accounts, I booked a one way ticket to Canada. He stared at me in disbelief. I believe I didn't need to stare at him.

"Time to take control of my own life again", I said as we walked back to our desks, "I'm off backpacking!" I was now sitting opposite Graham Day and beside Lisa Brailsford. We had a good laugh and I dropped the bombshell that I was leaving at a TAM (Thursday Afternoon Meeting). It was no big deal, to me, or to anyone. I was off backpacking. I was 26, I had no degree, I had about 30 dead end jobs behind me, I had done my time working in London and loved it. But it was time to get out and see more than just Europe. The bigger journey was about to begin.

On my final week working for Bite, I worked pretty hard though. I didn't see the point in letting things peter out. I had been inviting journalists to a PR event for Tiger Beer. We had a free crate of Tiger in the office and Graham and I would grab a few bottles towards the end of the shift. Something with Tiger stuck with me – it was Singaporean. Another place I hadn't been at that point. I was with the right people but in the wrong industry here. I was destined to be a global backpacker, not a PR executive. It didn't fit. I won't drink champagne from a tea cup.

On my final day in Bite, I was hungover – we had a major night out the night before (as some kind of leaving do) and I ended up sleeping on Graham's settee somewhere in West London. That morning I had been given a total of 10 tasks to carry out on my final shift at Bite Communications. Tasks that were a joke – like something funny in the office. It was common for anyone leaving to be given tasks to do on the last day at work. However, until this day, nobody, not even Ben White (who was a company legend and all round funny bloke) had completed all ten tasks. On hearing that nobody had ever done them all, I wasn't going to fail. This was my time. I probably wouldn't want to work in PR again, but I didn't want to be forgotten here at Bite. I'd do them all.

The tasks included mooning to the entire office during a business meeting, taking a shower and walking to my desk in front of the Managing Director, David Hargreaves, whilst holding a towel round my waist sipping a tin of beer. I was also supposed to e-mail my team and tell them I was going to the toilet to do a massive shit, copying in one of the directors "by mistake". That wasn't enough for me – I e-mailed the WHOLE company to tell them I was having a poo. Swedish and American staff I didn't know, they

knew this Ulsterman was ejecting brown substance from a
lower part.

I was single at the time too and I turned the "leaving top 5" into a
"sex league" at the final speech admitting that "I've done it as the 5
ladies who I would most like to bang in Bite". Sally Plant and Rhi
Morgan were on the list for sure. There was no inter-Bite shagging
with me. I fancied many of the girls but they wouldn't have had
me. I felt like a drifter. I even tried my luck with Mika, a Swedish
girl from the Stockholm office when we had a joint staff party. My
flirts with Sally fell on deaf ears, "you out tonight Sally?" to which
she'd reply, "so Jonny can you send me the newspaper scans?"
"Sure thing". I liked Sally Plant. Even the name. I fall in love with
names sometimes. Claire McKee, Vicky Everitt…they had
nice names.

"So Sally can wait, she knows it's too late" – Noel Gallagher.

As the time got to 5.45 p.m. and I was due to leave work on my
final day at Bite Communications in London, everyone in the
company gathered round my desk. It was a shock. They were
bearing gifts, giving a speech and showing a video of me singing
Blur's 'Parklife' in a cockney accent in the upstairs boardroom. Oh
my God – they had liked me! I expected they were glad to get rid
of me but it was the opposite! I was overwhelmed by the send-off
and I was in tears. They gave me a book saying, "We will miss you
JB – you have been an excellent PR person". The book was made
by Sally Plant herself and she had taken some time to craft it all
up. I didn't know it until that moment – but they had liked me there
and they had appreciated my work. I was really chuffed. I was
overwhelmed and emotional. I didn't want to leave the office on
my final day, but my mind had been made up and I had to pack my
bags for the adventure ahead. Life couldn't wait.

Within 48 hours, I was backpacking in Toronto on my own, loving the freedom of life on the road, with the office blocks and computer screens of Bite left far behind me. On my second night in Toronto, in the Planet Traveler hostel, life was about to change significantly once again. I really didn't have a clue how this would change my life back then, but you'll see.

They were good memories at Bite for sure and I learned a lot. It's over 13 years since I started that job and I'm glad I left when I did and I never returned to an office job. I do my own PR now. I'm top of my own pyramid. Oh, the irony…

Chapter 22
What's a Travel Blog?

Planet Traveler Hostel, Toronto, CANADA (July 2007)

"Maybe I'm on my own still, but at least I'm happy"
– Michael Tivey.

After leaving Bite Communications behind, I was backpacking in Canada again. I knew Toronto well from my 2001 visit and was glad to be back. It was of course, the city that had given me the phrase "don't stop living". This time I was attending the 2007 Under 20s FIFA World Cup and managed to get tickets for two of the group matches, including the highly anticipated Mexico v. Portugal clash. I also toured some more of the city, but it was a chance and significant meeting with two individuals in the Planet Traveler hostel in Toronto which turned my life on its head. It was ridiculous, and looking back years on, it just seems crazy that this chance meeting changed my life that much.

I headed for a beer and a walk through the city with my hostel dorm-mate, Lee Price. He was a lad from Essex in England and was on a one year backpacking round the world adventure. When we got to the bar, I pulled out my notepad and started writing notes after I had got my beer. He looked at me and said, "what are you doing?" and I told him "I keep a record of my entire travels. What I do each day, the names of the bars, attractions, streets. The price of things. Anything I want to make a note of, I write it down. I'm a writer, I love to write".

"Cool", said Lee, "I have a travel blog".

And then the truth came - I didn't have a clue what he meant. Not a clue. I had never ever ever heard of a travel blog. "What's a travel blog?" I naively asked.

When we got back to the hostel he showed me his online travel blog. It was brilliant. He had photos, he had his words and he had documented his backpacking trip so far online on this blog. "I'd love to do that" I said but I had no idea how to even get started. Nevertheless, I knew I should set one up. I could go public with my travels!

The same night, I met Mike Burkimsher in the hostel who was also an English guy, but he was returning from a few years in Australia and was taking the long way back to England. He also had a travel blog called "The long way home" and showed it to me. Again, I loved it. Another travel blogger! I knew this was something I had to do. I could write all my written notes onto the internet and even better add photos, and even better other people had a chance to read about it. How had I not heard of travel blogs before??

So, the next day, from the Apple shop in Toronto, Canada, I typed up my first ever "travel blog post" as an unsent e-mail, as a draft. I typed it and then e-mailed it to myself and I got into the habit of doing this once a day. I figured I'd work out later on how to put it all online and then I would already have all the content. It would be a case of copy and paste and add the photos.

Since I was in Toronto, I jotted down a note in my diary *"my new travel blog – don't stop living"* and that was that. I had the name for my travel blog – "Don't Stop Living, by Jonny Blair". Around the same time, my cousin Paul Scott was also backpacking. He was in South America rather than North America and also he had a blog. I liked it as well. I knew this was exciting, but I still had to be enjoying the moment. I didn't want to be backpacking and stuck behind a computer screen. I limited myself to an hour a day maximum typing this up and I stuck to it. If I knew then what I know now!

So, in Toronto in July 2007, I became a travel blogger. By the end of the month I had about 31 blog posts in e-mail format waiting to be uploaded once I worked the internet out. I later set up my blog on Blogspot.com from an internet café in Taupo, New Zealand and that was it. I was now online! People could read my stories and the first article on there after my welcome post, would be about Toronto in Canada. None of that early stuff will go properly into this book. The archives are online for you to check out. The USA was up next on my 2007 travels and the original version of the travel blog "Don't Stop Living" was born. In that hostel in Toronto, I also met Mike Tivey, a singer-songwriter from England. One night, Mike played us the song "Maybe I'm on my own still, but at least I'm happy" and the scene was set.

With all this in mind, I had completely forgotten about the job I left behind the week before. I was free and happy and I had forgotten about Bite Communications already.

Plus, I was now a travel blogger. Don't Stop Living was born.

Chapter 23
How Till Get Drunk For $10 US In New York City

Aces and Eights Saloon Bar, New York City, USA (July 2007)

"All free souls beware; a moon is in my head."
- Ian McCullough.

After re-discovering Toronto having left Bite, I opted to tour New York next. It was my first time in the USA for 10 years and my time to do it fully solo. Luckily this chapter doesn't need a warning notice with it. There's no sex, nudity, fraud or passport loss. There is no exam theft, smashed up cars or fake interest rates. I had learnt to be a better man, with merely minor faults by this stage of my life. This chapter is just a tale of me getting drunk with my travel buddies in New York City. FOR $10. Ten Dollars. That's drunk. New York City. In a Bar. For $10. Yes, I got drunk in New York City for $10 in a bar on draught beer and whatever spirits were placed in that magic glass!

For $10 US Dollars, myself and 7 others drank the bar dry on a special "All You Can Drink Night" in New York City. As this backpacking adventure reaches its 17 year anniversary, how the hell did I do it? How the hell can I remember it? Here's a full account of the night I...got drunk in New York City for $10!

I was on a backpacking world tour at the time and New York was one of the first cities on my hit-list that time so I made my way round all the sights the first few days and settled in - I had 8 days in NYC as I wanted to "do it properly but still on a budget". Nothing major in terms of spending - cheap and cheerful and have a few quiet beers. However, my best mate 'Millwall Neil' just happened to be working outside New York City at the time and was remarkably busy, but he could spare a night to come and visit me. "It had to be good" I remember thinking. I didn't want my mate Neil to come all the way to NYC for a drink and me, who was backpacking there at the time, have nothing planned or be too tight to scrape a decent meal or a beer together. So, I left the hostel for the afternoon and went for a walk looking for inspiration. On that walk, some kid hands me a flier for a $10 All You Can Drink Night!! Are you kidding? This was a gift from the Gods. Neil and I had no way to contact each other in those days, we didn't use Facebook (much – I had just started to use it) and certainly had no mobile phones, but my previous message to him was to meet in Mr. Bigg's Pub at 7 p.m. on the Thursday night. That plan remained and I knew he would be there. He knew I would be there.

Inspired by this flier for $10 all you can drink, I headed back to the hostel to chill for a bit then thought about just rounding up people from the hostel to come out and join the party. I mean there was no catch - I had been handed a flier for "**$10 All you can drink**". What drinking person (unless driving, pregnant or ill) would turn that down? There weren't a lot of people around late afternoon and time was getting on and I didn't want to be late for Neil so I rounded up a crazy Australian guy called Simon (who was in my room), and downstairs a Greek-Aussie called Zisis and a Welsh dude called Marc and we headed to Mr. Bigg's, which was on the corner of 10th Avenue and 43rd Street. Mr. Bigg's was just the venue I chose to meet Neil in (inspired by a previous buy one get one free beer flier), the venue with the $10 US all you can drink was a place called Aces and Eights Saloon. It was a short jaunt on the Subway I think.

That's when I told them the surprise. "Have you got $10?" I asked. "Yes, why?" "Oh, just that's all you'll need to get pissed tonight - we're drinking this bar dry". Have some of that and me and my new Welsh mate and Aussie mates high fived as we ordered a beer in Mr. Bigg's. Which by the way it was a buy one get one free beer for $1 at the time. That's right! Hence why I arranged to meet Neil there initially.

We were getting the beer down and loving it and then I told them - "oh my best mate's coming - haven't seen him for ages – I used to live with him in England. Hope he can find this place!" "Is he English?" they asked. "Yes!". "Then he'll find it". True to his word Neil my best mate wasn't even late, he saunters in with a Canadian mate, Justin and suddenly there are six of us. "Get these buy one get one frees down you lads and let's go to the next pub!!" It's an international drinking night. Simon says to me - Aussies, a Canadian, a Northern Irish lad, an Englishman, a Welshman - we'll drink them dry!!

We headed on the Subway to the Aces and Eights Saloon, the bar which had the "Shut Up and Drink" night. The Aces and Eights Saloon was on the corner of 1st Avenue and 87th Street. The "All You Can Drink" thing started at 9 p.m. I told the lads we were turning up on time and milking it. We got there at 8.58 p.m. . "You're two minutes early" says the doorman. "Oh, that's okay" I said to him "We can wait two minutes - we've all got our tenners ready!" And that was it - we paid $10 US at the door, got a stamp on our hand and were given a glass. We were told if you lost the glass you'd have to pay another $10 for a replacement. Bollocks to that said Neil and I as we just asked the bar girl for extra glasses. Nobody had to pay for another glass. The party was on.

We met some girls from the US and a Jamaican lad called Ricky, plus a few others. We played beer pong downstairs while continuing to drink and drink and drink. It was hardcore I'm telling you. We were all so happy and so young and free. It was easy! Then we played an international pool competition. There were about 8 or 9 nationalities by now - most of us from our group plus a few other groups. We had a bigger group now and probably 16 people in the pool competition with each round a knockout.

Despite being wasted, I remember getting to the semi-final of the pool competition and being beaten by Simon the Aussie. Neil lost the other semi-final to Ricky from Jamaica. Simon and I then went up to get another beer and another keg had run out so we were onto a new keg, another beer, it was endless. Still hadn't spent a penny or a cent inside. Only the $10!! We were milking it and it was a few solid hours of drinking! I think it's the most I have ever drank in my life.

Then the song "Land Down Under" by Men at Work comes on, Simon necks his beer, gets another one (free of course) and we head to watch him in the final against Ricky from Jamaica. The Jamaican lad must have been a dead cert to win having been a New Yorker now having emigrated from Jamaica. Home soil and all that. But we were all necking our beer and cheering Simon on. Ricky must have realised we were all supporting Simon!

One of the bar girls called Caitlin then brought down some shots. Simon the Aussie famously won the pool competition, the beer flowed and that's the last I remember...I got drunk in New York City for $10.

I woke up in New York City...I don't remember getting home to the hostel. Oh yeah baby!

As my travels progressed since then I later lived with Neil in Australia (Parramatta) caught up with Zisis in London for a beer once and also travelled round Taiwan and Korea with Neil. I spent almost 2 years living in Australia yet never met up with Simon – I promise he will be the first person I contact if I make it to Perth sometime. Since that night I have had a load of wild nights and more crazy stories will come, but come on, back in 2007 to get drunk in New York City for $10 must have been pretty damn good. I won't forget that night for as long as I live, which is ironic because the last few hours of it, I don't remember!

This USA journey also involved a tour of Hollywood, Staten Island, watching David Beckham's first ever training session at LA Galaxy and a wild night in the pub that George Best once owned – Bestie's by Hermosa Beach in Los Angeles. When that all calmed down, I boarded a flight from Los Angeles to Oceania. I was off backpacking in New Zealand, starting off in Auckland!

Chapter 24
Dust From a Distant Sun

Rotorua, NEW ZEALAND (July 2007)

"Give me something I can write about" – Neil Finn.

The summer of 2007 was the first time I visited Oceania and Asia. While that seems like I started it late, in the 13 years following that I'd visit almost every country in mainland Asia and a bunch of the Oceania countries. However, to begin with I backpacked through the North Island of New Zealand. I flew into Auckland from Los Angeles and got my plans in place while based at Auckland Central Backpackers. It was a lifetime ago now and it seems like I was such a novice backpacker in those days. In reality, I was young, hungry and vibrant and the time in New Zealand reflected this ongoing youthful zest which still hadn't deserted me. It was wild.

I'd been in the country less than 24 hours, I was jet lagged, I was tired but our hostel had a free bus tour of Auckland and up to the Bay of Islands so I got on-board. At the start of the tour, the guy at the front asked if anyone wanted to do a bungy jump. My hand was straight up, for whatever reason. When I looked around the other 20 – 30 backpackers on the bus, I was the only backpacker up for the Bungy Jump. It was only my hand that went up! This was slightly worrying of course, but I wasn't going to turn this chance down. I probably assumed everyone would have put their hands up. Wrong, I was.

We parked under Auckland Harbour Bridge and I got my gear on and we walked to the centre of the Bridge. It was brilliant. Was I scared? Yes, probably, but these are the things you want to do in life. I jumped off Auckland Harbour Bridge that morning, hoisting myself back on the rope to safety all to the tune of the Arctic Donkeyhead song "When the sun goes down". When I got back up, a hat-trick of Irish girls, Laura, Shauna and Ornella came up to me and asked me how it was.

I didn't want to tell them there was some crazy adrenalin like having an orgasm, but I said something to that effect and all three of them used my recommendation on the spur of the moment to decide they were jumping off too!

The actual bus had 20 – 30 backpackers on it and the only 4 of us that jumped off the bridge were 3 girls from the Republic of Ireland and me from Northern Ireland. The Irish air had clearly taught us to embrace these passions. I partied with the girls and a Californian lady that night in downtown Auckland and a few days later, I was in the town of Taupo, over a dreamy lake.

It was here, in the town of Taupo, that I left some dreams hanging around. Life had actually been a bit shit for me. I'm being more serious now. I have suffered from depression on and off from the age of 14. Anyone can get depressed and I've always been excellent at dressing up bad times. I polish poo poos. Everything has to be amazing, as happiness and having fun keep us alive and kicking. The bad times always overshadowed the good though and I had a need to belong. I was a lonely backpacker, new to New Zealand.

As you do, on my first day in Taupo, I got my haircut, I got some vouchers for cheap beers and I put my name down for a 9 a.m. skydive the next day. That night, I drank in Mulligan's Irish Pub in central Taupo because I had a free beer voucher.

I was up early the next day and I waited with hostel buddies David, Les and Stacie. The three of them would be joining me in a limousine to the airfield where we would do our sky dive. I got on well with Stacie Jayne. She was a hot girl. Essex lass, raunchy, wild, outspoken, fun and attractive. When we got to the airfield, the three guys, we stuck together and we let Stacie go in the plane before us, so the three lads could do our sky dives from the same plane. I was second in our plane to do the sky dive. If you've ever done a sky dive, you'll know it's a mind blowing, crazy experience. It was brilliant!

Stacie and I toured more of the area together that day and we headed with a hostel crew down to the pub quiz in Mulligan's Irish Bar in Taupo. I think I went there three nights in a row – you do that type of thing when you are a backpacker. When you travel the world, you sometimes think and feel you can do what you want as you won't be here again, in this town. In this place. And certainly not at this time again and not with these people again. Everything in life happens once. We were all cheap backpackers at our table and there was another couple Tom and his girlfriend Yvonne who joined us.

Beers were $3 NZD but we had vouchers for free beers. When those vouchers ran out, the quizmaster had announced some dares for free beers. I was straight up there. First challenge was to be faster than another dude to bring up a ladies bra. That was easy – Stacie took hers straight off and I handed it in. Free beer for Stacie and I. Stacie then had to find a pair of boy's boxer shorts for a dare. Again – easy – I whipped mine off quickly right there at the table and gave them to her. She won. Another 2 beers each. We had no shame. Then the clincher…

Then they asked for couples to go up in a challenge against each other. Stacie and I saw the free beer sign flashing so we pretended to be a couple for the night. We weren't. When we got up there,

there would be free beers for the first out of the three couples to successfully swap their entire clothes with each other.

But remember, she had no bra on now, and I had no boxer shorts. We simply hadn't time after the previous dare to go back to the toilet and get fully clothed again. Thus, for Stacie and I this meant full nudity of course and the other couple would probably have underwear. She had already given me her bra and I'd given her my boxer shorts (in the days before I got wise and travelled with tighter and lighter y-fronts/briefs).

No shame from Stacie and I as we realised the quickest way to win this competition was not to do it bit by bit like the other 2 couples, but to whip everything off each other, be naked and then whack everything back on. So that's exactly what we did. We both stripped fully nude, did our merry dance, put each other's clothes back on and boom! We had won the dare easily. Strangely and perhaps gracefully, no photos of us both nude exist - smart phones weren't prevalent in those days, a Godsend? We were loving it and we did a nude dance in the bar that night on route to getting our next free drinks.

We won a few more free beers, we won the quiz thanks to the other ones in our hostel team and I'd seen Stacie wild and nude. After Mulligan's we headed to a nightclub where Stacie and I danced. She confessed to having a boob job, she was the first girl I had met with implants and copped a good feel.

On leaving the town of Taupo, I had many dreams about Stacie and I wondered what could, would and should have been. I fancied her a lot. But we parted ways that day, at the bus station and it was on with each other's respective shows. I never saw Stacie again. I know I fell in love with her that night. I just know it.

However, this chapter is about New Zealand and on my travels I made two separate visits to the country. In 2007, I concentrated on the north island and in 2010, I concentrated on the south island.

There were some wild experiences in sulphuric Rotorua too. We saw Kiwi birds, I met the Irish girls from Auckland again and we had some more nights out.

There was also a visit to Tamaki Maori village where I was selected a chief of our tribe and had to come face to face with the Maori in a jungle resort. I met an English couple, Andy and Ali and we toured together for a few days. Another highlight was the zorbing experience where we were rolling down the hill inside a ball. New Zealand winters were colder than I expected them to be.

The next stop on my whirlwind trip however was to be Beijing in China. I had sorted out my Chinese visa in London and pencilled in a tour to the Great Wall of China and checking out Beijing, it was the first ever Asian country I visited and is currently still the one that I have travelled in the most (well, Hong Kong aside). I have since made over 20 visits to Mainland China and I'll reflect on those journeys a little bit more throughout the book and forthcoming books, if I haven't already bigged China up enough on my travel blog.

But when I left New Zealand, like I said before, I left some dreams hanging around Lake Taupo after that wild night. Those thoughts still linger with me day by day. I knew the backpacking lifestyle was now the manner of living for me. There was no going back

"Dust from a distant sun, will shower over everyone"
– Neil Finn.

Chapter 25
A Fast Flight to China

Beijing, CHINA (July 2007)

"Things have gone wrong too many times before, so take a slow boat to China" – Manic Street Preachers.

After New Zealand, I boarded a flight to China for the first time, with a stop-over in Kuala Lumpur. I was on a late notice round the world trip, almost as a taster to something bigger and better ahead. These days I tell travellers to avoid Beijing and Shanghai if they want to experience China and I base that on my own mistakes and experiences. I did the obvious on my first trip to China though – I flew in and out of Beijing. Textbook stuff. I loved it of course, but having now visited almost half of China's 29 provinces/regions, Beijing plays second fiddle to a lot of the unknown gems of this nation. China is a stunner. It's everything you dreamt of and more.

So, I booked myself into the largest backpacker's hostel in Beijing and I met a load of cool people there, including Rene, my Dutch mate who toured the city with me. We visited the Forbidden Palace, the Lama Temple, the Hutongs, Sanlitun Street. I did all the expected touristy stuff and I just remember being really inspired by China, but knowing that I didn't want to go to Beijing next time I visited this country. I visited the Great Wall – probably a bit mainstream but something that I felt needed to be seen and I did so at Badaling – probably the most touristic part of the entire wall! Overall, this fast flight to China, in and out of the same airport and staying just a few nights in a popular hostel gave me a taste, but my mind was on the old U.S.S.R. for now, I was on my long way back to Europe with Russia up next. I had a few days in Moscow, before one of my craziest journeys to date.

I was heading to Belarus to become the first ever Northern Ireland football fan to go there to follow the national team. And as I edit this chapter in July 2019, I am still the only Northern Ireland away fan to travel to Belarus to watch every full Northern Ireland international, men's or women's. In fact I will always be the only person that can hold that accolade as nobody else was at the 2007 game. It was me, myself and I. We played Belarus again in June 2019 and there were over 600 GAWA there compared with the one from 2007. This visit to watch Belarus v. Northern Ireland women's team was an event pre-arranged in the British Legion in Gillingham, England the previous May. Shaun Schofield and I had decided to go to another Northern Ireland ladies match. So, I got in touch with David Currie from the Irish Football Association (Northern Ireland – not the fake southern breakaway unit) and arranged to meet up with the squad in Belarus.

In fact, the buzz of the Belarus trip meant that Russia and China virtually passed me by, I almost forgot about them. I shoved them in as a shit B-side. In the next chapter of wacaday life, this Ulsterman headed to Minsk.

Shortest chapter maybe here, but China had plenty more in my backpacking cannon to come.

Later in life of course, I took many "slow boats to (and through) China", my destiny definitely was widening, broadening, extending beyond the wooden doors of my wonderful Marlo childhood bedroom.

Chapter 26
Multiple B: Beaten By Belarus In Belshina Bobruisk By the Berezina River

Bobruisk, Eastern BELARUS (July – August 2007)

"We're in the Army Now. We're in the Army" – Status Quo.

This chapter, which is brimming with "B"s, has been seen before, though it was edited for Shaun Schofield's book "Albania to America" in 2010. Therefore, I have stripped it back down to the original version here, in its entirety. This is the way the chapter on Belarus was meant to be for Shaun's book. It's a tad more personal and reflective than the others as I also fondly remember the 1980s and I've edited it again as of July 2019. You could also say that this chapter doesn't fit with the flow of the book. However, chronologically it completely does, so here it is, with belshynic aplomb.

My Dad had been going to Windsor Park to watch Northern Ireland for years and years – we are talking 50s, 60s, 70s, 80s... more stories about my Dad appear in the first few chapters. Dad provided my first memory of Northern Ireland and football. Aged two I was awoken by my Dad, Joe Blair placing a football programme on my bedside table. He had just got back from watching Northern Ireland beat the mighty West Germany 1-0, with Ian Stewart scoring our winner. He must have been buzzing but I didn't quite understand the significance of that win, or the programme until later in life. Four years later I was watching Northern Ireland versus Algeria on an old black and white TV – in the World Cup. It was fantastic to see people from my country taking on the likes of Algeria, Spain and Brazil. I was amazed! From then on I was in love with the Northern Ireland football team. My Dad had bought me a Mexico 1986 scarf, which I still have to this day and cherish as one of my top possessions. I also had two

Northern Ireland shirts from the 1980s (one of them has a faded badge but I still have it) and I lost my green and white Northern Ireland wristbands and wore out my green and white caser booting it against brick walls. I also completed the Panini sticker album for the 1986 World Cup, making sure I had doubles of my heroes Norman Whiteside, Pat Jennings and Alan McDonald (I sadly later lost the album and said doubles). Since then I have been to over 100 Northern Ireland matches, and various other under 19, under 21 and ladies matches. Supporting Northern Ireland for me is a drug, one of which it is a pleasure to be addicted to.

I had contributed to former Northern Ireland fanzine "Arconada... Armstrong!" in the mid-1990s, and set up "Here We Go...Again" fanzine with Michael and Gavin McClelland, which we sold alongside Marty Lowry's "Our Wee Country" (formerly TAWSIE) fanzine on match days from 1997 – 2004 (and we relaunched it in May 2016 ahead of Euro 2016; as a one-off). I had been aware, through Marty, of Shaun Schofield and his mental dedication to the Northern Ireland football team. I may also have spoken to Shaun or indeed sold him a fanzine over the years, however I didn't meet him properly until July 2006. I first met Shaun formally in Manchester of all places for the mainland NISC five-a-sides tournament, and have kept in regular touch since. Shaun was also one of only 15 Northern Ireland fans to turn The Isle of Wight into "The Isle of Green" in November 2006, when the South of England Northern Ireland Supporters Club (SOENISC) held the first ever NISC meeting on the English island. Crazy ideas and random-ness had become a regular trait since I helped set up the SOENISC in 2005. No-one could have predicted that this crazy-ness would reach a bizarre zenith in August 2007 in Eastern Belarus. Of all places. Of all places.

Only a handful of Northern Ireland fans turned up to watch Northern Ireland ladies play England away at Gillingham's

Priestfield on a wet Sunday in May 2007. In an almost identical match to Northern Ireland's (men's team's) defeat to England at Old Trafford in March 2005, it was a great day out in the Kent rain. At half time to be holding England's full-time pros to a scoreless draw was some feat and the Northern Ireland contingent where Shaun and I were sat, were buoyed by it and we gave a rousing singing performance in the second half. Unfortunately, we lost 4-0 in the end, but our wee ladies had played with pride and passion. It was in the pub (British Legion, Gillingham) after the match that Shaun came up with the idea of watching another one of the Northern Ireland ladies away matches. I was well up for it, Shaun and I were going to be the only two Northern Ireland fans at a ladies away match. Wacaday.

The thing that excites me about supporting a football team is that following a team is also an exposure to culture. It's more than just a 90 minute match. Going to away matches allows me to see new places and meet new people, football becomes the bonus, as ironical as Alanis Mozzarella or the Likely Lads would have you know. I enjoy this at both club and country level, as an AFC Bournemouth fan I have been to many away matches in England (and Wales) and of course Glentoran FC matches in Northern Ireland. Football helps us to see new places, experience different cultures, meet interesting people, discover strange traits, and to quote R.E.M. "with love comes strange currencies". It just so happened that Northern Ireland's next away match for the ladies was in Belarus. This made me even more eager to attend, as a Northern Ireland international football team had never before played Belarus in any shape, size, age or form. Landlocked Belarus is also (obviously) an ex-communist state, one of the most bizarre products following the break-up of the USSR. Shaun and I had decided – we were going.

Out of the blue, about a month later, Shaun informed me that he was unable to attend (for once) and would not be travelling to Belarus. I decided with no hesitation that I was still going. I would become the first Northern Ireland fan to ever watch any kind of Northern Ireland international football team play any kind of match in Belarus. I would travel alone like some kind of lunatic.

At the time I was working for a PR agency (Bite Communications) in London and had decided to take three months out to do a round the world backpacking trip in the Summer of 2007, before life and circumstances prevented me from doing so. Oh the irony of that. I arranged it so that I would be in Moscow, Russia the day before the Euro 2009 Northern Ireland ladies qualifier in Belarus. A spanner was then thrown into the works when I found out from David Currie that the match was not to take place in the capital of Minsk, but in the city of Bobruisk (Babyrusk). Where the hell even is Bobruisk?

Bobruisk is some 120 miles south east from Minsk, and less than 200 miles from the site of the 1986 Chernobyl Nuclear disaster in the neighbouring Ukraine. In fact, it's only 40 kilometres outside the sad and infamous "Chernobyl Exclusion Zone", which I visited separately on my Ukraine adventure in 2015. What a truly bizarre experience this was going to be.

Having sorted out my visas etc. in June and been in touch with the Irish Football Association, I was all set for a flight from Moscow (Sheremetyevo Airport) to Minsk International Airport. I did check the prices and times of trains as well, but it ended up being cheaper, easier and (of course) much quicker (though possibly less fun; I'll never know) to fly there. In my time in Moscow I had experienced some hostility and noticed how the peelers man the streets looking for foreigners to exploit, so I reckoned travelling alone to Minsk was also easier by air in them days. I didn't fancy being refused entry on my cross-border train, though I did often wonder how many Ulstermen had a Belarus Visa on their passport. Not that many, in those days, I'd imagine. But plenty of Ulsterwomen did – I'd be meeting at least 25 of them here! Without visiting the British Embassy, I found it virtually impossible to find English speakers in either The Russian Federation or in The Republic of Belarus so I generally tried to blend in and communicate by whatever means possible.

The route to the city of Bobruisk and the Northern Ireland ladies match began at 7 a.m. in Hostel Moscow (near Afanayevsky Boulevard). A quick breakfast and I caught the Blue Line 4 rapid transit system from Arbatskaya to change onto the Green Line 2 to Rechnov Vokzal, before somehow getting on the right bus to Sheremetyevo Airport Terminal 2. Fittingly the bus was green and white, although communicating with the driver was as hard as a 1970s Belfast terrorist. I got through customs and the like and made my way to the bar, I was shocked to see Harp on sale at an Irish bar at the airport. I'm not normally a fan of these "Irish themed" pubs made by the non-Irish, but I needed a cold pint and boy did that Harp taste good. It was quite refreshing to be in an Irish pub with English speakers (the three previous countries on my world trip had been Russia, China and Malaysia, where English speakers were few and miles between). It was at the airport in the queue for the flight that I met Dimitri, a Russian guy who spoke some English and was quite astounded that I would be travelling to Belarus, never mind round the world on my own! Due to an empty seat in the first class section of the plane, Dimitri somehow blagged me into first class, charming the attractive Russian air hostess in the process. I got a complimentary shot of brandy and some free food on a short flight (I think it was 1 hour at most). At the time I also had no idea how I would get from Minsk airport to the Hotel Tourist in Bobruisk (where I was booked in and the IFA team were due to stay). I am a spontaneous person and hadn't checked any bus or train routes, or any maps, never mind bought any tickets. What made the adrenalin pump even more was that I wasn't even sure that I would make it to Bobruisk; or find the Hotel Tourist; or if the IFA were definitely staying there; or if the match was even still on. When I look back now, over ten years on, I do feel like I was such a novice backpacker in those days, but it was the experience of going to places like Belarus that increased my experience and knowledge in the field of long term travel.

Once off the plane in Minsk, Dimitri and I considered the hourly bus option, but then he spoke to a taxi driver and managed to get us a cheap fare to Minsk Central Station, where hopefully I could find a train or bus to Bobruisk. Dimitri was on a business trip and his company paid for his transport. I thanked Dimitri and I think I gave him 20,000 Belarus Roubles (less than £5) as we said our goodbyes. I then had to hope for a train to Bobruisk. I stood out as a foreign backpacker by a mile in the middle of Minsk train station wearing an emerald green Northern Ireland shirt, as I started chatting to Taisa, a Belarussian lady who spoke NO English, but at least we both established that we were both by coincidence heading to Bobruisk. So I got my ticket (an elaborate brown and yellow two page effort) sorted and found the correct platform towards Homel or Gomel (which I was told would stop at Bobruisk). The trains were very infrequent in Belarus, and I had a wait of almost three hours. I had a very brief walk round the city (but knew I could do this again the morning after the match) before waiting with Taisa in the train station bar, where I got some pork-type roll and some gorgeous beer. I couldn't read the beer label, but Taisa pronounced it as "Boygopa" and "Krineetska"/"Greynitska". I think the beers cost me something like 18p and 23p in sterling (really!) and still rank as two of the cheapest beers from my journeys so far. Soon I was boarding a nice light blue train, journeying through some excellent countryside; and then, there I was at Bobruisk train station!

Here I was in Bobruisk amongst grey skies and local people. There wasn't another backpacker in sight, nor any information in English, nor any hostels or tourist information. I did feel lonely here when I arrived. At the time, it felt like I was lost and lonely on the other side of the world – I was nowhere. There was absolutely no way of me finding the 'Hotel Tourist' and in foreign countries I often find it hard to tell if a building is a hotel or not when I cannot read the writing. So, I asked Taisa to help get me there just before she left. In Bobruisk there didn't appear to be any decent bus system (or any taxis). It seemed to me that mates and families just give each other lifts all the time. Taisa then negotiated with a family (Mum, Dad, son) if they knew of this hotel or if they could take me there. Nobody spoke any English and I didn't speak any Russian or Belarussian (except please and thank you). Suddenly I was in the back of a 1980s style Lada and driven directly to the Hotel Tourist in Bobruisk. Again I tipped the family who gave me a lift. I think I gave them around a fiver (sterling), which was probably way too much and a lot of money to them but I was happy with it back then. The son was wearing a very old Barcelona shirt (think Ronald Koeman 1992) and kept looking at the Northern Ireland badge on my shirt. I kept trying to sing "We're not Brazil, we're Northern Ireland" to him. He probably thought I was a lunatic.

Even when I found the hotel, it didn't look like a hotel. I wasn't even sure and I remember the first door didn't open and was locked. I might even have been briefly scared. It was a yellow, grey and white building that looked like it was designed from a Soviet Textbook. But this was it. It was my hotel. Safely I had arrived in the Hotel Tourist, overlooking a sombre and picturesque Berezina River on the outskirts of the city. I hadn't a clue where I was, but I had my own cosy room for the night and I felt relaxed! Of course in those days, no internet, no smart phone, no Wi-Fi and I didn't call my Mum or Dad. In fact it was the first time I had my own room since I left my old room in the house in Dartford in England.

The previous backpacking had all been in shared rooms, beds, dorms, flights, buses or trains.

After a shower and a beer (the local brew) I finally saw relief when I bumped into David Currie of the IFA in the hotel lobby. The ladies soon followed and I recognised Una Harkin and Ashley Hutton (who had both played in the match at Gillingham). I had a dander round the central squares and parks, the bleak streets nearby and past the river, then I chilled out with some local beers before resting my head for the night. Match-day arrived and being on the IFA-organised coach, I was at the stadium a good hour before kick-off. I put the SOENISC flag up, soaked in the pre-match atmosphere, but was also attracting attention from the local peelers (the 'stewards' at the match being dressed in what I can only describe as Soviet style military uniform). Yes, it appeared the remnants of Stalin's communist legacy had not been completely phased out of this former USSR state. A peeler approached me complete with an English translator (!) asking where I wanted to 'sit'. Apart from Northern Ireland home matches in the 1990s where I mostly sat in the North Stand, I always stood at football matches. I wanted to stand behind my flag (which I deliberately put in front of the green seats) and give vocal support from there. However, I was made to watch from the seats and naturally I chose the green seated section to sit alone, with smile-less Belarussian stewards on either side of me! That was until just before kick-off when Australian Albert and Irish - Australian Owen plus a rather attractive (and large breasted) Belarussian lady turned up and decided to sit with me, so there were now four of us. I had met Owen and Albert the night before in the hotel bar and invited them down. Owen wore my scarf for the match, he was born somewhere in the Republic of Ireland and had since emigrated to Australia. Today he would be supporting Northern Ireland. I didn't actually expect them to turn up.

With Belarus ranked 40 odd places above Northern Ireland, we were majorly the underdog, however the Northern Ireland ladies had beaten Croatia 5-1 and Georgia 4-0 away in 2006, and in football anything is possible. On the day though, Belarus looked strong and composed, time and time again they tested Emma Higgins in nets. At half-time though we were only 1-0 down (with a Belarus goal disallowed for offside) and I did believe we could get a lucky break and sneak a draw. At half time, I was also made to move seats, as I had sung constantly for 45 minutes, giving the silent Belarussians an insight into what being a Northern Ireland fan is all about. Some of them assumed I was some kind of hooligan and even tried to approach me. The four of us moved at half time to higher up in the stand, by the Directors Box, close to where Norman Livingstone, the IFA official was watching from the box. The second half began and the Belarussians were much too strong, and they added four more, one a total screamer from 30 yards (which I did applaud amongst my tears). The final score was 5-0 to Belarus. On the day, on the pitch we didn't perform as team manager Alfie Wylie confessed.

However, in the stand I sang loudly, on my own, for 90 minutes totally eclipsing, out-singing and over-riding any Belarus chant. My range of songs were wide and varied, from "We're not Brazil, we're Northern Ireland" to "Wonderwall (after all...we've got Stacey Hall)" to "You're supposed to be at home" to "Alfie Wylie's green and green army" to "We've got that Una Harkin" to "All we need is Kimberley Turner". I even made up some songs on the spot as I was enjoying it so much! Almost every Belarus fan was watching me more than the match, totally overaud and flabbergasted at one man's passion for my country. I mean, who sings songs at a ladies' match? Not many fans, I'll tell you that. Being made to move seats at half-time made me sing more the second half, where I even gave a rendition of Pulp's "Common People", Status Quo's "We're in the army now" (a song which had been played a lot before the kick off and will stick in my memory of the day and in my time in Belarus), before slightly more controversial songs such as "Are you Russian in disguise?" attempted to get the home fans to sing. In the end, they just stared at me and even sang a "Northern Ireland du du du du de" for me. The local TV Cameras also filmed me (as did many kids on their mobile phones, yes some of them had video phones), at 5-0 down, when I started loudly singing "Five Nil; and you still don't sing". The Belarus fans still didn't.

After the match about 30 poorly dressed kids crowded round me as I waited in the tiny Sparta Stadium (home of Belshina Belarus, where I believe Portadown FC once played). I think they were aware of my "Western-ness" (I hate that term but others love it, which is the only justification I ever give for using it – but please note I'm NOT "Western" and I never will be, if anyone really wants to classify me geographically, I'm Northern) and assumed I was rich. They wanted gifts. In the end, all I had to give was a Northern Ireland keyring to a youngster who showed me he had a Spanish FA keyring from their visit, so he now had a Northern Ireland one to add to his collection. These kids were quiet and reserved. I felt sorry for them: watching this ladies match and filming my singing had been highlights in their day. One can only imagine what growing up amongst dreary grey and yellow buildings in Bobruisk would be like. Eighteen years on since the fall of communism, I noticed that parts of Belarus still had a lot of catching up to do with the "western world" (again, as much as I despise that term). Once the kids had dispersed into a fading sky, I re-joined the team bus and we headed to Minsk for the evening. The ladies were all shattered, but the team bonding and banter on the bus journeys were good, and they were quite upset by their performance on the pitch. All that mattered to me was that I was there to support Northern Ireland, win lose or draw.

I also got some time to see the sights of Minsk and Bobruisk, including the State Theatre, some Churches, the Berezina river, some Stalin-style buildings and Victory Square. I also noticed that Belarussians have a strange dress sense, I cannot really describe it, other than they wear what I'd consider as bland, boring clothes. No brand names, and not a lot of colour. The people in Belarus don't seem to smile much and their peelers seem to be obsessed and proud of their military uniforms, and the country seems to be quite immersed in the war related history. This is not surprising given that 25% of the Belarus population were killed between 1939 and 1945. Belarus and Ukraine also suffered the most from the Chernobyl disaster. Now that I have visited over 20 ex-Soviet Union states or Oblasts, Belarus still ranks as one of the most unusual and one that certainly gave me a flavour for backpacking further into the former Soviet Union. It was a totally bizarre place to visit and I have now been four times and even done a newspaper interview on my travels there (in Grodno).

The next day I would head to the Polish capital Warszawa (for the second time) and continue my round the world trip, having travelled all this way to Belarus to support the Northern Ireland ladies' team. Despite the result, it was an amazing trip to do and one which I will never forget. At the time of editing this in May 2020, I am still the only football fan to travel independently to Belarus to watch every Northern Ireland senior international football match of any kind. I also attended the first home match between the two sides in men's professional football – revenge was sweet – a 3-0 win for Northern Ireland at Windsor Park just before Euro 2016. But being the only Northern Ireland fan to travel to Belarus back then, it's a nice personal memory to have.

Chapter 27
Present

Warszawa, POLSKA (August 2007)

"This a present from Stalin's reign" – Artur Gorecki.

After the madness of Belarus faded out of view, I had the simple matter of a flight from Minsk to Warszawa. It was to be my second time to visit the Polish capital but I had no idea that it would be a sign of things to come. Nor that 10 years later I would actually live here.

What brought me to Poland this time? Well it was a concoction of many things really. Firstly, I felt that in March 2005 on my trip to Warszawa, that I had neglected the usual tourist things. I didn't really see the city. That was really a lads holiday and party to watch the football match (which Northern Ireland lost 1-0), but it felt that there was something more to it. The fact that I didn't really delve into Polish culture properly, yet came away loving the country, had lingered in my mind. Even more so given the sheer number of Polish people I had met between 2004 – 2007, including Piotr Oczkowski, the first ever Polish person I met in life. Secondly, I saw Poland as a cheap and easy stop-over after Minsk and Moscow. Thirdly, I would be hanging out with two good friends, Rafał Kowalczyk and Artur Gorecki and making many new friends over a short and sharp four day period.

The memories of this second visit to Warszawa are quite distant and faded now. I can tell you what we did in the day time and night time but there was something stronger here. A magnetism that would later influence my entire life. For now, Artur and Rafał turned up at Warszawa Chopina Lotnisko (airport) bearing an "Alan Connell" sign. It was, of course, an in-joke aimed at making me laugh and welcoming me to their country again. Alan Connell, or "Alan Connell Alan" was one of my favourite AFC Bournemouth strikers during my first few seasons watching the Cherries. Connell even left the Cherries for a few years and came back, and despite injuries, he remains some kind of cult hero to me. I hope other AFC Bournemouth fans agree that Connell played a big part in many happy moments down at Dean Court, scoring some important goals and generally running around the pitch always looking for a half chance to put away. For now, with blonde hair and a slim figure, I was Alan Connell on arrival in Warszawa. A nice joke from Rafał and Artur and a great introduction to Polish life, again.

From Day 1, the guys had planned my trip well. I remember they had mostly taken days off work just to see me and hang out. I had dinner and drinks with Rafał's family in the Bielany district, north Warszawa. That felt good, as it gave me a chance to see the raw and local Polish lifestyle, the real Polish hospitality and escape the tourist floods of Warszawa's city centre and old town (Stare Miasto). Of course, being an obvious tourist was also on the agenda and one by one, I ticked off a phenomenal amount of sights in the city, including one sentimental one.

We visited the Old Town, we went out drinking nightly in the bars in and around Nowy Swiat. I was trying Polish food and drink, falling completely for the dream hangover cure, Kefir. A product simply non-existent in my Ulsteric hometown of Bangor. Kefir is a dairy based milky, yoghurty, salty concoction, which is totally perfect for the morning after a night on the rip. Sightseeing wise, we toured Wilanow Palace and Łazienki Park, but it was the trip to "Stalin's building" that brought about the most significant part of that journey to Poland's stolica.

Warszawa just didn't seem as busy in those days. Gorecki parked his car on a hungover Thursday morning at the city's Plac Defilad. We alight and stare peakingly at the sky. A well-designed grey building pierces it. This was a building opposite the posh hotel (Intercontinental) me and the Northern Ireland fans had stayed at, back in 2005. This grey structure is known as Pałac Kultury I Nauki (The Palace of Culture and Science) and was ordered to be built by Jozef Stalin during the Soviet era. In fact, Stalin's Soviet regime had built similar looking buildings in a lot of the former Eastern Bloc / Soviet / Communist countries. I have seen similar buildings in Riga, Minsk, Kiev, Moscow and of course, here in Warszawa.

As he inhales a well-deserved draw from his cigarette, Artur Gorecki's words to me are simple, true, pure, slowly spoken and memorable. Unforgettable, I'd say. Harshly, with deep feeling and without remorse, Gorecki professed:

"Jonny, this, is our present from Stalin's reign".

Staring up at the monstrosity in a city that is changing gave me some kind of goosebumps. I don't know why, but this was deeper than visits to other cities, and to other buildings. I didn't know much about Warszawa, or Poland. I had read Stalin's book while at Newtownards Tech and I had studied the Soviet Union regime during the same history course. Suddenly a mixture of sadness and happiness came together all at once. It was quite sensational and indescribable. The Russians and the Polish were not good friends. The wars hadn't been kind. Poland was sandwiched in between Hitler's German Nazis and Stalin's Soviets. It was a country that needed to be strong and stand up for itself. And the thing is, it did.

Having worked with Artur and Rafał in England, I knew these guys. I knew their sense of humour, their way of communicating. There was a sense of hate, of love, of life, of honesty. There wasn't much bullshit with such guys. I could feel the fear in the three of us as we walked over to Stalin's "Palace", oxymoron that shit if you must. We were going inside to take the lift to the top floor to get a vantage point over the whole of the city.

I had my backpack with me and as the Polish security staff called to me on the way in, it was something they said like "Skąd jestes?" ("Where are you from?"). I had been taught about 20 words of Polish on this trip, and proudly could reply, when prompted by Kowalczyk "Jestem z irlandii polnocnej" ("I am from Northern Ireland"). A quick welcome and we are whisked in a Stalinic elevator to the viewing terrace to overlook the city.

I had a permanent marker in my backpack in those days. I often carried multiple pens of different sizes, shapes and colours. The pen is mightier than the sword and always one of my favourite inventions. This was a black permanent marker and at the top of Stalin's building, we had the chance to sign the wall. I signed it twice. Once with Jonny Scott Blair and the date. The second time, simply with "Alan Connell", my pseudonym for the trip, kind of.

We stopped for a beer at the top of this magnificent building and I liked that. Here we were at the top of a building given as a "gift" from a country that didn't exist anymore (USSR) to a country that took the gift, and still had it. Here I was with two friends I had made while selling cheeseburgers in England. You can't make this sort of shit up. We were happy. I think we were the winners here, the lucky ones. Stalin had been and gone, with a good riddance to his Soviet Regime. Poland had entered the European Union in 2004 and was revelling in a new sense of freedom, second wave if you like, after the post-1991 progression to a democratic republic.

Soon, we were back down on the terracotta. Artur parked his car and we headed to a bar which had cherry vodka shots. This felt like another telling point. Telling, not turning. From Bournemouth to Stalin, from Alan Connell to Cherries, from beer to vodka, it was a magical time. As we sat in that bar, I pulled out my paper and pen and started to write a poem, more a song really.

It was clear what the poem and song would be all about. It would be about Polish people, my friends here and my experiences in Warszawa. The main line of the song, was to be:

"This; a **present** from Stalin's reign".

Almost as if, I was envisaging Artur pointing to that building, while acting as a real life tour guide. After a few cherry vodka shots, I added the line "but you have your life again", and there it began. Within a few hours, the song had been written, no doubt over more Polish beers and maybe a meaty kebab. On my final day in Poland, on this trip we visited a pond somewhere in Warszawa (I still don't know where that pond is) and Rafał asked if I was going to throw a Polish coin into the pond, along with the rest of coins already in there. I wondered why.

Rafał said to me, "Jonny, if you throw a coin in, it means you will be back here again in Warszawa, one day".

It was a no brainer. I pulled out the nearest Polish złotówka coin I had in my pocket and flicked it high into the air above the pond. It landed, predictably in the pond. I didn't linger on the fact this meant I'd be back here. Life doesn't give us what we want, need or expect. We might not even get a tomorrow. Nobody is promised a tomorrow. But my coin was in the pond, and perhaps, maybe, one day I'd be back here. Who knew?

I was emotional at the airport too. We were joined by new friend Piotr Pawelski, who I met on this trip and we shared many a story about football and beer on some magic nights in the Polish capital. I boarded my flight from Warszawa to Prague in the Czech Republic and the Polish adventure was over, for now.

The coin told me that I'd be back in Warszawa one day, but really, nobody could tell…

Chapter 28
He Wears An Ulster Hat

Riga, LATVIA and Berlin, GERMANY (September 2007)

"Tony Kane is magic…he wears an Ulster hat"
– Northern Ireland football fans.

My first visit to Reykjavik in Iceland was also in 2007 and it was an odd journey we were on. I roomed with and travelled with three different groups of friends over a two week period, which included a trip to Riga in Latvia, a two day stop-over in Berlin and a hugely exciting tour of Iceland. This was the final part of my major 2007 travels and by now, I had become quite addicted to the budget backpacking field and expected I would travel for long periods of my life from here on in, money permitting. Plus, my travel blog "Don't Stop Living" was now a month old and I was documenting my journeys with more precision than ever before.

The money from my PR job in Bite Communications had now all been spent, with Iceland being the last recipient of my office work cash and I knew after that, I would be back in Bournemouth in England again to work in bars, pay off my debts (student and credit card) and try to finally complete my degree by May 2008. Once and for all.

But I'll start with Riga in Latvia in this chapter. It was a popular "stag night" spot in those days. They had their own currency, the Lat. Beers were cheap, the city was pretty and it seemed like a perfect place for the Northern Ireland football team to travel away to, win the match and keep up the hope of qualifying for Euro 2008. For once, Northern Ireland fans were hopeful of a result.

Myself included, we had a much stronger team than them, the result was never in doubt.

In the previous few years, we had beaten Spain, England, Sweden, Estonia, Finland, Latvia and gained draws with Wales, Denmark and Portugal. It certainly felt to me, for the first time since the 1980s that we would qualify. I roomed with Tim Beattie on this trip and we stayed in a decent hotel, Hotel Islande in Latvia's capital city, Riga.

Did I say that Riga was pretty, and cheap? Well soon, my opinion would change as local peelers arrested Northern Ireland fans, robbed them, ripped them off and tried to control our supporters with some kind of Soviet army style tactics. It was all a bit upsetting, but Tim and I arrived in the country on match day so obviously we missed the previous night's antics, so who is to know that Northern Ireland fans didn't also stir things up a bit. Either way, the trip didn't get off to a good start.

As Tim and I met up with Michael McClelland, Gavin McClelland, Ian McKinney and David Watson in downtown Riga, hopes had been dashed by the scene on the streets. Even the beer tasted awful, and it wasn't cheap. I said to the boys, "last month I was drinking 20 pence pints in Belarus. This ain't even cheap". For 2 Lats (£2) a beer, I could still have found a £1 beer in Bournemouth in those days, "Yellow Card" Nights down Inferno.

I met a few new and old characters on this trip to Latvia too. I bumped into "Bangor Boy" Michael Lewis outside the theatre, Mark Vanucci stayed in the same hotel as us, and downtown Riga, the North of England based Norn Iron boys and I exchanged banter late afternoon. Indeed, I met John Hart and Owen Millar and we chatted about Berlin – we were all booked on the flight to Berlin together the next day, and we had a dorm hostel there booked for a couple of nights.

Apart from my broken arm story, I haven't written about illness in this book yet. In Latvia, I started to feel ill. It was a dodgy burger and the rotten beer. I wasn't in good spirits as Tim and I entered the football stadium for the match. I felt really ill all day. During the second half, Chris Baird scored an own goal and Northern Ireland lost 1-0. Yes, we lost to Latvia in a match we were highly fancied to win and fully expected that we would go on to qualify for the tournament. The defeat was a kick in the teeth, but a look at the team line ups helped understand why we lost.

You don't change a winning team do you? Logic says only if there is an injury or suspension. Our defence had been the typical: Maik Taylor (Nets), Michael Duff (Right Back), Aaron Hughes (Centre Half), Stephen Craigan (Centre Half), George McCartney (Left Back). The only replacements would normally be Chris Baird (Centre Half) or Jonny Evans (Centre Half). However, on this particular night in Riga, manager Nigel Worthington had dropped the fully fit Craigan without any seeming justification. Aaron Hughes was unavailable. This meant a changed back four line-up. But instead of doing the obvious and putting Stephen Craigan on the pitch to be paired with Jonny Evans at centre-back, he messed with the system completely.

It got to the point where Northern Ireland fans were looking at a potential four full-backs playing centre-half roles or four centre-halves playing as four full-backs. At the time when I looked at our back four, I couldn't work out who was in which position. It even appeared that he had switched Michael Duff to centre half. Michael Duff had been our right back up until now in this campaign. Jonny Evans, a right footed player appeared to be playing at left back. Towards the end of the match Evans, from a deep left position missed an open net chance to make it 1-1, but on his left foot as he had been played on the left. We were down and out in Riga. Most fans couldn't believe that Stephen Craigan had been dropped. To this day, the dropping of Stephen Craigan remains a major talking point for Northern Ireland fans and so it should be. I believe Nigel Worthington made a major mistake here. We wouldn't have lost 1-0 had Stephen Craigan played. Our defence was solid with him there.

For the first time in years, I didn't drink any beer after a Northern Ireland match. I felt ill. I bought a sandwich on the way home to the hotel and was sick straight away in the hotel room. I took some pills and went straight to sleep. I didn't enjoy my time in Riga at all. About 3 a.m. Ian McKinney and Tim Beattie burst into my room and jumped on my bed filming it, I jumped up and started singing "We're Not Brazil We're Northern Ireland" at them. Looking back, it was probably the highlight of that trip. The memories of 2005's Dean Nutt-inspired "barfgate" came flooding back briefly. I realised now how Dean felt. It wasn't so funny when the joke was on your side.

The song for this trip however was related to Blackburn Rovers full-back Tony Kane. A player who had played for Northern Ireland at youth and under 21 levels but was spotted by the Republic of Ireland who poached him and capped him at under-21 level. Steve Staunton also approached him and asked him to play for the full Republic of Ireland squad. However, Tony saw the light and changed allegiance back to his birth country of Northern Ireland and was rewarded with a call up for the Latvia trip. The song was "Tony Kane is magic, he wears an Ulster hat. Steve Staunton said come play for me and Tony said fuck that. Tony is an Ulsterman who wears his shirt with pride. He plays for our wee country, green and white army on his side".

As we walked back to the hotel, having lost 1-0, some of us mused, "Tony Kane should've been on". I couldn't help think that Kane would have struck the unlikely winner in a 1-0 win for us. In the sadness of it all, Kane never won a full cap in the end and later returned to Northern Ireland to ply his trade for Ballymena United. But he became a cult hero on that trip for Northern Ireland fans, in the same way that Will Grigg did for the Euro 2016 tournament in France, without even kicking a ball. Northern Ireland fans still rightly class the un-capped Kane as some kind of hero from this Latvia trip. He's magic.

The next day I remember touring the sights of Riga city with Tim – the Old Town, Freedom Monument etc. and I had never felt less inspired by a city travel-wise. I almost felt bored as I clutched a predictably average 2 Lat "crappuccino" in central Riga. Luckily, John and Owen arrived at my hotel in a taxi and reminded me we were booked on a flight to Berlin so it was time to go and leave unmagnetic and unforgiving Riga unregrettably behind.

At Duty Free in Riga Airport, John Hart gives Owen and I a Mexican style hat each – he'd brought them just for us and we became the "three amigos". The three of us get on the plane acting like George Best in Madrid all those years ago with a Mexican hat hat-trick. The food poisoning and illness I had in Riga had now been forgotten and we left behind the dreams of the three points for a return to Berlin for two nights. It was same again lads – I had been in Berlin in 2005 as well and with John and Owen on route to Poland that time. We were back again in Berlin.

I remember distinctly that John, Owen and I occupied the three seats at the front of the plane on the left (as the plane flies) and John had brought a bottle of 1 litre bottle of whiskey on-board. We started mixing it with cola and the three of us drank it during the quick flight to Berlin. There is no chance we were sober on arrival, and probably the air stewardesses wondered why those three Mexicans kept ordering Coca Cola! On arrival in Berlin, we headed straight to the DaxPax hostel to check in and then we went out drinking. Looking back, we drank a lot on those trips.

Those times were ridiculously crazy and not always planned. You just never knew who you would meet or what would happen next. Michael and Gavin McClelland were also in Berlin that night as were David Watson and Ian McKinney. It was like a total repeat of the 2005 trip to Berlin, and weirdly that was in between two Northern Ireland away defeats (0-4 to England, 0-1 to Poland). Not a good omen really as we had already lost the first match of the two, (0-1 to Latvia).

We got smashed in the local bars and drank and sang the night away, ending up in some Irish pubs too including Kilkenny and Oscar Wilde. It was in Kilkenny while the band was playing that I met German girl Iris Röder. I pulled out a George Bush wig out of nowhere. I remembered I had bought it in London before leaving my PR job and I put it on and danced in the bar as George Bush.

I took Iris outside, took the wig off and we kissed passionately in the Berlin barnight starlight. It was to be another whirlwind romance with a German Damsel. John and Owen knew about Iris and we made our way separately back to the hostel that night. The next morning, I joined the free tour with Iris a bit late due to the hangover. Again, there was no texting, Facebook or Smart Phones at the time. I simply wrote on a bar napkin "meet me at Checkpoint Charlie at 12 noon".

In my dorm room, was not John and Owen however, I was rooming with a load of hot Canadian girls who were young and backpacking Europe for the first time. I'm not sure they liked the idea of dorm rooms or the backpacking lifestyle. I could feel their tension. When I danced around the room naked wearing a George Bush mask at 9 a.m., I expected it would cheer them up and they would love it. I mean, making fun of a US President, and they were Canadian.

But I'm not sure they liked it. One of them, Kyria Knibb took a photo of me in the buff with the Bush mask on and another, Caitlin Kirby told me it was crazy and disrespectful and I should consider my dorm mates. I was hungover and it was a good laugh to me, at the time. Owen and John came into the room to retrieve me from the madness and the Canadians had been welcomed to Europe. They never reported the "Bush dance" to the hostel staff though, and I arranged to meet Iris that day. Kyria Knibb later emailed me the nude photo she took of me, with a George Bush mask on with my willy out in a Berlin hostel!

Iris and I toured some of the city and had lunch together then we sneaked into a corridor and viewpoint by the hostel and got passionate. It was a fast couple of days though and we needed to be back at the airport that night, for the connection to Reykjavik in Iceland. In the madness, little Iris got on the train to the airport with us. This was a true lovewind lovestruck whirlwind romance. John, Owen and I needed to get our flight but I was still with Iris. I couldn't let her go. We wanted to go to Iceland together! As the doors swung open, John and Owen burst out of the train telling me we were at the airport and our flight was leaving in two hours prompt.

I snogged Iris passionately on the train and made a dash for the doors before they slammed gurningly behind me. I blew a kiss and a farewell to the sexy blonde Iris, her smooth breastage, her blueic eyes and her trim waistline. Alas, I'd never see her again. Fact. When I first met Iris, I was wearing my football shirt with the words "IRISh Football Association" on it. To date, she is the only girl I have kissed while wearing her name on my clothing. IRIS (h). Later in life, I wouldn't afford Slavic mistress Olcia Malinowa (of a later chapter in another volume) the same kind of luxury.

Within a few hours, the boys and I were now at the Aurora Guesthouse in Reykjavik in Iceland.

Chapter 29
Right Backs on the Left

Gullfoss Waterfall, ICELAND (September 2007)

"Don't go chasing waterfalls..." – TLC.

The 2007 tour continued from Berlin to Iceland. Before I headed back to Bournemouth, we were in Iceland for another adventure and the last money from my PR job had been milked and crushed to a pulp. I picked the most expensive country of the lot to finish in. Gavin, Michael and I had agreed to share a kind of mini-apartment in Reykjavik, though it was known as Aurora Guesthouse. We were joined by some lads from Lurgan including Davy who had been in Poland with us in 2005.

Similarly to the Latvia away trip, this was a huge anti-climax, yet Iceland as a country was beautiful. On match night, some more odd managerial decisions from Nigel Worthington and yet another own goal, this time from Keith Gillespie meant we lost 2-1. After the match, I drowned my sorrows in Belly's Bar in Reykjavik with the likes of Toddy, Louie and Jim McComish. It was in this bar that I met Tryggvi Johnson. He was happy that Iceland had beaten us of course and we chatted. The significance of this meeting took me on a ridiculously crazy twist NINE years later. I bumped into Tryggvi in Paris by coincidence the night Iceland qualified for the last 16 of Euro 2016! I'd see him again in 2019 in Munich!

In retrospect, the rest of our time in Iceland was cold, wet and windy; and uncharred by that result. We toured the Gullfoss waterfalls, the great Geysir and Pingvellir, where the Icelandic parliament was formed. There were a lot more good places to see on the sightseeing side of things.

I infamously turned up to the Blue Lagoon without any swimming trunks and had to buy a pair at late notice as nudity was forbidden. The only pair they had was a tight pair of female pink panties, that weren't even swimming shorts! Yippide Doodah, I was wearing tight pink girls' pants to the turquoise Blue Lagoon. The shape of my willy was damn apparent in the Icelandic September sunshine and I enjoyed it. But seriously, I was only going to be at the Blue Lagoon once in my life, so it was my only choice to actually swim in it. It had to be the pink pants or not go in at all.

I have covered some of my crazy Iceland times on my travel blog before. As well as the pink pants episode, I also stayed in Keflavik with Una Harkin of the Northern Ireland ladies' team and her friend Beth, and we went out drinking in a bar called Yello. So much so, that I slept late the day of my flight. And, I missed my flight. I had learned a lesson. This was the first time in my life that I had missed a flight and I was gutted. I finally left Iceland the following day and headed back to Bournemouth to work in the Pavilion Theatre and finish my degree in Public Relations. But I'm fast forwarding to June 2016 now for this crazy part of the story, to close the chapter.

I was in France in June 2016 for The European Championships and Northern Ireland had qualified. We beat Ukraine 2-0 in the group stage in a day known as the "Kings of Lyon", Gareth McAuley and Niall McGinn putting the Ukrainians to the sword. Then, the night after we confirmed our place in the Second Round (where we'd play Wales), I met up with Northern Irish friends Gavin, Wesley and Mark and we were drinking in O'Sullivan's Bar by the Moulin Rouge in Paris. Suddenly, Tryggvi Johnson turns up! It was incredible. He was wearing his Iceland shirt and celebrating as Iceland had just beaten Austria 2-1 that night to qualify for the Second Round. It is moments like this on my travels that just make it so phenomenal. To meet Tryggvi nine years on by fluke in Paris and with both of our teams through to the next round, well it was a crazy experience and we had a great night. Tryggvi is a mad Iceland fan and his girlfriend was also there on this occasion. It seemed like neither of us had aged that much, since that 2007 meeting in Belly's Bar.

My travels of 2007 had been well and truly milked however, and it was back to the hard work and study dreaming up my next adventure…

Chapter 30
SOENISC, The Glory Years

All over the south of ENGLAND (2005 - 2009)

"Insane in the membrane; insane in the brain" – Cypress Hill.

SOENISC. South Of England Northern Ireland Supporters Club. This part of my life has already had a chapter (Chapter 15's The Isle of Green), featured in a few chapters but now it really deserves one of its own to sum things up. An overview of what it was all about and a reflection on life in SOENISC, over ten years since I quit the club, after setting it up with Owen Millar and Tim Beattie in 2005. SOENISC was a cult. SOENISC was a culture. SOENISC was a fad. SOENISC was fun. SOENISC was lunatical.

So, what on earth was the SOENISC all about?

In short, having left Northern Ireland to live in the South of England, I did miss a wee bit of the craic I had back home with my Northern Irish friends. The idea was to start a football supporters club in the South of England for Northern Ireland football fans based there. I had no idea how big or ridiculous it would become!

In 2004, a supporter's club called the North of England Northern Ireland Supporters Club was set up in Manchester. Later in the same year, the London Northern Ireland Supporters Club was set up. But being based in Bournemouth, their meetings would have been a bit far for me to travel to. I had often flown on the same flights from Belfast to Southampton with footballer Chris Baird and chatted at length to him. Also, on those flights was Marshall Gillespie (a journalist) and Bean (Jason Cunningham). Having lived in Bournemouth from 2003 – 2005, it wasn't until the Poland away match in March 2005, that the seeds began to be sowed to start this new club. On route to Warszawa, we ended up in Berlin. In a bar in downtown Berlin one night, I met both Owen Millar and Tim Beattie. At the time, Owen lived in Bristol, and Tim was in Basingstoke. So, it made sense for us to agree to call the club "The South of England Northern Ireland Supporters Club" (The SOENISC). The plan was hatched and then in Belfast later in the year, we decided to go ahead with it.

It was the night that Northern Ireland beat England 1-0 in Belfast. A truly unforgettable night for us, September 7th 2005 when David Healy's 74th minute goal clinched the three points and we were in elation. It was like the moment I had waited for all my life as a Northern Ireland fan. All those home defeats and away days were now worth it. We had beaten England at home and I was there with my friends that had been there for every match with me for the previous 15 years. We deserved that night of success. In the Red Panda Restaurant in Belfast that night, the decision was also made to hold the first proper SOENISC meeting in Weymouth, Dorset later in 2005. By November 2005, Tim and I had got the club flag made, with the slogan "Good times never seemed so good" on it, because we all met in Berlin and the song for the trip had been "Sweet Northern Ireland, woah oh oh, good times never seemed so good!" (to the tune of Sweet Caroline by Neil Diamond).

In the first week of December 2005, we held our first official meeting as the SOENISC. With Owen now based in Torquay and myself in Bournemouth, we agreed on Weymouth as a good "half way house" and so we launched the club there. There was Tim, Owen and I to start the club. Also attending this historic first meeting was Richard "Richboy" Ingram, Alan "The Rabster" Brown (also known as the "Saucemaster") and Simon McCully from Bangor who I had met by chance while working in Tesco in Branksome in Poole! Simon came in to do his shopping and I was on the till. We were also in the same year at Bangor Grammar School but in different classes and we never really knew each other yet were now both living by chance in Bournemouth. So, there were six of us to kick off the club on a crazy day out in Weymouth. We launched the club and formed a six man committee in Finn McCool's pub in Weymouth, a pub named after a Northern Irish giant. It all seemed so apt. We played football on the beach, launched the club with cheap Champagne and had the never to be forgotten sing song in the Black Dog Pub. A pub which at the time somehow had 6 beers for less than £10, and with change as well. The club went from strength to strength and we held meetings in Torquay, Bristol and Southampton over the following six months. We now had around 30 members, though they were scattered all over the south of England so there was never full attendance at any meeting and in my four years as club chairman, I remained the only ever present.

The club days out normally involved an early meeting at a silly time. It was always something like "Meet on Green Street at 10.47 a.m.". The meetings would involve some serious chat at the beginning to discuss club events, tickets, merchandise and away trips. As chairman of the club, I basically ran the club from 2005 until early 2009. It's no exaggeration to say it was a lot of work and took up too much of my time. But I wanted to do it. I had an unquestionable and insatiable passion for it. I'm glad I played my part in the club's success, with media outreach being one of the key elements to my management and leadership. I had the club featured on TV, Radio, newspaper and in match programmes of almost every match we attended as a club. Second best was never good enough.

Of course, if you read Chapter 20 (The Isle of Green), then you'll get an idea about what a club meeting really entailed. It was all a bit of banter and stretched further than Northern Irish people who were passionate about football. From December 2005 until February 2009, the club had meetings in the following places:

- Weymouth (x4) – Our WAGM (Weymouth Annual Green Meeting) was held annually in December in Weymouth
- Bournemouth (x2)
- Poole and Brownsea Island
- Colchester
- Southampton
- Gillingham
- Torquay
- Bristol (x2)
- Bath
- Weston Super Mare
- Oxford
- Cowes, Isle of Wight
- Cheltenham
- Exeter
- Brighton
- Portland
- Yeovil (Cancelled due to adverse weather, later held in Pisa, Italy)

We also attended about 10 Northern Ireland away matches together, had club merchandise made such as fridge magnets, pin badges, two club flags, polo shirts, and t-shirts. In the club, I was chairman, Owen Millar was secretary and Tim Beattie was the treasurer. Graham Anderson later became secretary when Owen left England.

I'll just share some more of the club's highlights in this chapter now as there was way too much that happened to possibly write it all. SOENISC: The Glory Years would be a book of its own you know. At Weston Super Mare in 2007, we were there the day that Weston sadly got relegated. After the final whistle, the chairman of the club invited us onto the pitch to sing a song and make a quick speech. We launched into a chorus of "We're not Brazil, we're Northern Ireland", which was captured on video somewhere.

At the meeting in Bath in 2008, we had a Crossbar challenge at half time, drawing 0-0 with Bath City FC fans. We later got interviewed for local radio and appeared in the town's local newspaper and made some impression on the people of Bath. That day, we met in the Green Pub on Green Street and turned it green!

At the meeting in Oxford in 2007, we met former Northern Ireland internationals Jimmy Quinn and Darren Patterson. Jimmy Quinn wore my velvet green hat and signed it. He was one of my heroes in my teenage years and was given the title of Honorary Secretary of the SOENISC. Jimmy later became manager of AFC Bournemouth but failed whilst also being a catalyst for Eddie Howe coming in during the unbelievable 2008-2009 "Minus 17" season, where we stayed up after a 2-1 home win over Grimsby Town on the penultimate day of the season.

At the meeting in Exeter in 2007, we had a half time pelanty [sic] shoot-out on the pitch at the match between Alphington and Okehampton Argyle. This was two sets of teams from within SOENISC and created some huge banter and rivalry at meetings to come. Just to remind them – Tim Beattie missed his pelanty, Squid hit the crossbar, Graham (wearing a George Bush wig) had his saved and Richboy put his wide! But the craziest part of this day was that Alphington were 2-0 down at half-time and looked dead and buried. But we urged them on second half and sang songs about them, and they eventually scraped a 2-2 draw in a thrilling second half!

So now for the sad news, it all came to an end didn't it? Yes, my time as chairman of SOENISC came to an abrupt end and while I might mention it in later chapters, here is the real truth of why, how, where and when I quit.

In December 2008, we had a successful meeting in Weymouth and I was voted in as chairman for the fourth year in a row. Everyone assumed the club would continue to grow from strength to strength and that nothing would change. In February 2009, I organised a meeting in Yeovil. It was meant to be our first meeting in Yeovil, a team who play in green and white and we were featured in the club programme and website ahead of the meeting. I booked my train tickets and was still based in Bournemouth.

The day before the meeting, the club (Yeovil Town FC) personally phoned me to say that the pitch was waterlogged and the match was being postponed. It was amazing that a local football club cared enough to give me a personal phone call. Thanks, Yeovil Town, a team supported by my university coursemate and friend Chris Giddings. I got straight on the phone to Graham Anderson, the secretary and we decided to cancel our meeting. There was no point in taking our supporters club on a wet day to Yeovil if there was no match on. It was the first time we had cancelled a club meeting.

When I sat down and thought about it that night, I realised I didn't actually want to do this anymore. I had worked hard as chairman for almost 4 years, we had fun but it had run its course with me. I was 28 now and had been dating an English lady, Helen in late

2008, but more significantly, yet unknowingly, I had now fallen in love with a Hungarian dancer, Noemi. You will read more about Noemi in chapters to come, she was a little heroine. It felt like the nights of football, singing and alcohol had really taken their toll on me and I needed the change. It was time to settle down.

But there was a forwardlash - I had already booked a trip to Italy and San Marino in February 2009 for the Northern Ireland away match so I didn't cancel that of course. I went on the trip and admitted to the lads Graham Anderson, Alan Scott, Jono Crute and two of our English mates Ollie and John that I wasn't doing any more away matches for the foreseeable future. I was deadly serious, but they didn't believe me. It was true though; San Marino was to be my last Northern Ireland away match for almost 5 years (I would not return until Azerbaijan away in late 2013). It was such a lifestyle change for me at the time, most of my friends didn't believe it.

While officially I was still club chairman, I didn't do any more "work" for the club until the 1st April 2009. It was April Fool's Day. I was deeply in love with Noemi, I had been off the alcohol for two months and I was saving money hard for a new adventure. I sent an email around the club on April Fool's Day to say I was quitting.

I did that because I was sure everyone would think it was an April Fool's joke and not true. Within a few hours of receiving the email though, everyone realised it was over for the SOENISC and I. I withdrew from everything. I didn't even want to be a member of the club. I wanted to quit completely and so I did. That was it for me. And I never looked back.

I later met up with Graham Anderson, Andrew Gilmore and Jono Crute in Belfast to hand over the club flag and merchandise and that was it. I have so many fond memories from my time in the

SOENISC and was moved when Richard "Richboy" Ingram once wrote to me that "SOENISC was your legacy, Jonny. Safe travels". I am 99% sure I cried when Portadownczyk Richboy told me that. Richboy – you're a superstar.

Life moved on for me and it did for SOENISC too. I have been back in touch with the SOENISC members quite a lot in the more recent years and despite wanting to arrange a "10 years of SOENISC" meeting in 2015, it never materialised and I think the club will never be the same again. We had our good times and our peak and let's leave it at that.

Good times never seemed so good.

Chapter 31
Ulster Cherry

Dean Court, Boscombe, ENGLAND (October 2003)

"Wise men say only fools rush in, but I can't help…falling in love with you, Bournemouth" – Cherries fans.

Supporting a football team is about turning up to watch them – nothing else. It's as simple as that. You can't sit in an armchair and claim to be a genuine fan. You just can't. Restrictions aside of course - if you have restrictions on being able to move, or for medical reasons cannot attend then fair dos. But otherwise, health aside, there is almost no excuse anymore for being a fake fan. I would always rather be in the stadium than watching on television or on my laptop; a choice not always possible of course, but the sentiment remains.

From 1990 – 2003, I had been a regular supporter at Windsor Park in Belfast for the Northern Ireland national team and also at the Oval in the same city, to support my local team Glentoran FC. But when you grow up in Northern Ireland, as a kid you also usually end up supporting an English team. To me, this is logical enough – as Northern Ireland often have players plying their trade in England. I write this with no disrespect to the Northern Irish League, but the standard of football in England is more exciting to watch, those Northern Irish players earn more money in England and the English league attracts international players from all over the world. The Irish League, as much as I love it and support it, sadly doesn't. When Northern Ireland qualify for major tournaments, most of our players are playing in England at the time. It's no coincidence – the standard of football is better there. So, from a footballing perspective, it's acceptable to me for Northern Irish people to support three teams – our local team (Glentoran FC), our national team (Northern Ireland) and an English league team (AFC Bournemouth, you'll learn). Some also support a fourth team, usually a Scottish team - mostly Rangers, Celtic or Aberdeen. I went even deeper and chose teams in Poland, Uruguay, the Kong and Australia. I have a plethora of teams I support, in different countries. It's all for the love of the game intertwined with my personal nomadery.

For me, it could (and my Dad might argue should) have been Tottenham Hotspur. Yes really. My Dad is a massive Spurs fan and I have cousins from North London that have been season tickets at White Hart Lane - my second cousin Ashley still goes to watch Tottenham Hotspur and indeed he was in Madrid in 2019 for the Champions League Final. In the 1980s in Northern Ireland, almost everyone at my school supported either Everton, Liverpool or Manchester Untied. I hated that hat-trick but for some reason, in the 1980s when football kits were not popular, those were the only three English club shirts available in my local sports shop.

Yes, believe it or not, the third football shirt I ever owned was a Manchester Untied shirt, in 1987. The first was of course a

Northern Ireland shirt, given to me by my Dad (a 1970s Northern Ireland shirt) and I simply loved it. The second was also of course a 1980s Northern Ireland shirt which I since lost, and I believe it was given to me by Neil Fitsimmons, son of my Dad's friend Raymond. But, in 1987, I refused to wear the Manchester Untied shirt that my Dad bought me and he knew it. I don't know if that was a bad thing or just an honesty thing, I just couldn't bring myself to wear it. Sure, I liked Norman Whiteside (he was my hero) and George Best was also a hero but I felt no connection with Manchester at all. I just didn't like them. My Mum and Dad only bought that shirt for me because at the time, the shop had no other club football shirts except Everton, Liverpool, Rangers or Celtic ones. I was grateful they bought me it though as it certainly gave me that first feeling of realising, I could make my own decisions in life. I refused to wear the shirt and I have no idea what happened to it – I think they gave it to my brother Marko who also refused to wear it! Catastrophe! There was no mission in hell any of us would support Manchester Untied so for the time being, I focused on three London teams – Millwall (who were playing brilliantly in Division One at the time), Wimbledon (who won the FA Cup in 1988) and Spurs (not just for my Dad, but I loved watching Paul Gascoigne). In 1990, believe it or not, but Mum and Dad also bought me a Manchester City shirt; by 1992 I also had a Tottenham Hotspur shirt. Nothing seemed to suit me. Manchester and London teams eventually fell by the wayside. Bournemouth was where it was all at. Cherries were the team for me…but the journey to Ulster Cherry was far from smooth.

"Up the Cherries; in all departments"
– AFC Bournemouth fans.

To date, I have never shared my journey to becoming a proper AFC Bournemouth fan in 2003 as I never felt the need to. However, it has been a crazy journey which had more logic and screams of "real football fan" than people think. It still annoys me when I am abroad in some bar wearing an AFC Bournemouth shirt or scarf and somebody claiming to be a football fan says to me "Bournemouth?! Why the hell do you support them??" It just annoys me. You don't have to be from a town to support its football team. But you do have to have some real passion for that team. Normally I'm more a genuine football fan than the asker.

In honesty, I have more reasons for supporting AFC Bournemouth than I could ever write in here. I'm a proper fan of my club despite being nomadic. I am an AFC Bournemouth supporter, not because "I went to University there" or "I worked there" or "we have Eddie Howe as manager". There's a shit load more logic to it than that. Incidentally when that said football fan abroad asks me the aforementioned question, I always ask them back "what team do you support then?" and normally their answer makes me cringe. One guy in a bar in China once said, "Manchester United" and when asked why he said because they're always on TV, because they always win. They're not and they don't. AFC Bournemouth beat you guys 2-1 in 2015, and again 1-0 in 2019, ironically both times on live TV. I also met a Northern Irish guy abroad who claimed to support Liverpool. He could not back up his decision with a reason and had never lived in Liverpool or gone home and away to watch them. Plastics. I still despise them but here's my story on supporting my beloved AFC Bournemouth. Cherries are the team for me. There is no other.

For the record, I never felt any affinity towards Manchester United, or Manchester City, or the Netherlands. Yet in the late 80s and early 90s I had shirts of those three teams. The first English teams I actually 'liked' were Wimbledon FC, Millwall FC and Tottenham Hotspur FC. Wimbledon as they were the underdogs in 1988 and nobody liked them. Everybody in school anticipated the 1988 FA Cup Final and supported Liverpool. So, I told them all I'd support

Wimbledon and they would win. Nobody believed me. Wimbledon won 1-0 and a Northern Ireland international, Lawrie Sanchez, scored the winner. My team could easily have been Wimbledon and I still openly admit, I have a soft spot for the old Wimbledon and the new AFC Wimbledon.

"It's a weird and wonderful world if you come from Wimbledon" – John Motson.

I liked Millwall because they had Teddy Sheringham and Neil Ruddock and held their own in the top flight as underdogs in the late 1980s (at one point, Millwall were top of what is now the Premier League). I also liked Spurs naturally because of Dad, and Paul Gascoigne. I loved watching Gazza play and actually saw him live twice – once at White Hart Lane and a second time at Ibrox in Glasgow for Rangers. I loved watching Spurs when Teddy Sheringham and Jurgen Klinsmann played. And believe it or not, I owned Spurs shirts and watched almost all the matches on TV with my Dad. But I lived in Northern Ireland. I wasn't a real Spurs fan. I also wasn't a Wimbledon fan. I couldn't be a real fan of an English team unless I was watching them regularly live at the stadium, or living there. Another shock to some might be that, I did visit White Hart Lane about five times, with Dad, my brothers and cousin Ashley. But Spurs never felt like my team. I never felt in love. It was Dad's team. It was never my team. I never once had a shiver down my spine walking into White Hart Lane. I only really liked them because of Dad, Paul Gascoigne and Teddy Sheringham. I had already taken my Dad's Northern Irish team, Glentoran, so I didn't need to copy his English team too, I needed a team of my own. I also hated the system of clubs like Spurs. I felt smarter than to fall for the commercialism of clubs like that, at one point I wanted a Spurs shirt with Dumitrescu 8 on the back. Spurs informed my parents that Dumitrescu was number 19. They ordered me a shirt. It had Dumitrescu 19 on it. When Dumitrescu made his debut, he was wearing number 8. I had been right all along as a young teenager, and the club refused to change the shirt. I wanted to set it on fire. I never wore it again. But I did like Ilie Dumitrescu – he was a cracking player. So, despite owning Manchester United, Manchester City, Netherlands and Tottenham Hotspur shirts when I was a child, none of those four would be getting any support from me as an adult. I knew what I wanted... from Panini books to Match and Shoot magazines, there was always a little part of me checking the results of a team I just "liked the name of". It was AFC Bournemouth and as a 10 year old, I cut out a Cherries poster from Match and had it on my bedroom wall.

Aside from the name and my refusal to fall to commercialism, it was easy to fall in love with AFC Bournemouth...and three Northern Ireland based reasons also helped start this love affair...

1.Colin Clarke scored Northern Ireland's last World Cup goal in 1986, he was playing for AFC Bournemouth at the time.
2.George Best's last English League club in 1983 was AFC Bournemouth.
3.In my teens AFC Bournemouth had a seemingly never ending string of Northern Irish players – Keith Rowland, Jimmy Quinn, Neil Masters, Stevie Robinson...I watched them all don the red and black.

In reality...my AFC Bournemouth journey all started in 1994...

July 1994 brought about my first trip to the town of Bournemouth. It was a life changer. I was just 14 you know and Mum and Dad just took us there for a few days that summer. Something stuck with the town in my mind. I liked it more than London, I felt I could live there when I was older, it was always in the back of my mind. I could move there and I could watch the local team, the Cherries. But I wasn't a Bournemouthian. Thus, the only way I could justify this was to continue to support Glentoran and Northern Ireland in my home country and later become a real fan of AFC Bournemouth when I moved there. It was more like an "if I moved there I would feel like a real fan", but with retrospect, it felt like it was only a matter of time. Did the football club come before the beach and the university? I very much believe so. It's really hard to know looking back now, but for sure fate and luck played a part too. Bournemouth University picked me though and there was more fate to come.

Therefore, my idea to become an AFC Bournemouth fan was not down to as much fate as people think. My love affair with Bournemouth began in 1994, and when I finally moved there in 2003, within a week I had made my debut as a real fan of an English football team. I was genuine at last. An even bigger irony was perhaps that Bournemouth University dictated the location of my first house in Bournemouth. It was 256 Holdenhurst Road in the district of Springbourne. It was near two local pubs – The Cricketers Inn and The Dolphin. It was 20 minutes walk from Dean Court, home of AFC Bournemouth. They were more my local team than either Glentoran or Northern Ireland ever had been!

I now lived here, in sunny sunny Bournemouth and supported my local team, AFC Bournemouth – The Cherries. At the time, we were in the third division (then called Division Two, later League One). Overnight, Ulster Cherry was born and I was a hardcore AFC Bournemouth fan from here on in. The Ulster Cherry nickname was self-monikered and named after an actual type of cherry. Ulster Cherries do really exist. You should try them. This was my team now and nobody could take it away from me. I never looked back. I love watching my team, AFC Bournemouth.

But a few chance encounters enhanced my journey from Bangor in Northern Ireland to Dean Court in Boscombe. None more so than my first ever night on the rip in Bournemouth. I was stood at a queue for Dylan's bar in the Student's Union at Bournemouth University and I was getting a tad irate at the queue and the time it was taking me to get served for a beer. It was like the first proper night out at university and I wasn't used to queueing for a pint. The bar was packed and I was being shoved left right and centre with a frustrating delay to buy a single pint of beer. I turned to the guy next to me, who I didn't know. He was English, and I said to him:

"Fuck sake, Is it always like this in England? This would never happen to me in Belfast!"
"Yeah mate, but you'll get served man, hang in here! You're not in Belfast now."
"I'm Jonny by the way."
"Austin."
"Cool mate, let's grab a beer together."
"Yeah man."
"Do you like football?"
"Yeah mate – big Cherries fan!"
"Are you kidding? I'm only new to the town but I want to go. Can we get tickets for the next match?"
"Yeah mate no problem, leave it with me. Hartlepool United at home on Saturday, you down for it?"
"For sure…is Warren Feeney playing?"
"Yeah – star man these days – he just hit the winner against Rushden and Diamonds last week."
"Great. Do you want to meet in the Dolphin pub near the stadium (and near my flat) around 1 p.m. for the 3 p.m. kick off?"
"Cool mate, see you there." Said Austin.

And that was it. Austin Sheppard was my new friend and a lifelong Cherries fan. It was a stroke of fate. I was in. There was no going back. I was now a proper fan of an English League team, AFC Bournemouth. I was Ulster Cherry. When you saw a passionate

Northern Irishman at Dean Court singing "Alan Connell Alan" or "We've got Wade Elliott, he's f*cking brilliant!", that was me. I still think it was written in the stars for me to meet Austin that night, a copycat phrase from Steve Fletcher in the AFC Bournemouth "Minus 17" documentary.

From that day until May 2006, so for three full seasons, I only missed about 3 home matches and went to a load of aways. The Cherries were my team, it would have been amazing to have followed them in the 90s of course, but I'd have had to have flown over as a teenager every week to England to watch them, and I had no friends there until I made the move. So, it was nice to finally be a Dean Court regular and season ticket holder.

My home debut as a Cherry was a pulsating 2-2 draw with Hartlepool United in October 2003. It was unforgettable, it was a brilliant match! We started badly and went 1-0 down and despite pressure, we couldn't grab the equaliser! There were only about 20 minutes left. It was at this point that fellow Northern Irishman Warren Feeney came on as a sub. I was there with Austin and my flatmate Steve also came for the day, though he is a Chelsea fan. I told them both, Feeney will change the game. I was kind of joking, but Warren Feeney came on and that is exactly what he did!

Warren Feeney scored one and set one up for Derek Holmes as the Cherries went 2-1 up! I was ecstatic! I started dancing like a buck eejit with my Northern Ireland flag in the North Stand and a few local lads were loving it, chatting about Feeney and Northern Ireland to me. I had teenagers grabbing the flag as this Northern Irishman in the crowd was loving the Bournemouth team! Bournemouth is an educated town, quite proudly British and Conservative too, which meant the locals here knew about the situation in Northern Ireland, and when they saw my flag, they also knew what it was. "Warren Feeney's flag" somebody shouted, "must be an Ulsterman", "he's one of us" another remarked.

Hartlepool United in their light blue and dark blue mixed kit, had the last laugh on the day though, with an injury time equaliser from Gavin Strachan – an excellent free kick. We drew 2-2, but I was hooked!

My first home win as a Cherry was a 1-0 FA Cup victory over Bristol Rovers, Wade Elliott scored the winner, followed by a 1-0 League win over Brentford, also Wade Elliott. When we beat QPR (Queen's Park Rangers) 1-0 in January 2004, Warren Feeney grabbed an emphatic winner in one of the best games I have seen at Dean Court. QPR came down to the south coast, top of the league and the Cherries were just outside the play off zone. They bombarded our goal but couldn't score and we were singing like maniacs that day. "Top of the League you're having a laugh!" was ringing through my head for weeks. A few weeks later, on Pancake Night (Shrove Tuesday) we were at Dean Court and Cherries were 3-0 up against doomed Wrexham. 3-0 up and cruising. It couldn't get much better than this could it?

On came substitute James "Jamie Ayta" Hayter and he scored a hat-trick inside 2 minutes and 20 seconds, a record! It was crazy. We just couldn't believe it. We won the match 6-0 and Cherries were on course for the play-offs. When we won away to Sheffield Wednesday on St. Patrick's Night 2004, we walked out of Hillsborough believing we could get promoted. That Sheffield Wednesday away match is still one of my favourite away trips and was my first Cherries away day! Back then, we were in the third tier, known as Division Two, with the leagues above us called Division One and The Premiership. The next season, Division One was re-named the Championship and the Cherries were in League One.

Despite a great winter 2004, Cherries faded in April and May and we missed out on the play offs in 2004, but I had now over 30 home matches under my belt and a few aways, as we charged for the play-offs again the next season. Highlights of the following season included our trip to Blackburn Rovers (then Premier League) and we bate them 7-6 on penalties with Eddie Howe scoring the winning penalty after a scintillating 3-3 draw. It's the only time I have ever seen any of my teams score 10 goals away from home. We also beat Port Vale 4-0 and Doncaster 5-0, smashing teams aside with aplomb at Dean Court. I was living the dream. We were top 6 again! Cherries were on fire!

In 2005 – 2006, I made it to a few more cool away venues including winning at Brentford 2-0 and a last gasp 1-0 win at Layer Road, Colchester. A 1-1 draw at Nottingham Forest that season kept us in what was now called League One. At that match, we met up with Lock-In Lee Adams in Nottingham, my mate who features a lot in my stories, and a big Nottingham Forest fan. I introduced you all to Lock In Lee Adams in Chapter 11's "The Lock In".

In 2006 – 2007, I moved to London so I didn't renew my season ticket at Dean Court, but I went to all the away matches in and around London that season including new venues like Gillingham, Millwall and Leyton Orient. I made the trip back down to the south coast to stay with Austin and Neil and went to a few home matches too. We survived relegation in 2007 but a tough season was ahead in 2007 – 2008.

Over the first 4/5 years of becoming a Dean Court regular, our friendship group for Cherries matches had expanded and these are some of my best friends in the world – Austin Sheppard, Dan Darch, Patrick Hogan, Chris Sheppard, Richard Rowland. "Millwall Neil" also came along often when he wasn't watching Millwall. We always have a good time together and we have been all over England (and Wales and Scotland) watching AFC Bournemouth. 2007 – 2008, I got a half season ticket instead, as backpacking and travel had kicked into my journeys. Shout outs also to Dawn Rothwell, Helen Bird, Neal Bird, Craig Wells, Steve

Hill, Sandra Jones, Steve Brown, Tom Dowthwaite, Ben Stanley Clarke, Carey Paton, John Garard (Nonny), Chris 'Bouts' Manning, Chris Millar, Dave and Serena Stone and just all the cool Cherries fans that I met in those pre-Premier League days. I'd probably argue the best times were when we were younger and in the lower divisions.

But sadly, football experiences are just the same as real life – they are up and down. In May 2008, we travelled up to Carlisle on the last match of the season where a 1-1 draw was not enough to save us from relegation and the Cherries went down to the basement division again, from where we had come up in 2003. It was a sad day up there, but was also the reason why we all booked our season tickets straight away for the next season 2008 – 2009. We were on this journey together and we would bounce back stronger the next season.

However, the FA docked us 17 points as the club went into administration, the previous season we had only been relegated because of the docking of 10 points. 27 docked points in 2 seasons was harsh but those were the rules. At the start of 2008 – 2009 season, we went to the first away match at Aldershot together and scraped a draw. We continued to lose or draw almost every home match and by December 2008, we were second bottom on minus one (-1) point and the club wouldn't be around much longer. It was over – we would be relegated and liquidated. Kevin Bond had gone as manager, we had Jimmy Quinn in, but Jimmy was sadly unpopular and useless (yet also a hero of mine from his playing days when he scored for Northern Ireland in front of my 13 year old eyes against the Republic of Ireland at Windsor Park in Belfast).

We lost 2-0 at home to Barnet in our last home match of 2008 and we were toothless. It was Jimmy's last home game as manager – we were completely shit that day. Going to Dean Court became a frustrating and sad place to be, but we hung in there and sang our hearts out, in vain. Dan said that we would turn it round and he booked himself in for 5 or 6 away trips in early 2009, inviting me.

I didn't go. It was the same time of my life that I had fallen in love with someone. This is a story to be covered in Chapters 35, 36 and 37, apologies for the chapter jumping but a lot of my stories are intertwined. I lost my way with the football for a few months. I quit the SOENISC (South of England Northern Ireland Supporters Club, which I was chairman of), I leant my season ticket to others and I didn't go to Cherries away matches. You could tell I wasn't feeling myself when I turned up for a 1-0 home win against Shrewsbury and found it hard to raise a smile. The Cherries were playing brilliant again, under young manager Eddie Howe.

I didn't know it then, but ridiculously, at the Shrewsbury match in February 2009, this would be my last HOME AFC Bournemouth competitive match for almost FIVE years. Yes, really. It was January 2014 before I was at Dean Court again for a competitive fixture. Five years, staggering! But at the time I would never have known that!

In between times, I lived in Australia, Uruguay and Hong Kong and travelled to over 50 countries. I still followed all the results online and wore my shirts and scarves around the world. In 2012, Mick Cunningham (who passed away in 2015), club photographer contacted me and asked for some Cherries shirt photos from around the world. I sent him some from places like China, North Korea and Vietnam, which featured in the match day programme. I also wrote a few articles for two AFC Bournemouth fanzines down the years – A View from the Tree and The 8.44 to Waterloo.

Travel had taken over my life, but I craved some lads' time and a few Cherries away trips, so I booked two away matches in between times and a further one I had to cancel due to working in Hong

Kong. Hereford away in 2009 was my last Cherries away match for 2 seasons and I returned for Bury away only in that time, in 2012. We lost 2-1 to Hereford and 1-0 to Bury. Expectedly the match that I cancelled was Preston North End away, which we won. Yeah – I was in Hong Kong having a few quiet beers and texting Dan Darch that day, we knew we would win. The day Eddie Howe took the Cherries from League One to the Championship had me crying in China. I was crossing back across the border from Shenzhen into Hong Kong and Dan and I Skyped in tears to each other. We beat Carlisle 3-1 that day, which contrasted to that dark day about 5 years earlier when we got relegated at Carlisle. It was so ironic that it was Carlisle again, such a spooky full circle. Now we beat them, and we were in the Championship, the second flight, the second division. It was amazing! This was as good as it will ever get for us. That's what we all thought. We'll give the Championship a good crack.

I made it to my first AFC Bournemouth Championship match against Huddersfield Town in January 2014 and we won 2-1. Despite having done a few aways in between, this was my first home league match in 5 years, and my first Cherries win in 5 years and life had gone full circle on me again. I admit I over-use the term "full circle" but I like the term, and it's my book remember! It felt good to be back at Dean Court again and I knew the lads had deserved this moment more than me. I had missed so many matches the last 4 or 5 seasons due to being abroad and now I was back – same seats in the North Stand, same pre-match pub (The Portman), same crazy players, same manager (Eddie Howe was back after a spell at Burnley) and same style of football. In fact, we were class. We turned on the style and lit up the Championship. We played the way we always did. With flair and passion. Pass and move. Real football. AFC Bournemouth play real football. At least in my mind, this is how football should be played. Passion, finesse and with a bit of style. In fact, I did go to two matches at home in those five years – but one was a pre-season friendly and one was the FA Cup match with Liverpool, the previous Saturday.

Now, I had seen the Cherries play, win, lose, draw, score and concede in every cup competition and in three of the top four divisions. The only thing missing was a second flight away win and a Premier League dream (only a dream in those days). It was time to put that second flight away win right the following season as I flew into Birmingham for the Birmingham City away match. I wasn't expectant, but the lads were. "We'll smash them" said Darch in the pub the night before the match. If you were in Birmingham that day, you'll know the score and that Dan was spot on. We "smashed them 8-0!"

More to come on life as an AFC Bournemouth fan of course, but this chapter should tie things together for you – a high speed insight into our journey watching the Cherries. So, in 2014-2015 we were in our second season in the Championship. It cannot, surely, get any better than that. We're living a dream.

This is just a brief overview of the AFC Bournemouth times I've enjoyed and I've condensed it quite a bit here. It was a lot crazier and more dramatic than just a few mates supporting a team. I have attended over 150 Cherries matches since 2003 despite an almost 3 year gap at one point and I'm immensely proud to be an AFC Bournemouth fan.

My mates that go to watch the Cherries with me – they're the best lads and lasses in the world, and I love them all dearly. I'll see you again boys and girls, Portman pre-match (though it's shut now – 2020 update), back row, Dean Court, singing our hearts out. Nothing changed through the four divisions.

Up the fucking Cherries! Boscombe, back of the net!

Chapter 32
The Day We Got Relegated

Carlisle, ENGLAND and Glasgow, SCOTLAND (May 2008)

"Down, down, you bring me down" – Stone Roses.

One pint in Charminster for Neil Macey, Dan Darch and I turned into 6. Then we headed back to Dan's for a few hours sleep. We didn't get it. Patrick Hogan had come home with a threat that he would drink fabric conditioner if the Cherries stayed up. We hadn't stayed up yet, but the idea was too good to pass so we made him drink it. Patrick Conditioner. In the meantime, if the Cherries didn't stay up, at least we had.

We got our gear ready for the flight and Neil and I grabbed a beer in Dan's and a quick 2 hours sleep (correct me if I'm wrong Neil - but we must have had some sleep right?).

My friend from Northern Ireland, Gemma, drove us to Bournemouth airport and the car was packed. At the airport we met up with Serena and Dave, Steve Brown, Chris Manning and some other AFC Bournemouth fans. We were the team everyone wanted to love. Except Carlisle fans, Leeds fans, Scum fans and those in the relegation scrap. Our manager was Kevin Bond and honest truth - I had a hunch we would go to Carlisle and win 3-0 to stay up. I was so sure we would do the 'Great Escape'.

We bought champagne in the airport and were allowed to take it onto the plane. We had dressed up for the occasion, all in fancy dress.

It all began in February 2008. Cornish Cherry Dan and I had decided we were going to the last AFC Bournemouth away match in Carlisle no matter what. After research, we realised we could actually get there for cheaper and via Scotland on the flights from Ryanair. If we were saying goodbye to the third division (why the fuck is it called League One?) it was going to be in style. We began to plot the "party plane", using the internet and a website belonging to Ryanair.

A click of a few buttons and suddenly we were confirmed on the early Saturday morning Ryanair flight from Bournemouth Hurn to Glasgow Prestwick and the Sunday evening flight back, all for less than £30 including taxes and what have ye. Not bad for an away trip and especially via a different country (or if you disagree, a different region of the same "country"; Scotland, UK). At that stage it was just the two of us, and relegation was staring us in the face. We advertised it as a "relegation party" to all of our mates. However, an inspired turn in fortunes for the Cherries over the next two months kept the dream alive till the final day, 10 points stolen by the FA or not, we were making one hell of a fight. This fight had reached a telling pinnacle when Sam Vokes ran clear of the Railwaymen's defence on April's final Saturday. We were at home to Crewe Alexandra that day, who themselves were in big relegation trouble. Vokes made no mistake against a North Stand which erupted like a red and black volcano ready to make a famous great escape (part two). As the match entered injury time, with the Cherries 1-0 up, we waited patiently and agonisingly for the ref to blow the whistle. And there it was. We had a dream now. We were heading to Carlisle, not to make up the numbers, but to win the match and stay up. I can tell you this, as a football fan, your life doesn't get any better. The beer was sweet that night, we got muellered and Vokes had become a brief hero. Kevin Bond was our boss at the time - these were in pre-Eddie Howe manager days of course.

By this stage in the season, a few more mates had jumped on the bandwagon party plane and already the AFCB messageboards were full of people booking their flights up there. Some people were rumoured to have paid about £180 for the same flights that me and the boy Dan had booked for about £30 return on a Corona inspired web-browsing session three months earlier. The scene was set, the normal Airbus had been renamed a "party plane", the Cherries could still achieve a miracle, fancy dress was made an optional extra and plastic champagne flutes were bought in G and Ts in Winton (which reminded me of Wyse Byse in East Belfast, Northern Ireland). The story begins on the Friday evening...

It was the night before the big match and a few of us had finished work and got a wee carryout (that's a Northern Irish term for beer/alcohol you take away). The carryout wasn't quite enough so we headed into "downtown Charminster" where we wore our Bournemouth tops on a lively evening. We drank long into the morning, then realised our flight was at 6.22 am (or some bizarre time like that). Only 1-2 hours sleep would be had before Gemma and Swiss Cherry Corinne picked four of us up in fancy dress for a "party car" to Hurn airport. In those days it was acceptable to add the word "party" as an adjective to almost every method of transport, or indeed every noun. If you don't get it, it's because it's not funny and it was our crazy world at the time. If you get it, it's because it wasn't funny, but you enjoyed yourself in the lack of funniness of it. Either way the barrel of laughs began when three of us decided that the £1.99 bottle of cheap Cava from Asda was NOT the champagne we had craved to start the day off. Still, it didn't stop us drinking it as a wakeup call.

The fancy dress was as follows and in keeping with the theme of the day: myself in Tartan gear like a wannabe Scotsman (it was only fair since we were going via Scotland – I had a kilt on and no underwear just so I could show my willy to the girls later on), Dan dressed like a robber (we were looking to get out of jail), Neil dressed as Elvis Presley (Elvis isn't dead and we hoped the

Cherries wouldn't be) and then there was Patrick dressed in a blue pullover. "What have you come as you eejit I screeched at him?" No answer was given as it was obvious that one of your mates always has to wear the opposition's colours on the day of a big match. And for no apparent reason. We still wonder why Patrick did that. Perhaps he'll read this and have an answer. Even the females in our immediate group also joined in, if not in full fancy dress at least Swiss Corinne and Northern Irish Gemma donned Cherry colours for the day. Then was the story of the Shep. Shep had been to most of the previous matches with us, but since he was not based in Bournemouth at the time, he decided to get his own breakaway "party train" and meet us in Carlisle. His cowboy hat added to the day's party atmosphere, but not before we had arrived at a busy Hurn Airport.

Once through security - first time I'd been frisked in fancy dress, and sadly not by an attractive Russian female - we grabbed an early morning beer, well most of us, some sipped on water and tea, which I found rather disturbing and in bad taste. Soon Paul Williams and Linux had joined us and a group of red and black shirts were gathering by Gate 3, which included Steve Brown, and Serena and Dave, some of the Portman/Percy Shelley regulars. The flight was on time and the party plane dream was happening. The flight was full and at a guess I'd say at least 57 Bournemouth fans boarded it. Not all were wearing shirts and drinking champagne, but chants of we are "staying up" and "flying high up in the sky" were given blank glances by Latvian air hostesses, whose only saving grace were oddly-obvious decent sized breasts for the old men behind us to glance at. And yes, I mean, oddly-obvious.

Once we had hovered somewhere over urban Coventry I popped open the party champagne (I bought a higher quality one this time - £18 in the airport, as obviously you can't get it through security). The glasses were raised and Cornish Cherry sat by the window, luckily avoiding my dodgy opening of the champagne bottle. Only about one shot of champagne was lost, and it was nestled onto the tartanic crotch my Scottish kilt anyhow – one of my cheap champagne flutes proved to be bottomless. We had hoped Nonny AKA John Garard would be on our flight for a highest ever rendition of his iconic popular two word chant "Red Army".

But John was already in Scotland by this stage. The party plane had a great atmosphere and everyone who didn't like football asked us where we were going and wished us good luck. We'd need it, we were playing a team with an amazing home record. We exited the party plane and soon headed for our party train, which would see us change at both Troon and Glasgow on our way back over the border into England. This saw us also get on a "party bus" as the train system was off for the weekend. I cranked up a bit of Belinda Carlisle on the old iPod, only for the irony of her surname and not for the quality of the music, although those who grew up in the 1980s will remember her "Heaven is a place on earth" tune and more cringeworthingly her (blushes, awesome) nude Playboy shoot.

I'd always wanted to be entering Carlisle at some point in life. Belinda, or otherwise.

We stopped at Glasgow for a Scottish breakfast aye. Scottish accents reminded us of diversity as Neil and I chose cold Scottish Tennents over Coca Cola. The fried breakfast was beezer and set us up rightly for the next train, on which we enjoyed a short sing song and the views of Scottish countryside. This was sightseeing, partying and football all in one. On life's short corridor, I wouldn't have it any other way. Looking back now, it feels like one of the last crazy weekends I had with these lads, I'm sure they'll agree as our lives went on separate paths after that. Just over a year later, I'd be living in Australia, Corinne would be in Switzerland, Gemma would be in Northern Ireland with her new-born baby and

Millwall Neil was out in Taiwan! This was the last big one, though at the time, we wouldn't have known it.

A lovely Scottish train steward then came down the aisle selling alcohol. That was the cue for another beer and a loud "cheers" as the party train crossed the border into England. Nobody checked our passports, and although one of us was dressed as a robber, we hadn't smuggled any illegal goods across the border. The train seemed to be a short journey and soon we were confronted with the train station sign "Carlisle". Though in this strange English world of no pronounced "t" in the word water, the "s" goes unpronounced, giving it a "Carlile" sound. I still pronounce the "s", if you were that "s", how left out would you feel? You'd be like the "d" in Pernod if you were French. It was still only 11.19 a.m. Four hours to kick off, some pubs to find, Cherry fans to mingle with and to check in to the Travelodge, pre booked by Cornish Cherry. In fact, a diverse group, this set of Cherry fanatics, polling ourselves from Switzerland, Cornwall, Northern Ireland, London and even a guy from Corfe Mullen just to remind us that this was our local team as well. If anyone looked least like a Bournemouthian, it was actually Poole's very own Patrick. Cornish Cherry had his Cornwall fleg, I had my Northern Ireland fleg and there was Patrick pretending to eat a piece of out of date Dorset Fudge...dressed all in blue.

Once checked into the Travelodge, we waited for Shep and his cowboy hat to arrive at a wee bar on the main street. In there we played pool and found out that everyone supported Newcastle. There's still glory hunters in football. Though where I come from, Newcastle is an unknown team in the lower amateur leagues of Northern Ireland. I assumed they meant Newcastle United, the English side. On route to the stadium we found another bar and then Carlisle Rugby Club seemed to be the place for the rest of the Cherries hardcore. Over 1,000 Cherries fans had made the trip, it was a real party atmosphere. Palm trees, inflatable sharks, red face paints and stupid fancy dress were all in evidence as we entered Brunton Park 15 minutes before kick-off. The good old terrace was packed and in good voice already. The match itself was the only reason we were here though. The next 90 minutes would decide our fate, that coupled with hearing news of Gillingham (who to be fair, looked doomed before the match), Cheltenham (who would surely have no chance against O'Driscoll's Doncaster) and Crewe (who most expected to beat Oldham at home).

Our message was simple. Let's win this match and make it seven in a row (I think it would have been seven in a row anyway – memory is hazy) and then see how the other results go. In a nerve-wracking first half we went close a few times, but sang loud and proud behind a net that we wanted to see bulge. Sadly, when it did, it was the second half, and Carlisle sneaked a 1-0 opener at the back post. Dejection hit all round and it seemed in some ways that a dream may just have died. We don't go down that easy I'm afraid (unless it's faced with a naked Kylie Minogue in the darkest corridors of suburban Belarus). Then, in doom and desolation, up popped our favourite Channel Islander to make it 1-1. Equaliser! The place erupted. Brett Pitman had grabbed us the lifeline and we were drawing 1-1 but possession wise, suddenly we were on top. Real news and fake news kept filtering through the stands. We pretty much knew that Gillingham were down, but we were more than shocked at the Cheltenham news. Everyone had expected Doncaster to get at least a point that day as they were in with a shout of automatic promotion for second place. But the Robins were 2-1 up. We stopped caring about the Crewe v. Oldham score when we realised all we needed was a win and Crewe were going for a Burton (who, they could even have played had Burton came up from the Conference that year).

Okay I'll spoil it now before I cry. If you're reading you might know the fucking story. We didn't get the 2-1 win. Cheltenham held on as if their balls were getting cut off and the Leeds sent Gillingham down, while still none of us cared how shit Crewe were. Nobody was doing us a favour and even a draw was now not enough. Suddenly a referee was blowing a whistle which meant 1-1. We all knew it was over. We were so close to doing the great escape, but yet so far. Nice fucking dream, we had drawn away to Carlisle on the last day of the season and it wasn't good enough. We'd given it a shot. We were worthy of staying up anyway on points and performance and in the end the only reason we went down was from the 10 point administration deduction. Any other time, a 1-1 draw there was a good result. Today, it sent us down.

Tears were shed and a quick salute from Danny Hollands was enough to bring a fake smile. Former World Cup star Darren Anderton was also in a sombre mood, he hadn't seen or experienced relegation before as far as we could tell. Cornish Cherry was stood at the back with bright red hair which had run in the heat and a slow red tear down his cheek told the whole story. With this sort of passion for football, is it any bloody wonder why we love our club? An old mate from Radio Solent then popped by, it was Chris Latchem and I hadn't seen him since a 1-0 defeat at Millwall in 2006. Shep, myself and Cornish Cherry all gave our post-match thoughts and interviews to the Radio Solent microphone for immediate broadcast. Despite being the in-form team in England, we had just got relegated. We were down. Yes, we would be in Division 4 for the next season. We played like a team in the top half for the previous 10 matches. Ifs and buts were not important, and we then heard that Nottingham Forest had somehow gone up, pleasing Lock In Lee of course but Doncaster Rovers couldn't even do us a favour by winning. No thanks to Sean O'Driscoll, their manager, a former Cherry.

We headed to the pub, and on the way I was stopped by the Carlisle News and Star where I posed for photos and gave yet another interview as Neil posed by an Elvis sign. Though by this stage Elvis was actually kind of dead and the Cherries were down with the Luton, Gillingham and Port Vale.

Whether we were depressed or not, we drank long into the night and discussion turned to how we would book yet more party planes to places such as Darlington and Morecambe. I read recently how a group of Manchester City fans got a "party fishing boat" to an away UEFA Cup match in the Faroe Islands (though the story goes that it broke down and they had to turn back and fly anyhow...) and it is these types of lunatic ideas which make supporting your football team the most passionate non-sexual hobby in the world.

I wouldn't have it any other way. The next time you see me I'll be dressed as some kind of red and black cartoon hero or something boarding an aeroplane to a Cherries away match in somewhere as bizarre as downtown Hartlepool or outskirtic Bratislava. Come join our party and don't forget yer carryout...anyone's welcome and one's well if any come. Those days were pure madness and when I head back to England to watch AFC Bournemouth it's the same crowd of friends, but we've all mellowed, or maybe just got older.

Again, Cherries are the team for me, I love it.

Chapter 33
Walletless in Trieste

Trieste, ITALY (October 2008)

"Where do you go...buttoned in your favourite coat, stepping out to a different world, and you might be home late?" – Ocean Colour Scene.

I don't remember getting off the plane. I don't remember getting on the plane. Basically, I was a disgrace and I relied on my comrade Graham Anderson to get me through it. But I got through it, and yes I got on and got off the plane. I stepped out into a different world; unaware I was even there. The thing is though, life had been building up to this one. My predictable European jaunts, the days watching Northern Ireland, the vodka nights in Moscow (he spews up), the crazy activities in New Zealand, the Bournemouth relegation and my China visit to trek the Great Wall were all cool and I'd written about them, but one place close to home was missing. I had never been to the former Yugoslavia. In fact, take the word former out of that. I had never been to Yugoslavia. Current or former is irrelevant. My shoes had never stepped foot on that land. A few days down the park in Bangor pretending to be Darko Pancev was as far as it got. Besides, Darko Pancev and Robert Prosinecki annoyed me in the end. They beat Northern Ireland 2-0 at Windsor Park in Belfast on my home debut as a Norn Iron Supporter. The World Cup quarter finalists of 1990 displayed a footballing masterpiece and as a naive 10 year I kind of expected Kingsley Black and Mal Donaghy to show them how it's done. Yugoslavia changed though. War happened. The borders moved around, the country ceased to be called that, we had seven new countries (and a further few debatable regions including Liberland, Glagolia and Enclava) and yet my wandering heart had never been there.

Then an e-mail from John Hart goes something like "who wants to fly into Italy and cross the border into Slovenia for the away match?" No 28 year old Northern Ireland football fan with money to do it has ever said no to such a proposition. I barely even had the money for it. By now, I spent my days working on the Isle of Wight ferries between Yarmouth and Lymington. Yes, the same Isle of Wight that featured in Chapter 20. I now worked here and I loved it. All day I was travelling and being paid. At night I was your boring bar man in the elegant Pavilion Theatre in Bournemouth. In the intervening years, I had finally graduated and now was working in two jobs on the south coast.

I'd saved up enough cash from those jobs for a few trips around Europe to watch Northern Ireland, a renewal of my AFC Bournemouth season ticket and a few nights out. I was pretty tight and skint in those days. And almost always single now – girls hadn't really featured for a while (little did I know, this was to change so dramatically, soon). I had become too much of a lads lad really and that was an odd time of my life from 2005 – 2008 where I wasn't really dating many girls at all, or meeting any I even liked.

Anyway, Slovenia was a tad crazy. We flew into Trieste in Italy. John Hart, Andrew Milliken, Nial Coulter, Graham Anderson and I. We all met at 5 a.m. at Birmingham Airport. The only issue was that I had drank vodka the night before. Why did I do that? I don't drink vodka. I hate vodka. I can't stand vodka. Vodka destroys me. I cannot drink it and I hadn't had a shot of vodka for at least 6 years when I wrote this in July 2016. Yes, my Polish life would soon change things, but for this chapter we are now in 2008.

The night before, in Birmingham had been another reunion with Lock In Lee. Graham Anderson and I stayed at Lee's place and partied in a club where it was £9 entry and "All You Can Drink". That is where it all went wrong and the vodka came into play. I was sick everywhere and only thanks to Graham I made the flight. It was actually my first time in Italy and after getting a bus from the airport in Trieste to our downtown hostel, Affiti Ghega, I konked out – straight to sleep while the lads headed into the city to eat some pizza and drink some beer.

It took me a few hours to materialise and when I woke up, I must admit, I did not know what country I was in. I am serious. I was in a dark, drab, grey room. I was alone, in a trance. With a bottle of fizzy water to sip on. I thought I was still in Birmingham, England. I opened the door of the twin room Graham and I were sharing and it was into a dark corridor. It was grey and spooky. It felt like I was back in East Berlin. Then I checked my pockets. Passport – yes! Camera – yes! Mobile phone – no. Wallet – no! Wait! What? No wallet?? That's right I had no wallet, no money, I had no credit cards, I had nothing. I didn't even have money in any other pockets. I had managed to get from Lee's flat in Birmingham to a hostel room in Trieste, Italy without any money and without my phone. I couldn't remember where I had lost my wallet either. Oops!

Was it in the £9 all you can drink club? Was it at Birmingham airport? Trieste airport? Was it on a bus in Trieste? A bus I have no recollection of taking! I hoped that either Graham or Lee had taken my wallet off me to keep it safe. In that situation, they were better carers of it than me.

Some important things I had though - I had a map of Trieste in my pocket and somehow (I still have no idea how in those pre-Smart Phone days) I got in touch with Graham in an internet café to confirm they were in a pizza shop round the corner. I got there and the lads were all in good spirits – John, Andrew, Nial and Graham. They had taken good care of me and then I asked them, "I'm hoping one of you guys has my wallet?" I was about 100% sure one of them would have had it. None of them did, and they weren't even joking. Oops. So, I have a few days now in Italy and crossing into Slovenia and I have zero money or credit cards. But at least I have four friends. I asked Graham to lend me some Euros, which he did immediately without hesitation. Thanks Graham!

My memory of this trip is a little bit clouded. As I recall, Graham had a working phone and he texted Lock In Lee in Birmingham to enquire if he had my wallet. As I ordered a "chef's special pizza with an egg on it" and a reluctant beer in the city of Trieste, good news filtered through from Lee. Lee had taken my wallet off me the previous night so I didn't lose it and it was safe and well in his flat in Birmingham waiting for me on my return! Okay cool, now I relaxed, we got into the mood and toured some of the sights of Trieste before darkness set in and we headed to get a carryout. John and I went in search of a corkscrew and we bought some cheap Italian wine.

We spotted a fountain which changed colour often and had a good view of the city. I was bright, awake and lively again. The hangover had gone, I wasn't worried about not having a wallet, or any money and we chatted and drank. Again, it was a lads trip.

The plan was simple – get a train the next day across the border to the city of Ljubljana in Slovenia, the former Yugoslavia. Graham and I were spending two days in Bled by the Lake to go white water rafting and drink in the "George Best Bar" and then we were heading to Ljubljana for the football. Actually, the football match was in Maribor in Slovenia, so we had another double bus ride to organise once we got there. It feels now that we were so young, well organised and vibrant back then. We went with the flow and we squeezed a lot into these trips. We did our sightseeing, we watched the football, we drank a lot, we sang a lot, we got countless trains, buses and trams. We never wasted any time in life, and I still don't. I hate wasting time.

This particular night in Trieste also brought five of us together. Five friends that all knew each other through supporting Northern Ireland down the years. We were actually all quite independent people, yet as a team of five on this night, it was quare craic! You had Andrew "Moby" Milliken who is an Aghadowey man living in Glasgow and helps run the Scottish Northern Ireland Supporters Club. You had Nial, a Bangor man and John from Saintfield, both living in the North of England, Manchester United fans and guys who run the North of England Northern Ireland Supporters Club.

Graham Anderson lives in Bristol and alongside myself, we ran the South of England Northern Ireland Supporters Club in those days. All five of us were buck eejits if truth be told. We really weren't Dennis.

We had a decent quantity of Italian wine by the fountain that night, some in-depth chat and then we took our carryouts to the castle. Trieste is an ancient city with a fortress. On the castle walls, we meet some Korean and Chinese people holding a barbecue so we gatecrash it and get some food with them. We are interrupted by the police at this point who try to question us all. The five Northern Irish lads however make a dash down the hill and suss out a bar.

In my hungover state earlier, I somehow spied a "cool German Bar" so I showed the lads where it was and in we went. In this bar we ordered large Steins of German beer and Andrew got his phone out (he must have owned a modern one as it played music!) and we started singing "Killaloe". It was good banter. Talk turned to football and our chances in Slovenia. All of us felt we could get a draw, but would probably lose. Nigel Worthington was still manager at the time, if you remember back, I criticised that manager in chapters 28 and 29. I liked Nigel as a player – a hard working left back who played at the World Cup in Mexico 86 and in the Premier League for Norwich City and Leeds United. As a manager, I wasn't his biggest fan.

After a few jars in this bar, we headed to a wee poky pub in the city centre, not too far from our hostel. In here, Nial and I started drinking Mojitos and we were out until about 3 or 4 a.m., there was a Romanian girl in there I kept chatting to. Next morning, Graham and I had espresso coffees and cake in Trieste square and we toured a bit of the city before deciding to get on a "train" across the border to Slovenia.

It was actually me now who was organising everyone to get this "train". I got everyone to meet at the "train station" for the "train". What happened next was we bought our "train" tickets for a direct "train" to Slovenia. Lost in translation and because I am an eejit, they were actually bus tickets and we would be heading on a bus to Trieste! Either way, it was cheap and cheerful. There wasn't even a border check on entering the former Yugoslavia for the first time. We were now in Slovenia, another new country on my journey and we arrived safe and well (and I was still wallet-less of course) in central Ljubljana. The Slovenian capital. And the madness didn't end there.

Chapter 34
Wegoslavia

Bled, SLOVENIA (October 2008)

"These are crazy, crazy, crazy, crazy nights" – Kiss.

Well we were now in Slovenia and Graham and I left Ljubljana on an actual train (not a bus) this time for Bled. This was a sublime countryside venue which boasts a beautiful lake, castle and also meant a chance to feature in a BBC Northern Ireland documentary. Please note that some names in this chapter have been changed to protect identities.

I had got in touch with the BBC to arrange to meet them in the aptly named George Best Bar (and Backpackers) in Bled that evening for some banter. When we got there, the BBC film crew were in high spirits and we checked into our dorm, Graham and I. We headed straight to the bar for a beer and a bite and were also greeted by John, pub owner and a Belfast man. Nigel and Warren from the BBC were filming a documentary for BBC Northern Ireland fans on how members of the Green and White Army were getting to Slovenia and the antics we were getting up to. We met

Neil Burnett in here – he was based in Hong Kong and a Charlton Athletic supporter. Again, this was such irony, as within four years I myself would be not only living in Hong Kong but meeting up with Neil as part of Hong Kong NISC events!

When life gets this good, you have to pinch yourself sometimes to check it's real. Looking back this adventure in Slovenia will linger long forever in my memory. In many ways, my obsession for football and lunacy reached a combined peak here in Bled, Slovenia. A peak which would have been a good time to call it a day and bow out on. I found myself becoming part of a BBC hyped up documentary following Northern Ireland football fans on route to a match. But not just that. The things we get up to on route to these matches, which in this case was an amazing experience which will never be replicated.

So, after the crazy time in Trieste (and still without a wallet) we filmed the first part of the documentary for the BBC in The George Best Pub in Bled, Slovenia. The morning after that story is where the "green and white water rafting army" lunacy began. It was Friday 17th October 2008, and myself, Graham Anderson, Alan Garforth and Tina Garforth were about to be filmed by the BBC while rafting down a river in deepest Slovenian countryside. Dressed in green. Wearing wigs. Hungover. Having had less than an hour of sleep. As we all agreed at the time "this is total carnage". It was, but nobody stopped to complain. So, the story continues...

I grabbed about 38 minutes sleep as did Graham in our small hostel room on the top floor at The George Best Bar and Hostel. We had been drinking the previous day in two countries, on trains, buses and in bars. Not to mention being invited by 'Holly' back to her wee flat for more beer and wine in the early hours. Graham and I hung around there till 7.38 a.m. Or so the video reveals. We were due to start the rafting at 10 a.m. There was no time to be late. So, we both got our 38 minutes of sleep and then I got up, fresh and got a quick shower, walking half naked down the hostel corridor not worrying who saw my Northern Irish body. It could well have been the BBC, but it wasn't. They had already filmed me briefly first thing, topless, by the hostel bedroom, looking half asleep. It was a nice "real" moment for the documentary, it was unstaged.

Everything was spontaneous, everything was unplanned. The night before Alan and I had sung "Northern Ireland's green and white water rafting carryout army". In the morning we had drank so much we didn't need a carry out as we were still hungover from the night before! I have no idea where the strength to raft would come from when I got out of bed.

We made it to the front of the hostel, where Warren Bell and Nigel McAlpine from the BBC were waiting. There I lost my wig, then John, the owner found it, in the bin, in the bar. It smelt really bad so I put it on briefly and decided to ditch it. That sparkly green wig had backpacked about 10 countries with me for Northern Ireland away matches! It bled and died in Bled, ironical. Graham and Alan donned their own special wigs for the day. I wore the blue Northern Ireland away shirt for a change. We boarded a small minibus bearing the words "white water rafting - bled" on it. We met the two guides - Mika and Robbie the rafting experts. One of them drove us up the mountains, past Lake Bled and many rivers and trees. The countryside and the minibus journey was amazing. We weren't too hungover to appreciate that. We even had time to sing songs about the mountains "it's nice but it's not the Mournes" came out (Northern Ireland's very own mountain range obviously being superior to this one...at least in our biased nationalistic minds).

Another moment was captured by the BBC when Alan and I looking totally dazed and in false reality sang "you are my Donard, my Slievey Donard, you make me happy when skies are grey. So sod Ben Nevis and Mount Everest, please don't take my Donard away..." - the original version of this tune was sung by myself and Richboy in Vaduz, Liechtenstein in 2007, and included the word "fuck"; at the last minute, for the BBC edit and to make it on, we omitted the sware word. Just as well! The bus took less than 15 minutes, and the journey involved random banter and we showed no nerves before the rafting experience. Soon Alan had his Ulster fleg up on the window and we were out in the chilled open air with a Slovenian sun belting through awesome trees, idyllic countryside and nameless mountains down on these four lunatic Northern Ireland fans now living in the South of England.

The silly comedy continued "Canoe believe it?" I said calmly pointing an oar at Alan. "There's Jonny Evans" shouted Alan over towards trees where the only sign of life was a Kingfisher bird. Soon we got changed into the wet suits, they weren't green and white, but blue and black. The green was still apparent though from Alan and Graham's wigs. Graham's wig was reminiscent of that from Doc from "Back To The Future". This was the present, there was no sign of a Delorian, and fate had brought us four together, in a raft with Mika, the cool Slovenian guide. More filmage was done, before we lifted the raft and hoisted it into the water, jumping into the raft straight after. I had been placed at the front with Alan, and I had the "raft cam" attached to my forehead so I accepted some sort of responsibility for the carnage. I didn't dare fall out of the raft with the "video camera" even though they told me it was predictably waterproof.

Within minutes we were oaring our way down the slow, steady river. We all savoured the views and enjoyed the relaxation of it. There were three types of speed, as explained by Mika. Fast was when we wanted to go faster through the dips and rock areas, normal was just light rowing and no speed was when the water current took us down on our own. It wasn't too strenuous at all.

None of us ever looked tired or knackered. Surprising, given the total lack of sleep the previous 4 nights, not to mention the indulgence in alcohol! Every now and then at various points, Warren and Nigel from the BBC would pop out in the scenery with their cameras. We sang many songs on the way down through the mountains. The journey took a total of almost 2 hours! But you wouldn't have thought it. It was calm and peaceful and the best moment was the "bodysurfing" part.

At one point, around the half-way mark there was a strong current and Mika slowed the raft down and took it over to the side. One by one then we all jumped into the cool water to surf down with the current taking us down. A lifejacket attached as part of the wetsuit meant there was no need to swim. We just sailed automatically down the river. It was so fresh, so relaxing and the perfect way to delete the hangover from the previous night (and current morning) of Union beer from The George Best Bar. I was second into the water, after Graham. I remember Alan shouting "there's his wig!!" "watch him go, the doc's away..." and that was Graham Anderson floating through Slovenian rivers into a wilderness on a dream which doesn't end. We all followed down the stream, before Mika called us back over and into the raft again to continue the white water rafting. Which for the day we had changed to "green and white water rafting".

Soon a heron was following us down the river on a gorgeous day, spotted by Tina. We often link things back to Northern Ireland and we christened it "the Buttercrane heron", after an old symbol and advert for the Buttercrane Shopping Centre in Newry, which Tina later mentioned on BBC. That was a nice moment of nature and beauty in another cultured football trip. We continued to row down the river singing more ridiculous songs and sobering up. We forgot we were on camera and being recorded the whole time though, as Graham often told stories of a sexual nature that he could have kept to himself. It all added to the humour and at the very end, we rowed the raft over ashore to where Robbie had driven the van to. We all jumped out of the raft and into the cool river. It was clean, it was calm. We sang "Good times never seemed so good" as we floated in the Slovenian mountain water. Very soon though the white water rafting experience was over. It was refreshing, thoroughly enjoyable and a relaxing way to spend a few hours.

We sat down by the trees by the river where we did interviews and match predictions for the Slovenia v. Northern Ireland match. It's a very nice wee documentary the BBC did actually, which really captured the spirit and happiness of it all. We all got given a free blueberry alcohol shot at the end of the rafting, before getting a DVD and CD of photos. Now that carnage was over and done with we had to get ourselves off to Ljubljana for some rest before the big match the next night. It was all part and parcel of being part of Northern Ireland's GAWA (Green And White Army), and doing something a bit different on route to an away match. I, for one, enjoyed every moment...

The video can still be viewed on the BBC website on this link -

http://news.bbc.co.uk/sport1/hi/football/internationals/7665629.stm

After the BBC documentary, we headed back to the capital city. I was still travelling without a wallet and Graham and I stayed at the quirky Hostel Celica in Ljubljana – a converted former prison. We appeared on Slovenia TV too, in the city of Maribor when fellow SOENISC member Jono Crute and I were interviewed. Crute famously proclaimed that Slovenia will win 2-0. When the match ended, Alan gave me an extra 30/40 Euros as he knew I didn't have a wallet. As a sign of the times, I eventually paid him back by cheque. It was the last time I have ever written a cheque! If anyone cares, we lost the match 2-0, as predicted by Jono Crute and we were filmed on BBC dancing to the Oasis hit "The Shock of the Lightning".

Northern Ireland lost 2-0 at home to Hungary again the following month, and it was after this match that life got weird and mangled my head up for good. I had no idea that a crazy double romance was on its way.

At the time, I needed a change in lifestyle. Life as a single male was not that great. I spent too many hours watching football, partying, drinking, dancing and singing. Yes, they were good times looking back, but I kept hoping for something new to happen in my life. I kept wanting to travel more. I never expected love. This is when things got really bizarre and my life changed dramatically. I didn't see this one coming.

Chapter 35
Cod and a Good Romance

London, ENGLAND (October 2008)

"Love, love will tear us apart. Again" – Ian Curtis.

It was my last ever Oasis gig as a paying spectator. I'd later work at an Oasis gig on the bar at the BIC in Bournemouth, but this night was a mad one. Nobody knew it was the end of Oasis of course, but something was brewing and the Gallagher brothers didn't last much longer in their rock'n'roll band.

I had been working flat out on the Wightlink ferries as well as in the Bournemouth Pavilion Theatre, but two days off led me to London to watch Oasis at Wembley Arena. I agreed to stay with my New Zealand friend Steve Jones on the night of the gig and two other friends, Michael McSparron and James Condron joined us for the Oasis concert. The gig rocked along, let's not dwell on the music, which was as ever taintless, but afterwards there was a moment that was going to change my life again. Ridiculously so.

After the Oasis gig, we called in for a good old English fish and chips (cod), and the lads and I decided on a late night final pint in a bar somewhere near Liverpool Street. I have no idea what bar it was and could not find it again now if I tried, but I started chatting to a lady in here. This lady was Helen. I seemed to be perpetually single in those days, often having flings and never ever settling with anyone. It probably got rather predictable and frustrating but I was a busy guy so I never really pondered on it. From the start, Helen and I got on well. To take it onwards, we decided to date for a while. Helen was a professional artist, a mother of two and a Blackpool FC fan. Helen was also a lot older than me as she was 44 to my 28. It didn't seem to worry either of us at the time. She looked younger than 44.

Helen came to visit me in Bournemouth a few times and we had great nights out. I also took her to watch the Cherries with me – a dour 0-0 home draw with Blyth Spartans in the FA Cup was my idea of a "date". That is still probably the worst game of football I have ever seen! And nothing to do with Helen or the date! 99 Cherries fans went to the away replay but we lost 1-0 late on, in what was regarded as the worst ever few months as a Cherries fan.

But things were peculiar in my life at the time, and these three Chapters 35, 36 and 37 will take my journey through a double romance, neither of which over-lapped, I must say. Though Helen may have thought there was an overlap with Noemi, there wasn't. There was a slight gap. I never double dated. I need to be clear about that.

But I messed things up with Helen and I never forgave myself for it. I was a nightmare to her, I got lost. It was a great romance with Helen though – we had really fun times and she remains the only girlfriend that I never argued with. Not once – we never argued about anything. That's zero arguments! Something quite rare in any relationship.

I didn't want to drag the past up too much in this chapter, as it doesn't seem right, and I cannot believe it, but I lied to Helen about a few things. Looking back now, I cannot believe I was dishonest to her. I was a disgrace. It pains me, the reason I did this was only because my emotions were all over the place and I wasn't thinking straight. During the romance with Helen, I had fallen in love with someone else by complete fluke and I didn't even know it. But as I said, I had no overlap here – I just happened to meet that lady while I was still dating Helen. The love was un-noticed by me – it was blind at the start. It all happened so suddenly.

Somehow though, I knew my days in England were now numbered (with a low number) and I didn't realise where the hell life was taking me. Later on in life, I blamed my depression on the karma given to me as I knew that I had lied to Helen. However, I later admitted and apologised for my lies to Helen and am doing so again here and will do so again anytime – I will meet Helen face to face and admit it all anytime. I have no qualms to help others in depression or mental illness in their hour of darkness. I know how it feels – I'll do what they ask if it is something simple that saves their life – I'll do that for anyone.

Sadly, for me, those lies for sure came back to bite me. One of the reasons for the delay of this book was my own depression. That depression was caused by the lies of a girl that I had the misfortune to meet later in life. I believe in karma now. All the bad things I did in life, came back to haunt, destroy and depress me. I was victim to my own misdemeanours - The Great Exam Heist (Chapter 5), The OXI One (Chapter 7), My Favourite Mistake (Chapter 9). Those blemishes on my past came back as bad karma. I thought that by being honest and admitting my mistakes, that it would negate them. That wasn't to be. More of that will be revealed in the subsequent chapters in later volumes of Backpacking Centurion.

I had lied to Helen and reckon I deserved karma later in life as a result. I really believe in karma now, and I got it back real bad. New people will be introduced to my story in due course including Noemi, Panny and Olcia. That won't all be good and things will become clearer before they go awry again. Segments of my journey make more sense when pieced together.

As I write this now, some 12 years on after meeting Helen, I realise how cool a person Helen had been. How nice a person she was and how I was an asshole at times to her. I can't really explain it other than bad timing. We never argued but I did ignore and neglect Helen in her time of need. In the next chapter, I'll try and tie it all together a bit better, perhaps in a way I never explained to Helen. There will be a story about a Hungarian dancer.

To conclude though, I got back in touch with Helen and I met her again in 2014 on my first trip to London for 5 years and we had a drink together, which was nice. Neither of us will forget the times we had but ultimately my destiny lay further afield and within months, I'd be plotting my departure from England, where to date, I haven't lived in since.

The next few chapters will be destructive in more ways than two. The Hungarian dancer story is to be continued in Volume Two, Chapter 36…I'm not sure it would have made a fitting end to the "Don't Look Back in Bangor" volume. We never know what's around the chimney corner…

Backpacking Centurion: A Northern Irishman's Journey Through 100 Countries

Volume 1: Don't Look Back in Bangor

by Jonny Blair

Rough translation guide from Northern Irish and Jonny Blairish intill English:

bake – face

bake on ye / look at the state of yer man / see yer bake – you do not look happy

beg – bag

Bournemouthian -a person from Bournemouth

Bournemouthic – typical of Bournemouth

brave – really good

bate – beaten, lost

belshynic – of Belshina Belarus

breath thefter – something that takes your breath away

buck eejit – cultured idiot

buckie – tonic wine (95% time it's the brand 'Buckfast')

carryout – takeaway alcohol

caser – leather football

craic – banter so it is

crappuccino – a very bad quality cappuccino

Cremola Foam – a popular fizzy drink in Northern Ireland during the 1980s

dandered, a dander, to dander – walked, a walk, to walk at a normal Northern Irish pace

datily – in order of date

Dennis – wise, clever

docken leaf - rumex obtusifolius, a leaf that helps after a nettle sting

eejit – idiot

eejitiotic – like an idiot

electionic – resembling an election

feg - cigarette

fillim - movie

fleg – flag

footballic – of football

forwardlash – exact opposite of backlash

GAWA – Green and White Army, Northern Ireland football fans

geg – funny person

here's me till im – after that, I said to this man

intill - into

jamember – do you remember

Jurassic Park – it's a fillim about dinosaurs

look at the bake on yer man – look at his face

lunatical – crazy

musicly – musically

nat – not

nets – goals, goalkeeper, keeper

pelanty - penalty

photy, photies – photo, photos

Portadownczyk – a man from Portadown in Northern Ireland

quare geg – a right laugh/something funny

Quoile – a river in Northern Ireland

see him? – look at that guy

shap - shop

shar - shower

so it is – no meaning, can be replaced with a blank space, but that would be boring

spake – speak, dialect, style

stolica – capital city

tap - top

that there – meaningless Northern Irish garbage

themmuns – those people

thingy – that person, you know that person right?

thon – that wee one

till – to

Ulsteric – adjective describing 'of Ulster'

unchaptertitled – that was not the title of the chapter I gave

UTCIAD – Up the Cherries, in all departments! (AFC Bournemouth fan chant)

Wacaday – copyright of Timmy Mallet, crazy, lunatical

wee – term of endearment, often signifying small

whackpacking, whackpacker – to go backpacking in a crazy way, a crazy backpacker

whatcha – what are ya

whoppaday – crazy low amount

worldic – global

ya, ye - you

yer Da woulda stuck thatun away – your father would have scored a goal

yer gegging me – you are joking about with me

yer man – that male person

yer woman – that female person

yoghurty – creamy like a yoghurt

yous, youse, yousens – you people

If there are any other unknown words or phrases that are used in this book, you can email the author Jonny Blair for clarification, as he often uses his own phrases and confuses others with his peculiar use of language.

The Backpacking Journey of Jonny Blair March 1980 – 2020

This is a list of all the continents, countries, disputed regions, wacaday republics, exclusion zones, uninhabited islands, unrecognised countries, micronations, metropolises, cities, conurbations, towns, villages, hamlets and deemed significant places visited by Jonny Blair from 1980 – 2020. The list may not be 100% accurate or complete and is listed in alphabetic order.

Continents Visited (8/8)

Africa Antarctica Asia Europe Middle East North America Oceania South America

Places Visited

On this list I have included everywhere I have been narrowed down to cities, towns, villages or what I deem to be a significant place. These are listed under the same categories as the countries or regions that I personally class them as belonging in. Those places in brackets mean I was only there in transit (the bus stopped, the train stopped, I changed flights etc.).

Adammia Jagstonian Plains, Tytannia Province, Maternia Province
Afghanistan Aybak, Bactra (Bactria), Balkh, Hayratan, Masar e Sharif, Samangan, Tashkurgan
Algeria Algiers
Andaman Islands Port Blair, Corbyn's Cove
Andorra Andorra La Vella, Escaldes Engordany, Ordino
Angola Luanda, Panguila, Viana
Antarctica Admiralty Bay, Aitcho Islands, Barrientos, Cuverville Island, Deception Island, Drake Passage, Elephant Island, Foyn Harbour, Gerlache Strait, Jougla Point, Half Moon Island, King George Island, Neko Harbour, Neptune's Bellows, Neptune's Window, Neumayer Channel, Port Foster, Port Lockroy, Telefon Bay
Argentina Beagle Channel, Buenos Aires, Puerto Iguazu, Ushuaia

Armenia Garni, Geghard, Goght, Haghpat, Khor Virap, Noravank, Sanahin, Tatev, Yerevan

Austenasia <u>Wrythe</u>, Orly

Austria Anif, Braunau Am Inn, Grodig, Linz, Neumarkt Kostendorf, Salzburg, <u>Vienna</u>

Australia

Australian Capital Territory - <u>Canberra</u>, Casuarina Sands

New South Wales - Blackheath, Blue Mountains, Byron Bay, Cann River, Coffs Harbour, Coolangatta, Jenolan Caves, Kiama, Nowra, Narooma, Katoomba, Maclean, Newcastle, Ourimbah, Parramatta, Port Macquarie, Sydney, Tweed Heads, Ulladulla, Wollongong, Woodford Island

Queensland - Beerburrum, Brisbane, Glasshouse Mountains, Logan, North Lakes, Scarborough, Surfer›s Paradise

Tasmania - Bagdad, Bangor, Bangor Farm, Batman Bridge, Bishopsbourne, Bruny Island, Carrick, Cataract Gorge, Cradle Mountain, Cressy, Devonport, Don, Dove Lake, East Sassafras, Forth, Georgetown, Glenorchy, Great Lake, Hobart, Isle of the Dead, Kettering, Kindrid, Latrobe, Launceston, Lillico, Longford, Lower Landing, Makintosh Dam, Moonah, Moriarty, Penguin, Poatina, Queenstown, Rinadeena, Ross, Sheffield, Stanley, Strahan, Swansea, Teepookanna, Tullah, Ulverstone, Wesley Vale, Wineglass Bay, Zeehan

Victoria - ١٢ Apostles, ٩٠ Mile Beach, Bairnsdale, Brighton, Great Ocean Road, Leongatha, Marlo, Melbourne, Peterborough, Yarram, Yellow Pinch Dam

Azerbaijan Baku, Balakan, James Bond Oil Fields, Mud Volcanoes, Qobustan, Quba, Seki, Xinaliq, Zaqatala

Bahrain Manama, Umm al-Na'san, Riffa, King Fahd Causeway, Oil Field, Sitra, Muharraq Island

Bangladesh Chittagong, Dhaka, Uttara

Basque Country Bilbao, Donostia (San Sebastian)

Bavaria Munich

Belarus Bobruisk, Barysaw, Grodno, Minsk

Belize Actun Tunichil Muknal, Ambergris Caye, Belize City, Belmopan, Benque Viejo del Carmen, Caye Caulker, Placencia, San Pedro, Spanish Lookout, Xunantunich

Belgium Antwerp. Bruges, Brussels, Eupen, Ghent, Kettenis, Saint Ghislain

Benin Abomey, Cotonou, Ouidah, Porto Novo

Bolivia Colchani, Desaguadero, Incahuasi, La Paz, Oruro, Potosi, San Cristobal, San Juan de Rosario, Santa Cruz de La Sierra, Uyuni

Borneo (see separate country sections for Malaysia, Brunei and Indonesia)

Bosnia Neum, Mostar, Sarajevo

Bosnia-Herzegovina Sarajevo

Botswana Chobe, Gaborone, Kasane, Kazungula, Tlokweng

Brazil Belem, Belo Horizonte, Fortaleza, Foz Do Iguacu, Juquitiba, Macapa, Oiapoque, Recife, Sao Paulo

Brunei Darussalam Bandar Seri Bagawan, Kampong Ayer, Muara, Serasa

Bulgaria Gorna Oryakhovitsa, Plovdiv, Sofia, Veliko Tarnovo

Burundi Bujumbura, Lake Tanganyika

Cambodia Angkor Thom, Angkor Wat, Baphuon, Bayon, Chau Say Tevoda, Preas Dak, Phnom Penh, Poipet, Siem Reap, Thommanon, Trapeang Kreal

Canada Niagara, Toronto, Winnipeg

Catalonia Barcelona, (Andorra Border)

Channel Islands Guernsey, Herm, Jersey, Lihou Island, Little Sark, Sark

Chernobyl Exclusion Zone Chernobyl Town, Pripyat, Reactor Number 4, Kopachi

Chile Cape Horn, Hito Cajun, Santiago

China (incomplete)

Anhui – Huangshan, Nanping, Yuliang

Beijing - Badaling, Beijing, Forbidden City, Tiananmen Square, Great Wall of China

Chongqing - Chongqing, Foreigner Street, Yangtze River
Guangdong Province – Chikan, Da Lang, Danxiashan, Dongguan, Guangzhou, Jin Jiang Village, Kaiping, Majianlong, Mount Daxia, Ruishi Lou, Shaoguan, Shenzhen, Yao Tang, Zhuhai, Zili
Guangxi Province - Baisha, Guilin, Li River, Yangshuo
Hunan Province - Changsha
Jiangsu Province - Pingjianglu, Suzhou
Jiangxi Province - Jiangling, Jingdezhen, Little Likeng, Likeng, Nanchang, Sanqing Shan, Shangrao, Wangkou, Wuyuan, Xiaoqi, Yushan
Fujian Province - Gaobei Hamlet, Gu Lang Yu, Hong Keng, Shancheng, Ta Pa Tsune, Taxia Village, Tian Luo Keng, Xiamen, Yongding
Shanghai – Shanghai
Liaoning Province - Dandong
Yunnan Province - Gejiu, Gum Guy, Jianshui, Jin Ji Cun, Jinjiang Waterfalls, Kunming, Lijiang, Luoping, Nansha, Screw Tin (Yellow Fields), Shilin Stone Forest, Shuhe, Shangri La (Zhongdian), Tiger Leaping Gorge, Upper Trail Hike, Yuanyang Rice Terraces, Xingjie Zhen
Zhejiang Province - Hangzhou, West Lake
Christiania Christiania Freetown (inside Copenhagen, Denmark)
Colombia Bogota, Chia, Cucuta, (Duitama), Guasca, Guatavita, Santa Ana Alta, Sopo
Costa Rica Alajuela, Cacao, Grecia, Penas Blancas, San Jose
Croatia Dubrovnik, Split, Zagreb
Cyprus Limassol, Larnaca, Nicosia, Tseri
Czechia Prague, (Decin), Olomouc, Ostrava
Democratic Republic of Congo Bukavu, Kahuzi-Biega National Park
Denmark Copenhagen, Helsingor
Don't Stop Living http://dontstopliving.net/
Druze People Isfiya Village
East Timor *Atauro Island* - Beloi, Vila *Mainland* - Cape

Fatucama, Dili
Ecuador Ciudad Mitad del Mundo, Quito
El Salvador Barra de Santiago, Chalchuapa, Joya de Ceren, Las Chinamas, Mangrove Forests, Nejapa, Puerta del Diablo, San Andres, Anguiatu, San Salvador, Santa Ana, Sonsonate, Tazumal
England (incomplete) Aldershot, Alnwick, Bath, Bideford, Birkenhead, Birmingham, Blackburn, Blackpool, Blandford Forum, Boscombe, Bournemouth, Brighton, Bristol, Burnley, Bury, Carlisle, Carshalton, Cheltenham, Christchurch, Colchester, Crawley, Crayford, Dartford, Derby, Doncaster, Dorchester, Durdle Door, Eastbourne, Eton, Exeter, Fleetwood, Gatwick, Gillingham, Gloucester, Gosport, Gravesend, Heathrow, Hereford, Lake District, Lancaster, Leeds, (Leicester), Liverpool, London, Loughborough, Luton, Lymington, Lytham St. Anne's, Manchester, Mansfield, Milton Keynes, New Forest, Newcastle Upon Tyne, Newhaven, Nottingham, Oxford, Pease Pottage, Poole, Portsmouth, Preston, Rochester, Salisbury, Sheffield, Southampton, Southend, Southsea, Stansted, Stonehenge, Sunderland, Torquay, Truro, Wakefield, Weston Super Mare, Weymouth, Winchester, Windsor, Woking, Worksop
Isle of Wight - Cowes, Newport, The Needles, Yarmouth
Islands - Brownsea Island, Portland
Estonia Parnu, Tallinn
Ethiopia Addis Ababa, Asbe Teferi, Dire Dawa, Harar
Faroe Islands
Bordoy - Klaksvik, Norddepil
Fugloy - Kirkja, Hattarvik
Eysturoy - Gjogv
Streymoy - Kirkjubour, Saksun, Torshavn
Svinoy - Svinoy
Vagar - Gasadalur, Bour, Sorvagur, Vatnsoyrar, Midvagur, Lake Sorvagsvatn
Vidoy – Hvannasund
Fiji Nadi

Finland Helsinki, Järvenpää, Suomenlinna

France Campeigne, Cherbourg, Dieppe, La Roche Sur Yon, Lyon, Marseille, Nantes, Nice, Paris, St. Gilles, St. Jean de Monts, St. Malo

French Guyana Cayenne, G.S.C., Iracoubo, Kourou, Organabo, Sinnamary, St. Georges de L'oyapock, St. Laurent du Maroni

Frestonia Freston Road, Bramley Road (London, England)

Gambia Banjul, Barra, Brufut, Serrakunda, Bakau, Kololi

Georgia Batumi, Davit Gareja, Gergeti, Gori, Kazbegi, Lagodekhi, Sighnaghi, Tbilisi, Uplistsikhe

Germany Bah Harzburg, Berlin, Bremen, Dresden, Frankfurt, Hamburg, Hannover, Leipzig, Magdeburg, Marburg, Munich, Nuremberg, Oker, Osterweddingen, Simbach Am Inn, (Trier)

Gibraltar Gibraltar City, Europa Point, Top of the Rock

Gorno Badakhshan Khorog, Vanj, Kalai Khum

Greece Athens

Rhodes - Afandou, Faliraki, Rhodes Town

Guatemala Anguiatu, Antigua, Coban, El Florida, Flores, Guatemala City, Huehuetenango, Lago Atitlan, La Mesilla, Lanquin, Melchor de Mencos, Nuevo Valle, Panajachel, Quetzaltenango, Rio Hondo, San Marcos La Laguna, San Pedro La Laguna, Santa Clara La Laguna, Valle Nuevo, Volcan Santa Maria, Volcan Tajumulco

Guyana Bartica, Corriverton, Falmouth, Georgetown, Kaieteur Falls, Molson Creek, Parika, Sloth Island

Herzegovina Kotor

Honduras Copan Ruinas, El Florida, El Guasaule, La Ceiba, Puerto Cortes, Rio Cangrejal, San Pedro Sula, Tegucigalpa, Utila

Hong Kong (incomplete)

Hong Kong Island - Aberdeen, Admiralty, Causeway Bay, Central, Chai Wan, North Point, Sheung Wan, Stanley, The Peak, Wan Chai

Kowloon – Austin, Cheung Sha Wan, Diamond Hill, Hung Hom, Jordan, Kowloon Bay, Kowloon Tong, Kwun Tong, Lai Chi Kok, Lam Tin, Mong Kok, Olympic, Prince Edward, San Po Kong, Tai

Kok Shui, Tsim Sha Tsui, Yau Ma Tei, Yau Tong
New Territories - Fan Ling, Kwai Fong, Lok Ma Chau, Lo Wu, Sai
Kung, Sha Tin, Sheung Shui, Tsuen Wan, Tsueng Kwan O,
Yuen Long
Outlying Islands - Lantau Island, Ma Wan/Park Island, Mui Wo,
Tai O, Tsing Yi, Tung Chung, Yi O
Hungary Budapest, Debrecen, Szolnok
Iceland Blue Lagoon, Geysir, Grindavik, Gullfoss, Keflavik, Kerio
Crater, Pingvellir, Reykjavik
India
Delhi - New Delhi
Gujarat - Ahmedabad, Aralaj Vav
Maharashtra – Elephant Island, Mumbai
Goa - Harvali, Mapusa, Vagator, Vagator Beach, Anjuna Beach,
Panaji/Panjim
Other - Agra, Chennai, Hampi, Karnataka, Mathura, Taj
Mahal, Vrindavan
Indonesia
Bali - Denpasar, Kalibukbuk, Lovina, Munduk, Singaraja, Ulun
Danu, Ubud
Java - Borobudur, Jakarta, Prambanan, Yogyakarta
Iran Alamut Valley / Alamut Castle, Bandar e Golmaniyeh,
Bayaziye, Bazargan, Chak Chak, Dakmeh, Esfahan, Gazor Khan,
Kaluts, Kandovan, Kerman, Khalate Talkh, Kharanaq, Khoor, Lake
Orumiye, Maku, Marvdasht, Mashhad, Mahan, Mesr, Nasqh-e
Rostam, Orumiye, Osku, Persepolis, Qazvin, Rayen, Sadegh Abad,
Salt Flats (near Khoor), Shahr-e Kord, Shiraz, Tabriz, Tarjrish,
Tehran, Yaseh Chah, Yazd, Zarad Band
Iraq *Kurdistan* - Amadiya, Dohuk, Erbil, Sulav, Sulimaniyeh
Other - Kirkuk, Mosul
Italy Bergamo, Faenza, Florence, Milan, Pisa, Rimini, Rome,
Treviso, Trieste, Venice
Ivory Coast Abidjan, Grand Bassam
Japan Tokyo

Jordan Amman, Aqaba, Irbid, Petra, Rum Village, Wadi Musa, Wadi Rum

Kaliningrad Kaliningrad City

Karakalpakstan Nukus

Kashubia Gdunsk, Gdynia, Kartuzy, Pomlewo, (Wejherowo)

Kazakhstan Almaty, Ile Alatau, Korday, Shymkent, Jibek Joli, Turkistan

Kenya El Doret, Lake Nakuru, Malaba, Maasai Mara National Park, Nairobi, Nakuru, Narok

Kiribati Tarawa

North Tarawa – **New Jerusalem, Abatao Island**

South Tarawa – **Bonriki, Bairiki, Betio, Bikenibeu, Eita**

Kosovo (Blace), (Kulla), Pristina

Kurdistan (see Iran, Iraq and Turkey)

Królestwo Dreamlandu Dreamopolis

Kugelmugel Kugelmugel

Kuwait Kuwait City: Sharq, Salmiya

Kyrgyzstan Ala Archa, Bishkek, Cholpon Ata, Issy-Kul Lake, Ruh Ordo, Petroglyphs

Ladonia Nimis

Lagoan Isles Baffin's Pond, Beeney St. Georges

Laos Don Det, Pakse, Nong Nok Khiang, Thanaleng, Vang Vieng, Vientiane

Latvia Riga

Lebanon Beirut

Lesotho Maseru, Thaba Bosiu

Liechtenstein Vaduz

Lithuania Kaunas, Kryziu Kalnas (Hill of Crosses), Siauliai, Uzupis, Vilnius

Luxembourg Luxembourg City

Lovely Eel Pie Island, Westminster, Leicester Square, Bow (all within London, England)

Macau (Macao) Coloanne, Macau Old Town, Taipa

Northern Macedonia (formerly FYR Macedonia) (Blace),

Gostivar, (Kulla), Ohrid, Skopje

Malaysia Batu, Beaufort, (Gemas), Kota Kinabalu, Kuala Lumpur, Labuan, Mamutik Island, Mount Kinabalu, Sapi Island

Malta

Comino Island – **Blue Lagoon, Comino, Cominoto**

Gozo Island – **Ewkija, Mgarr, Victoria**

Malta Island – **Il Birgu (Vittoriosa), Birkirkara, Cirkewwa, Floriana, Il Mellieha, Luqa, Mdina, Mosta, Paceville, Popeye Village, Rabat, Sliema, St. Julian's, Valletta**

Maasai Tribe Maasai Mara National Park (Kenya), Rabat Village (Tanzania)

Marshall Islands *Majuro Atoll –* **Majuro City, Eneko Island, Delap, Uliga, Djarrit**

Mexico Agua Azul, Ciudad Cuauhtémoc, Mexico City, Misol Ha, Monte Alban, Oaxaca de Juarez, Palenque, San Cristobal de las Casas, Teotihuacán

Moldova Butuceni, Chisinau, Orheiul Vechi

Monaco Monte Carlo

Mongolia Ulaan Baatar

Montenegro (Budva), Kotor, Niksic, Podgorica, (Rozaje)

Morocco (Agadir), Casablanca, Marrakesh

Myanmar Amarapura, Bagan, Inwa, Mandalay, Sagaing, Yangon

Nagorno Karabakh/Artsakh Agdam, Askeran, Gandzasar, Stepanakert, Vank

Namibia Duesternbrook, Sandwich Harbour, Walvis Bay, Windhoek

Narnia Aslan, CS Lewis's Wardrobe, Holywood Arches (Belfast, Northern Ireland)

Nauru Anabar, Anetan, Anibare, Aiwo, Arenibek, Arijejen, Arubo, Baiti, Boe, Ewa, Ibwenape, Ijuw, Makwa, Meneng, Nibok, Orro, Ronave, Topside, Waboe, Yangor, Yaren

Netherlands Amsterdam, Delft, Edam, Madurodam, Noordwijk, (Rotterdam), The Hague, Volendam

New Zealand

North Island - Auckland, Hamilton, Huntly, Mount Manganui, Paeroa, Palmerston North, Papamoa, Rotorua, Taihape, Tamaki Maori Village, Taupo, Taurangi, Waihi, Wellington
South Island - Belfast, Christchurch, Cromwell, Dunedin, Franz Josef Township, Greymouth, Lawrence, Makarora, Oamaru, Otago Peninsula, Picton, Queenstown, Wanaka
Nicaragua El Guasaule, Granada, Leon, Managua
North Korea DMZ, Kaesong, Panmunjom, Pyongyang
Northern Cyprus Turkish Nicosia
Northern Ireland (incomplete) Aldergrove, Antrim, Armagh, Ballintoy, Ballyclare, Ballygowan, Ballyhalbert, Ballymena, Ballymoney, Ballyskeagh, Ballywalter, Ballywhiskin, Bangor, Belfast, Benone, Broughshane, Bushmills, Carrick A Rede Rope Bridge, Carrickfergus, Carrowdore, Carryduff, Castlerock, Castlewellan, Cloughy, Coleraine, Comber, Conlig, Craigavad, Craigavon, Crawfordsburn, Crossgar, Derry, Donaghadee, Downpatrick, Drumahoe, Dundonald, Dundrum, Dungannon, Dungiven, Eglinton, Galgorm Resort, Ganaway, Giants Causeway, Glengormley, Glenshane Pass, Greyabbey, Greysteel, Groomsport, Helen's Bay, Hillsborough, Holywood, Kearney, Killinchy, Killyleagh, Kircubbin, Kirkistown, Larne, Limavady, Lisburn, Londonderry, Loughgall, Magherafelt, Milford, Millisle, Nendrum, Newcastle, Newry, Newtownabbey, Newtownards, Portadown, Portaferry, Portavogie, Portballintrae, Portbraddon, Portrush, Portstewart, Raffrey, Ringhaddy, Scarva, Seahill, Strabane, Strangford, Tandragee, Trim Trail, Tullymore, Warrenpoint
Norway Bergen, Flam, Gudvangen, Myrdal, Oslo, Rygge (Airport), Voss
Oman Muscat, Mutrah, Riyam, Ruwi
Panama Miraflores (Panama Canal), Panama City
Papua New Guinea Port Moresby
Paraguay Asuncion, Ciudad del Este, Luque
Peru Aguas Calientes, Cuzco, Desaguadero, Juliaca, (Lima)
Inca Trail - Machu Picchu, Ollantaytambo, Runkurakay,

Sayaqmarka, Wayllabamba, Warmiwanuska, Winaywayna, Phuyu
Pata Marka, Intipata, Intipunku, Q>Orihuayrachina, Miskay,
Patabamba, Llactapata, Hatunchaca
Philippines Balicasag Island, Bohol Island, Cebu City, Manila
City, Panglao Island, Tagbilaran, Virgin Island
Podjistan Four Gables, The People's Palace, Rural Podjistan
Poland (incomplete) Auschwitz, Białystok, Białowieża,
Biskupiec, Bochnia, Bydgoszcz, Chorzów, Chotyniec, Elbląg,
Gdańsk, Gdynia, Gliwice, Gręblin, Grotowice, Jaroslaw, Kalwaria
Zebrzydowska, Katowice, Kętrzyn, Kielce, Kokoszkowy, Kościan,
Krajenka, Kraków, Krzyz, Kuklowka – Zarczeczna, Lanckorona,
Łeba, Łęczyna, Leszno, Łódz, Lubiewo, Lublin, Majdanek,
Malbork, Międzyzdroje, Mory, Nieciecza, Nowa Słupia, Nowy
Wies, Ojców, Olsztyn, Opole, Pawłowice, Pelplin, Piaseczno, Piła,
Plock, Poznań, Pruszcz Gdański, Radom, Radymno, Rywałd,
Rzeszow, Szczecin, Słowiński National Park, Sopot, Starogard
Gdański, Stutthof, Swidnica, Poznań, Radom, Tarnów, Tarnowskie
Góry, Tczew, Toruń, Trzcianka, Warszawa, Wilczy Szaniec
(Wolfschanze / Wolf's Lair), Włocławek, Wólka Milanowska,
Wrocław, Zakopane, Zakrzewo, Zalipie, Zamosc, Zielona Gora,
Zlotoklos, Złotów.
Portugal Alvor, Faro, Lisbon, Portimao, The Algarve
Qatar Doha
Republic of Ireland Arklow, Blarney, Cashel, Cork, Donegal,
Drogheda, Dublin, Dundalk, Dun Laoghaire, Muff,
Rosslare, Wicklow
Romania Bran, Brasov, Bucharest, Cacica, Campulung
Moldovenesc, Marginea, Moldovita, Sucevita, Suceava
Romkerhall Kingdom of Romkerhall
Russia Kaliningrad, Krasnodar, Moscow, Saint Petersburg
Rwanda Cyangugu (Rusizi), Gitarama, Kigali
Saudi Arabia Dir'aiyah, Ha'il, Hrabat, Jabal Umm Sanman,
Jeddah, Jubbah, Mashar NP, Riyadh, Shaqra, Ta'if,
Tawarun, Ushaiqer

San Escobar Swidnica San Escobar Embassy, San EscoBAR (Warszawa)

San Marino San Marino City, Serravale

Scotland Ayr, Cairnryan, Edinburgh, Glasgow, Gretna, Irvine, Kilmarnock, Stranraer, Troon

Senegal Dakar, Foundiougne, Karang, Lac Rose, M'Bour, N'Gor Beach

Serbia Belgrade

Singapore Singapore City

Slovakia Bratislava, Don Valley

Slovenia Bled, Ljubljana, Maribor

Solomon Islands Honiara

South Africa Bloemfontein, Cape of Good Hope, Cape Town, Golela, Groot Marico, Johannesburg, Kopfontein, Montrose, Nelspruit, Pretoria, Robben Island, Simon's Town, Soweto, Sterkfontein

South Korea DMZ, Imjingak, (Incheon), Paju, Panmunjom, Seoul, Suwon

Sovereign Military Order of Malta Private Residence in Fort Saint Angelo, Flag Square in Vittoriosa

Spain

Basque - Bilbao, Donostia

Catalonia - Barcelona

Menorca - Mahon, S›Arenal

Majorca - Magaluf, Palma

Mainland - Alicante, Madrid, Malaga, San Martin, Seville, Torrevieja, Valencia

Sri Lanka Adam's Peak, Colombo, Dambula, Dellhousie, Galle, Haputale, Kandy, Kurunegala, Mirissa, Negombo, Pinnawala, Sigiriya, Tissamaharama, Yala National Park

Suriname Albina, Concordia Plantations, Marienburg, New Amsterdam, Nieuw Nickerie, Paramaribo, South Drain, (Zanderij)

Swaziland / Eswatini Ezulwini, Mahlanya, Malkerns Valley, Mantenga, Manzini, Lavumisa, Lobamba

Sweden Angelholm, Gothenburg, Helsingborg, Malmo, Solna, Stockholm

Switzerland Basel, Zurich

Taiwan Anping, Changhua, Chiayi, Eluanbi, Guanshiling, Hualien, Kaohsiung, Kenting, Lotus Lake, Shinying, Taichung, Taipei, Taidong, Tainan, Tailuga/Taroko Gorge, Taoyuan, Tiansiang

Tajikistan Dushanbe, Hissar, Kulob, Khorog

Tanzania Arusha, N'gorongoro Crater, Rabbatt Maasai Village, Tarangire National Park, The Serengeti

Thailand Aranya Prathet, Bangkok, Nong Khai, Udon Thani

Transnistria (Bendery), Tiraspol

Trinidad and Tobago Piarco, Port of Spain

Tunisia Monastir, Sidi Bou Said, Tunis, Kairouan, Teboulba, Carthage, Mahdia, Sousse

Turkey Adana, Agre, Ankara, Cappadocia, Dogubayazit, Goreme, Gurbulak, Istanbul, Kaymakli, Nevşehir, Sumela, Trabzon, Ürgüp

Turkmenistan Abdullah-Khan Kala, Anau, **Ashgabat, Darvaza Crater, Dashoguz, Diyar-Bekir, Jerbent, Konye-Urgench, Mary, Merv, Ruhubelent**

Uganda Entebbe, Jinja, Kampala, Tororo

Ukraine Lviv, Kiev (see also Chernobyl Exclusion Zone: Chernobyl Town, Pripyat, Reactor Number 4, Kopachi)

United Arab Emirates Dubai, Sharjah

United Kingdom (see England, Northern Ireland, Scotland and Wales)

United States of America Atlanta, (Dallas), Kissimmee, Hollywood, Los Angeles, New York, Orlando, (Philadelphia), (Pittsburgh), (San Francisco)

Uruguay Casapueblo, Colonia del Sacramento, (Maldonado), Montevideo, Punta del Este

Uzbekistan Denau, Samarkand, Bukhara, Karshi, Termiz, Navoi, Nukus, Tashkent, Khiva, Urgench

Uzupis Uzupis Neighbourhood in Vilnius (Lithuania)

Vatican City State St. Paul's Square, Sistine Chapel,

Vatican Museums
Venezuela <u>Caracas</u>, San Antonio del Tachira, San Cristobal
Vietnam <u>Halong Bay</u>, <u>Hanoi</u>, <u>Lao Cai</u>, Lao Chai, <u>Sapa</u>, <u>Ta Van</u>
Wales <u>Abergavenny</u>, <u>Cardiff</u>, Fishguard, Holyhead,
Mardy, <u>Swansea</u>
Wallachia Hranice, Valašské Meziříčí
Western Sahara El Aaiún
Zambia Kazungula, Livingstone, Victoria Falls
Zimbabwe Kazungula, Victoria Falls City, Victoria Falls

<u>**Places I have physically been to but don't count on the list:**</u>
<u>**(Mauritania)**</u> (Nouakchott Airport)

* Those places in brackets are because I have been in that place but
not left the vehicle (transit on a bus, train, plane etc.)

<u>**Acknowledgements**</u>

The author wishes to thank the following people for their help and
assistance on this journey and for being there on my travels and
playing a big part in my life.

All fellow pupils and members of staff at Kilmaine Primary School
where I attended from 1984 - 1991.

My parents Muriel and Joe Blair who have loved me on every step
of my journey.

My brothers Marko Blair and Danny Blair and my sister
Cathy Blair.

My ex-girlfriend, Panny Yu.

My best friends in life Rafał Kowalczyk, "Millwall Neil", Michael
Whitford, Dan Darch, Austin Sheppard, Sandra Kabasinguzi,

Daniel Evans, Lock In Lee Adams and Richard "Richboy" Ingram for always being there for me in times of need.

Authors and Writers Deacon Blake, Richard Morgan, Michael Miller, Niall Doherty, Carlo Cretaro, Matt Kepnes, Derek Earl Baron, Gunnar Garfors and Paddy Campbell for inspiring my journey, all people who I have met in real life.

My backpacking friends Chaz Fitzsimmons, Fifi Rushfield, Russell Sneddon, Natalja Tsumakova and all other honest people who I went backpacking with.

My Polish backpacking buddy from India, Ilona Skladzien.

My childhood sweetheart, Claire McKee.

The Slavic lady who slept in the bunk bed above me in Bucharest, Olcia Malinowa.

The Hungarian dancer, Noemi Linzenbold.

Scott Eldo at Eldo Design for the book formatting and cover design.

The Green and White Army, the GAWA, Northern Ireland fans.
All supporters of AFC Bournemouth.
All supporters of Glentoran FC.

Footballers Gerry Armstrong, Pat Jennings, Norman Whiteside, George Best, Teddy Sheringham, Gary McCartney, James Hayter, Eddie Howe, Steve Fletcher and David Healy, all of whom I have seen in real life either in a shopping mall or on a football pitch.

Musicians Tim Wheeler, Mark Hamilton, Rick McMurray, Noel Gallagher, Liam Gallagher, Nicky Wire, James Dean Bradfield,

Sean Moore and Neil Finn, whose words and songs have inspired me along the way.

All the readers and followers of my one man travel blog, Don't Stop Living.

All the readers and followers of my Poland based travel blog, Northern Irishman in Poland.

This book is dedicated to everyone (past, present and future) at Kilmaine Primary School in Bangor, Northern Ireland.

Stay beautiful.